Institutions, Communication and Values

Also by Wilfred Dolfsma

CONSUMING SYMBOLIC GOODS: Identity and Commitment, Values and Economics

ETHICS AND THE MARKET: Insights from Social Economics
J. Clary and D.M. Figart (*co-editors*)

FIGHTING THE WAR ON FILE SHARING
A. Schmidt and W. Keuvelaar (*co-authors*)

GLOBALISATION, INEQUALITY AND SOCIAL CAPITAL: Contested Concepts, Contested Experiences
E. Dannreuther (*co-editor*)

INNOVATION IN SERVICE FIRMS EXPLORED
J. de Jong, A. Bruins and J. Meijaard (*co-authors*)

INSTITUTIONAL ECONOMICS AND THE FORMATION OF PREFERENCES: the Advent of Pop Music

KNOWLEDGE ECONOMIES: Innovation, Location and Organization

MEDIA AND ECONOMICS
R. Nahuis (*co-editor*)

MNCs FROM EMERGING ECONOMIES
G. Duysters and I. Costa (*co-editors*)

THE ELGAR HANDBOOK OF SOCIAL ECONOMICS
J. Davis (*co-editor*)

UNDERSTANDING THE DYNAMICS OF A KNOWLEDGE ECONOMY
L. Soete (*co-editor*)

Institutions, Communication and Values

Wilfred Dolfsma

palgrave
macmillan

First published 2009 by
PALGRAVE MACMILLAN

Palgrave Macmillan in the UK is an imprint of Macmillan Publishers Limited, registered in England, company number 785998, of Houndmills, Basingstoke, Hampshire RG21 6XS.

Palgrave Macmillan in the US is a division of St Martin's Press LLC, 175 Fifth Avenue, New York, NY 10010.

Palgrave Macmillan is the global academic imprint of the above companies and has companies and representatives throughout the world.

Palgrave® and Macmillan® are registered trademarks in the United States, the United Kingdom, Europe and other countries.

ISBN: 978–0–230–22379–0 hardback

This book is printed on paper suitable for recycling and made from fully managed and sustained forest sources. Logging, pulping and manufacturing processes are expected to conform to the environmental regulations of the country of origin.

A catalogue record for this book is available from the British Library.

A catalog record for this book is available from the Library of Congress.

10 9 8 7 6 5 4 3 2 1
18 17 16 15 14 13 12 11 10 09

Printed and bound in Great Britain by
CPI Antony Rowe, Chippenham and Eastbourne

She ate a little bit [of the cake], and said anxiously to herself 'Which way? Which way?', holding her hand on the top of her head to feel which way it was growing; and she was quite surprised to find that she remained the same size.

Lewis Carroll, *Alice's Adventures in Wonderland*

Contents

List of Tables and Figures

Tables

Figures

Preface

Institutions indicate what kinds of interactions between human beings one may expect, how these take shape, and what effects they may be expected to have. Science, social science, and within these (institutional) economics are also shaped by institutions. Such institutions, needless to say, both constrain and enable certain kinds of personal action. Which of the two is the case may be difficult to determine, especially when one is an actor oneself. Archimedean positions are not easy to take. When working on the ideas brought together in this book, a number of institutions have played a role.

Papers that form the basis for the work in this book were presented on various occasions. Annual meetings of AFEE (Philadelphia 2004; Chicago 2006; New Orleans 2008), EAEPE (Bremen 2005), EBHA (2005) and the ASE (Amsterdam 2007; Boston 2007) and the research conference on 'Studying path dependencies of businesses, institutions, and technologies' at the Free University of Berlin in February 2008 are among them. In addition, seminars at Utrecht School of Economics and the University of Aberdeen Business School have helped shape arguments. I would like to thank the people who have given feedback, comments, suggestions.

At such (lightly) institutionalized academic meetings, and separate from them, friends and colleagues have stimulated me by making suggestions, offering alternatives, or prompting me to go further than I then believed was warranted. I would like to thank all participants in these meetings, without implicating them in any way, but in particular I would like to thank Rick Adkisson, Kaushik Basu, Annette van den Berg, Paul D. Bush, John Davis, Rick Dolphijn, Jack Goldstone, John Groenewegen, Geoff Hodgson, Eric Jones, Jurjen Kamphorst, Piet Keizer, Stefan Kesting, Irene van Staveren, Jack Vromen, Pat Welch, Ulrich Witt.

The chapters included in this book are based to some degree on articles that have appeared in academic journals already, or that may do so in the near future, in revised form. This guarantees quality of the papers, since it involves extensive communications institutionally shaped in a way that offers the assurance that standards of quality are enforced, while at the same time these ways of communication constitute audiences (Dolfsma and Leydesdorff 2009). These journals include: *Journal of Economic Issues*, *Journal of Evolutionary Economics*, *Journal of Organizational Change Management*, *Knowledge Organization*, *Review of Social Economy*.

Some of these original papers are co-authored. I have learned a lot from working with the colleagues and friends with whom I have had the privilege of cooperating. Let me thus thank Hugo van Driel, John Finch, Robert McMaster, Antoon Spithoven and Rudi Verburg.

Still, what I present here is more than a collection of articles stapled together. Not merely the sequence of arguments makes a point, but the way in which they relate is aimed at conveying the message that institutions are man-made entities and that their workings, the changes they may undergo as well as how they need to be understood are fundamentally imbued in language and communication. This communication is highly symbolic, where the meanings of symbols to the people involved is provided by these same institutions. This, to me, is both a theoretical and an empirical claim.

1
Introduction

Relations within the economy are thoroughly standardized, or, as many economists and other social scientists would now have it, institutionalized. Institutions, including the fundamental institutions of language enable economic processes, and may even be seen to constitute them. Commerce and communication are inseparable. Connections within the economy can be thus conceived. Such a conception of reality implies a number of things that this book possibly only begins to investigate.

First is a change in the way in which one looks at how the economy relates to society: they may not be so strictly separable as some claim (Chapter 2). This always hotly-debated theoretical issue in the social sciences dates back to considerations of social order to which Thomas Hobbes, Adam Smith and David Hume were among the most important early contributors. The discussion has considerable ideological overtones, with the contribution of the market to welfare and well-being at stake. Welfare is usually conceptualized in material terms, and a changed view would imply that both market and society can contribute to well-being and to welfare. Social relations and (non-profit) social undertakings also help provide for a livelihood. There are spheres outside the domain of the market that contribute to well-being, and accomplishments in the market can make a contribution to well-being that is not captured in welfare. Taking the argument to the heart of economics, towards the end of Chapter 2, I focus on reforms in the health-care sector as a case in point. This is an area in which relations between market and society, and especially their highly symbolic nature, are inescapable.

The growing institutionalist literature on the concept of the institution and the understanding of institutional change has paid some attention to the role of language and communication, but not much. Even when spheres such as those between the economy and society may not be sharply distinguished academically, in daily business most people will understand what is referred to when these terms are used. This points to a dual role of communication. For social systems, in and through communication, which includes the use of spoken or written language but the use of signs in a more general sense too, distinctions are created, emphases are placed and connections and relationships emerge. Communication and language are thus centrally implicated in an understanding of institutions and institutional change. What then differentiates institutions, and how can institutions be identified through time and space? The analysis in Chapter 3 develops Searle's (2005) argument that language itself is the fundamental institution. Searle's argument is broadly functionalist, however, and does not convey the ambiguity of language. Institutions need to be reproduced continuously, mediated by language – which is a deeply contentious process. Moreover, ontologically language and understanding delineate and circumscribe a community. A community cannot function without a common language, as Searle argued, but language at the same time constitutes a community's boundaries, and excludes outsiders – or alien topics – from discussion, allowing for focused and effective communication. This is how institutions both constrain and enable. By drawing upon Luhmann's (1995) systems analysis and notion of communication, I underline the essentially vulnerable nature of institutional continuity within a context of change and reproduction.

Giving communication, language and their often symbolic nature their due offers new insights for the debate on structure versus agency (Chapter 4). This debate, among the oldest in the history of the social sciences, is uncompromising, emphasizing either agency or structure. Analysing the *process* of institutionalization, and the role of communicating symbolic meanings, presents a possible conceptual compromise. Institutional change is instigated by tensions arising from discrepancies between agents' valuations or perceptions of concrete institutional settings and the socio-economic values that underlie a setting. Agents who perceive such tensions can mobilize others by communication designed to instigate (or prevent) changes. Agency may manifest itself in different ways, however, changing an existing institutional setting. By focusing on the highly symbolic socio-cultural values supporting an institutional furniture, communicated through these institutions, the understanding of the processes of institutional change is enhanced.

Within the domain of economics, there are at least two general views on the proper role and meaning of institutions: original institutional economics (OIE) and new institutional economics (NIE). OIE and NIE hold differing positions on a number of issues. There is an ongoing discussion about the question as to whether these positions are categorically different (Hodgson 1988), are part of the same continuum (Rutherford 1994, 1995), or may indeed be reconciled (Groenewegen et al. 1995; Schmid 2004). These discussions tend to focus on methodological points of contention, and often draw heavily on the history of economic thought. In line with the argument throughout this book, I take a slightly different approach in Chapter 5 by analysing the phenomenon of 'silent trade'. Has trade without communication ever existed? What would it mean for economics? The theoretical possibility of silent trade and its supposed existence are a central tenet of mainstream economics and NIE. While this chapter has theoretical and methodological implications, the approach is primarily based in economic history, showing that 'silent trade' in the sense of trade with the most minimal communication has never existed. Given Searle's (2005) argument that language is the fundamental institution, the conclusion that silent trade does not exist will have implications for the discussion about the ways in which OIE and NIE relate to each other. Economic activity, trade, is predicated on the assumption of some sense of a shared set of institutions that reduce uncertainty, making it possible for people to align behaviour, expectations and interests. Communication, then, is not a fringe phenomenon, but rather a *sine qua non* for trade or exchange.

Economic value creation in general and knowledge creation in particular require coordination. What holds for trade, holds for economic interactions within the communicative boundaries of an organization as well. Coordination however can take several forms. In addition to markets, where prices coordinate, and hierarchy, where authority coordinates, other forms have also been suggested. Some have called these networks, others clans. Chapter 6 suggests that the notion of *gift exchange* allows for the middle ground between market and hierarchy to be explored more fruitfully. Assessing the three coordination mechanisms in the context of knowledge creation and diffusion is particularly relevant. Each has particular advantages, but those offered by gift exchange make it an effective and sometimes preferred alternative. Knowledge creation is seen by many to be central to economic dynamics. While symbolic communication occurs in each of these three kinds of communicative settings, one of them fits better with knowledge creation and diffusion than the others, as the theoretical argument of Chapter 6 endeavours to show.

Exchange of knowledge between individuals working in a firm, between and even within divisions, does not occur automatically.

Empirical evidence, some of which is presented and discussed in Chapter 7, further develops the earlier discussions. It is not obvious that people exchange ideas, direct one another to useful information or give feedback, even when they have no motives for not cooperating. As a firm's competitive advantage is closely related to its innovative capacity, largely based on how it uses knowledge that is already available, the question then is: how does *knowledge flow* within a firm? What explains when and how knowledge is put to work? In recent years, increasing attention has been given, by scholars in social sciences in general and in management in particular, to the networks of relations between individuals within firms. Consultancies too are scrambling to set up units that can analyse these networks for firms. It is on the analyses of networks of people exchanging knowledge that I will focus. In addition to the structural issue of who relates to whom, I will argue that there is a need to look at how relations are established and maintained. The anthropological literature on gift exchange provides opportunities for understanding the intricate, motivationally complex and highly symbolic exchange of knowledge.

Prevailing views of organizations – as, say, a hierarchy or as a market ('nexus of contracts') – take a generally mechanical view of interactions between agents bent on economic improvement. An alternative view is the concept of path dependence (Chapter 8). Disentangling the constitutive elements of the concept of path dependence (initial conditions and lock-in) in studying organizational change at Toyota, concerted communication of symbolic meanings is found both conceptually to provide necessary complements and to provide the more compelling story. External initial conditions are found to act less as 'imprinting' forces than suggested in the literature on the genesis of the Toyota Production System (TPS). A firm-specific philosophy in combination with a critical sequence of events shaped and locked Toyota into a course that led to its being heralded for its production system and as the biggest producer of cars in the world. *Meta-routines* conceptually connect the core elements of path dependence, that is, sensitivity to initial conditions and lock-in mechanisms.

Communication of economic import of course occurs in areas other than those of production. Fashion is the quintessential post-modernist consumer practice, or so many hold, where symbolic communication-through-consumption takes on a dynamics of its own (see Chapter 9). I argue that, contrary to what many hold, by approaching fashion as a means of communicating one's commitment to modernist values it is possible to understand its otherwise seemingly incoherent reality.

Using the framework of the Social Value Nexus to relate such values to institutionalized consumption behaviour enables an understanding of the signals sent through consumption patterns. Modernist values are not homogeneous, and are in important ways contradictory, resulting in the observable dynamics of fashion that have bewildered many observers.

From an evolutionary perspective bankruptcies may be seen as an important selection mechanism (Chapter 10). Bankruptcy has, however, not received much attention in the economics literature. Bankruptcy law is a highly formalized way of communication in economic settings and such laws differ widely across countries and even within a federalized country such as the USA. Filing practices within a country can differ substantially among social groups as well as across regions (Fay et al. 2002). Bankruptcy is, thus, not the uncomplicated selection mechanism in the economic realm it is sometimes perceived to be. Bankruptcy law is a social creation, set in language, and can have dire social consequences. Bankruptcy can be an unpleasant process for individuals, their families and for wider society. The question is how to *evaluate* bankruptcy regimes from an economic perspective, contrasting the instrumental rationality approach of the Chicago (law and economics) school with the instrumental valuation principle from original institutional economics in the context of personal bankruptcy.

What, in short, this book offers is an argument – conceptual, methodological and empirical – that communication conceived broadly or language more narrowly are inseparable from both the economy and from a meaningful understanding of institutions.

2

Market and Society: How Do They Relate, and How Do They Contribute to Welfare?[1]

As we observed in the introductory chapter, the relationship between market and society is a hotly debated issue in the social sciences. The ideological overtones of the debate concern the contribution of the market to welfare – usually conceptualized in material terms – and to well-being. I surmise that both market and society can contribute to welfare and to well-being.

2.1 Expanding and purifying markets

Views on how market and society relate to each other may be classified according to Figures 2.1 through 2.3. There are three broad ways in which to perceive of the relation between the two spheres. First is to see market(s) and society as two separate realms (Figure 2.1). Obviously, the neoclassical economic view, specifically the Walrasian approach, is an example of this.[2] Market and society remain separate at all times. Indeed, the view of the market one finds in this literature is highly abstract – markets are 'conjured up' as Frank Hahn expresses it – and the realistic nature of the market might be questioned. As the market encroaches on society, for some at least it might bring with it a sense of alienation, as envisioned by Marx. This might be the outcome of the differences in what motivates people in the two spheres; the different terms in which they view the world when perceiving of themselves in one sphere or the other (van Staveren 2001; Le Grand 2003). Another view captured in Figure 2.1 is the one that Parsons and Smelser (1956) present on the relation between market(s) and society. They argue that distinct markets (*nota bene*: plural) emerge at the boundaries between different spheres, such as polity and other sub-spheres in society, effectively insulating these spheres from one another (Finch 2004).

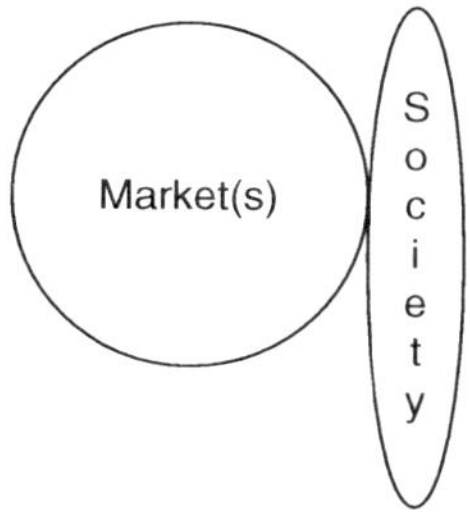

Figure 2.1 The 'separatist' view: market and society as separate

The second way in which to conceptualize the market in relation to society is probably best associated with the works of Polanyi (1944) and Granovetter (1985). The market in this view is perceived of as thoroughly and necessarily embedded in society at large, including in such institutions as money and the firm. Growth of the market domain may be interpreted as an increasing ellipse within the wider social boundary depicted in Figure 2.2. A growing market interacts with society, and the two change in the process; even when, conceptually, the market has generalized traits (Rosenbaum 2000). Establishing the effects of a growing market on society is not unambiguous. Indeed, drawing the boundaries between market and society is haphazard, as social and institutional economists acknowledge (Waller 2004; Dolfsma and Dannreuther 2003). Thus, the effects of expanding markets are not so clear-cut, even when usually the increase in material welfare may be obvious. Institutional and social economists would then, however, ask: at what cost? As society changes in response to a growing market, comparing the situation that has arisen with the previous one becomes more complicated. Certainly doing so in Pareto welfare terms is impossible as his framework entails the view of the relation between market and society as separate realms, such as depicted in Figure 2.1.[3]

The perspective underlying the Keynesian welfare state views the market as part of and regulated according to dominant social or societal values such as norms of distributive justice (O'Hara 2000; Fine 2002) – as in Figure 2.2. The process of liberalization and privatization ('reform') boils down to an attenuated role for the state, certainly in terms of distributive justice, and there is a shift in values towards those centring on the individual and towards negative freedom. The state is viewed in such a perspective as a coercive force, whereas the market is viewed as the domain of freedom (van Staveren 2001).

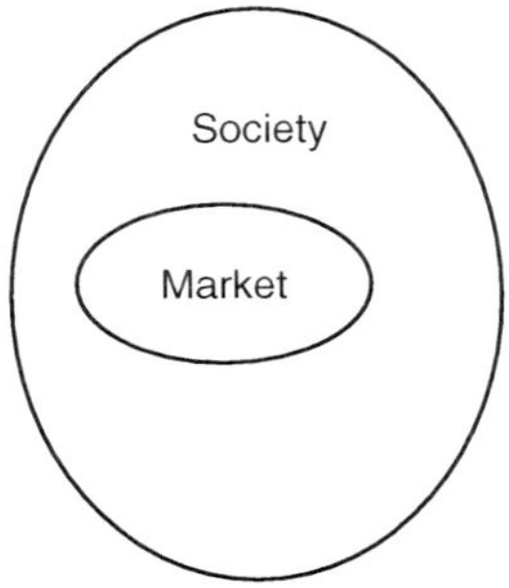

Figure 2.2 The 'embedded' view: market as embedded in society

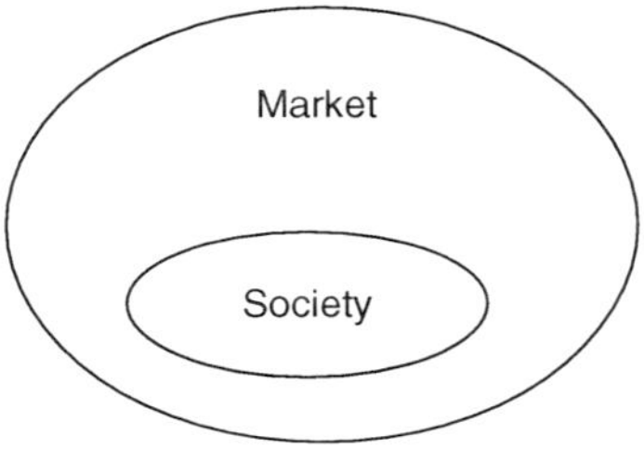

Figure 2.3 The 'impure' view: society within the market

Alternatively, the market may be perceived not as a pure entity, but as heterogeneous (Hodgson 1999).[4] Figure 2.3 clearly relaxes the Parsons-Robbins boundaries between the economic and social domains by arguing that non-market elements need to be present in a market context in order for the market system to function. Such 'societal' elements would not emerge from within the market, nor does this mean that society is completely subordinated or eclipsed by the market. This view strongly hinges on how one defines a market, and seems to entail a strict definition consistent with a 'contractual' view, where market-type relations between agents are presumed to be ubiquitous (Hodgson, 1999).[5] Growth of the market in this view is of a different nature than in the previous two views. The argument is not just about how concrete markets impinge on other domains in society, but on how market-like thinking expands into other domains with their associated ways of thinking and perceiving. Such an expansion, Hodgson and others argue, may occur but can never completely eclipse all elements of 'society' within the market without jeopardizing itself. Even when Hodgson does not define impurity precisely, or explicitly indicates what impurity refers to, I take this to mean impurity with regard to the motives of actors and the relations between them. This seems consistent with Hodgson (1999).

Views on the contribution of markets to welfare hinge on the conceptualization of the relation between market and society. A perception of the economy (the economic domain) as a sphere entirely separate from society would be accompanied by a belief that markets necessarily contribute to welfare. Given that markets are presumed to be ubiquitous in mainstream economics, I argue that the foregoing is a reasonable representation of economic orthodoxy. Mainstream conceptions of the market are functionalist – in appropriate conditions the market is an efficiency conduit, and hence generates welfare as well as well-being. Creating these appropriate conditions then drives policy. However, as I have argued, this 'separatist' view is not the only conceivable view of the relation between society and economy. There are two more views; views stressed and developed in the fields of institutional and social economics, as well as elsewhere. The three views of the relation between economy and society can also be used to clarify interactions between market and society.

2.2 Changing relations between market and society

We acknowledge that markets can increase both welfare and well-being. This has been argued on a number of occasions, and has been substantiated by empirical material. Rather than challenge this view, I point to the darker aspects of markets. In processes of change or reform, there is a distinct way in which the relations between market and society are presented by both sides of the argument. I focus on those advocating change. The example of reforms in health-care serves to illustrate and clarify our position.

In stable circumstances, actors involved in a particular practice recognize that the economic aspects of that practice are embedded in a broader social context; the view is that of Figure 2.2. They also recognize that motives that operate for themselves and others alike reflect a number of considerations, some of which are more materially oriented while others are more relational (Figure 2.3). Under conditions of change, advocates refer to a 'pure' situation, as in Figure 2.1, where market and society are presented as separated both in terms of spheres and in terms of motives. This is done by referring to the purported socio-cultural values underlying the market, values such as transparency, accountability and efficiency. Referring to these values, new institutional settings are sought (see Dolfsma 2004). As a new stable situation emerges, however, the changed practice needs to relate to the larger society that surrounds it, and impurities emerge. Nevertheless, the bifurcation between society and markets (to some) presents a strong *prima facie* (neo-liberal) case for the extension of the former into the realm of the latter. Even when evidence in favour of reform was not persuasive and evidence of the effects of reform is daunting, there may be a tendency to argue that this absence of effects is the result of the implemented reforms having not gone far enough. From this perspective the policy implication is obvious: extend the market domain to these non-economic, non-market domains, creating the 'appropriate conditions', and efficiency and therefore welfare (as conceptualized according to a Paretian/utilitarian frame) will be enhanced. This has certainly happened in the case of health-care reforms (Light 2001a), as elaborated below.

2.3 Health-care

In recent years the health-care sector has been subject to processes of ongoing market-oriented reforms in many countries. The economic rationale underpinning much of the market-oriented reforms to health-care systems is predicated on the presumption that health and health-care may be treated as commodities.[6] Indeed, any market-oriented reform necessitates an increasing recourse to contractualized relationships between parties, whether patient and clinician or, as in the UK, between vertically disintegrated units of the system. Especially given the promotion of an efficiency rubric, this increased codification is accompanied by a host of quantitative measures. Moreover, such measures revolve around generating monetized measures of value and economic evaluation techniques, pointing towards the commodification of health-care.[7] The value of the activity is concentrated on exchange value as opposed to use value, hence the requirement for measurement, encouraging a focus on outcomes through such indices as performance indicators. A consequentialist tendency and attitude is promoted.

In essence this involves 'the market', and references to the market, attaining greater prominence than other organizational mechanisms. Whatever one might think of these changes, they do show the value of the three views of the relations between the market and society in helping to gain an understanding of the process. In addition, and more prominently, the way in which the changes have been advocated and implemented, at least in the case of health-care, follows the sequence of banishing elements from the system that are considered non-economic and attempting to create a pure market *de novo* (Light 2001a, 2001b). What is apparent to institutional and social economists is that such attempts are bound to fail. In a new configuration, the subsystem will need to relate to other subsystems and society at large (Light 2001a). Boundaries between the two are never entirely clear, they change and are permeable. In addition, impure elements (motives) (re-)enter the very subsystem that was deemed in need of purification – if ever they had been expunged.

We argue that the inevitability of such a return to a 'contaminated' situation – in the minds of pure market theorists – can be shown in terms of the measures introduced by such advocates themselves in seeking to alter the system. Indeed, as outcomes foreseen by advocates did not materialize, new reform programmes tended to be proposed (Hendrikse and Schut 2004). The mechanisms and measures are re-embedded. As such mechanisms and measures can never stipulate every circumstance that might arise, and as such mechanisms and measures are necessarily complementary to related areas, the limited effects of the programmes were to be expected. These two arguments are even acknowledged in the mainstream (Milgrom and Roberts 1990). Individuals in the sector have, for instance, altered their behaviour such that they act in accordance with the stipulations of the pure market mechanisms and measures introduced, but in fact are able to circumvent their effectiveness. Sometimes this is done in direct violation of the stipulations, as in the UK, where meetings to coordinate activities of the different parties involved are called that government regulations and contracts explicitly forbid. Previously existing 'societal' ties are drawn on – ties with individuals who can be trusted (Light 2001a, 2001b).

Indeed, there is increasing importance attributed to *managing* health-care provision in particular ways that enhance the role of financial incentives (of clinicians) and the employment of pricing. Greater emphasis is placed on accountancy techniques and on the utilization of (mainstream) economic language and discourse (see for example, Fitzgerald 2004; Grit and Dolfsma, 2002). As the language and discourse of health-care provision changes, so new metrics become increasingly absorbed and embedded. As Kula (1986) has argued theoretically, and shown in a large number of cases in different settings, the newly introduced measures are quickly embedded in existing practices, partly undermining the use for which they have been introduced (see Light 2001a). Davis and McMaster (2004) argue that health-care reform, and the mainstream economics underpinning it, is likely to encourage a change in the nature of care in health-care systems. Clinician conduct and behaviour is, to some extent, influenced by the social obligations of their membership of, and embeddedness in, a professional group, which is predisposed to the Hippocratic oath. The trust that had underpinned the cooperation within health systems necessary for (effective) provision is corroded with the emphasis on measurability and efficiency (Gilson 2003; Hunter 1996). A high-trust environment is substituted by a low-trust environment in which different people with a different view of 'good care' assume control (Fitzgerald 2004; Grit and Dolfsma 2002). Professional discretion is marginalized. It is a moot issue whether this is entirely inimical to the social relations associated with an increased recourse to market-type arrangements, such as performance measurement, the monetization of incentives and contractualization of interactions. Nevertheless, some recent anthropological and ethnographic works have suggested that the nature of care is changing with changes in the arrangements governing the provision of health-care (see, for example, Fitzgerald 2004; van der Geest and Finkler 2004). Such studies appear to indicate that market orientation encourages health service managers to adopt a more abstract and homogenized view of the care process, akin to a Cartesian approach (Davis and McMaster 2004).[8] This contrasts with a more person-oriented focus of some, although not necessarily all, clinical services, which can lead to conflict and agent disorientation (Fitzgerald 2004) as well as to a narrower and more reductionist view of care.

The conceptualization on which the reforms were based, that of markets as separate, was overly restrictive, inadequate for the conceptualization of the potential effects of markets on society, welfare and well-being. To be more realistic, the contributions of Polanyi, Hodgson and Granovetter, among others, need to be used to conceptualize the relation between market and society differently. Such an approach broadens the notion of welfare beyond the monetized parameters of economic orthodoxy, and feeds into the policy debate by recognizing that a functionalist interpretation of the market is informed by a particular view of how it relates to society.

2.4 Conclusion: markets, society and welfare

In this short chapter, I have presented different views of how market and society relate: the market as separate, the market as embedded, and the market as impure. These characterizations seem to presume that boundaries between different domains can be drawn. This, however, may be problematic. When I discuss a growing market in this chapter, as in the reform of systems of health-care in a large number of developed countries, I actually refer to the market sphere expanding in a qualitative way, encroaching on other, adjacent spheres, and not necessarily to a growing market in a quantitative sense.

In processes of change intended to expand the market, one particular view (economy as separate from society) tends to be advanced, driving institutional change. I have argued, for health-care, that any such new measures introduced will not bring about the pure market context envisaged, but will necessarily be re-embedded in society, as 'other' non-economic motives (re-)emerge to 'contaminate' the system. Introducing elements of a pure market in a 'hybrid' context does not necessarily increase welfare, let alone well-being.

The notion of welfare, however, certainly from a Paretian perspective, seems to depend upon the concept of the market as separate. 'The market' in this view, is both a (necessary) concept through which to understand welfare, and also a requirement for aggregation across individuals so that we can speak meaningfully of societal welfare. This would seem to imply, for the purpose of measuring welfare, that society = economy. In order for society at large to be understood to contribute to welfare, this idea of the market needs to be projected into realms where at present there is no such idea. I argue, however, that such a conceptualization of the market, and certainly the way in which it is believed to relate to society, needs to be much more complex, allowing for changing boundaries between the two spheres, for a range of motives to come into play, and for a concept of welfare which comes closer to that of well-being. This undermines the mainstream, Paretian perspective on welfare (see Dolfsma 2008a) as well as the view of economy as separate. Well-being, more loosely connected with markets, is even less likely to be affected – positively or negatively – by how markets develop, expand, are contaminated or purified. Certainly, how well-being is affected depends on how, when the dust settles, the boundaries between market and society have been redrawn.

3
Institutions, Institutional Change and Language[1]

> Boundaries are an evolutionary achievement par excellence.
> (Luhmann 1995, p. 29)

By developing Searle's (1995, 2005) argument that language is the fundamental institution, this chapter contributes to the growing institutionalist literature on the conception of the institution and the understanding of institutional change. Language is ambiguous, however, and so institutional reproduction, mediated by language, is a deeply contentious process. Moreover, ontologically, language and understanding delineate and circumscribe a community. A community cannot function without a common language, as Searle argued, but language at the same time constitutes a community's boundaries, allowing for focused and effective communication. I develop the argument by drawing upon Luhmann's (1995) systems analysis and notion of communication, underlining the essentially vulnerable nature of institutional continuity with change and reproduction as meaningful information crosses a system's boundaries. This raises the question of how institutions may be recognized when they are vulnerable even when reproduced. Drawing from John Davis (2003) one may pose the questions: what differentiates institutions, and how can institutions be identified through time and space?

3.1 Introduction

In this chapter I elaborate on the work of Searle (1995, 2005) and others to argue that language is the central institution and at the same time conceptually an indispensable element of institutions. In particular, conceptualizing the durability and change of institutions is only possible through acknowledging the role of language. Durability is widely recognized as an essential dimension of institutions, but I add that durability only really makes sense if one also recognizes that it implies vulnerability. Language, considered as an institution, and its use in communication offers ample scope to investigate the recursive institutional conditions of durability and vulnerability. Hence, we may pose the following question:

> What makes institutional reproduction a vulnerable process, and how is institutional recognition retained through time and space?

John Davis (2003) poses similar questions in the context of assessing how the individual in economics is conceptualized in terms of individuation and re-identification. As detailed in Section 3.2 (below), institutionalist analysis has emphasized at least since Veblen the durability and reproductive qualities of institutions. Yet, institutional reproduction is not inevitable and institutions are indeed vulnerable. By vulnerability I refer to the potential for institutional reproduction to fail such that institutions may no longer be re-identified across time.

Of course this prompts questions as to the causes of institutional vulnerability. I draw upon Luhmann's (1995) social systems approach to refer to communication and language used within a community or system and across a system's boundaries. Human beings are also actors, such that action may be understood recursively as communication (Luhmann 1995; Leydesdorff 2006). Analysis of communication envisages individuals as actors drawing on rules and norms. Successful communication is in no way guaranteed as actors' understandings of the rules and norms drawn on in communication can be incomplete, or incompletely or differently understood, even within a single community. Communication is usefully described as experimental, rather than self-explanatory and unproblematic (as implicitly assumed by Searle), as involving a social process of 'limited inquiry and intelligent adaptation' (Flaherty 2000).[2]

Individuals acquire some understanding or representation of the contextual rules within which they are situated and act. Language and understandings of institutions are shared within a community if communication is to be successful and institutional reproduction is not to fail. Analysing that which separates or distinguishes *and so* connects institutions and institutional furniture (language) allows us to discuss institutional change and durability. I thus introduce the term 'boundary'.[3] Communication analysis shows how boundaries between realms are described, permeated, interpenetrated and changed. Further, boundaries maximize both the autonomy of systems and communication between them (Star and Griesemer 1989). Communication across system boundaries, as Luhmann argues, both yields meaningful communication and creates the circumstances for the failure of institutional reproduction.

We develop our argument across the chapter's remaining five sections. Section 3.2 briefly reviews literature on the concept of the institution, highlighting the status of language. Section 3.3 focuses on the ways in which institutions need not be durable and can instead be vulnerable. Drawing on Luhman in particular, Section 3.4 argues that the institutions within a system are particularly vulnerable to the incursion of information from across a system's boundaries. Communication, necessary for institutional reproduction, may thus also cause vulnerability. Section 3.5 addresses the question of how institutions can formally be re-identified through change. Section 3.6 concludes.

3.2 A résumé of the 'institution'

Interest in the concept of institutions has revived over the last three decades as evidenced by the significant growth in references to institutions in mainstream economics, primarily through the lenses of the 'new institutional economics' (Williamson 2000). There are, however, crucial differences between the 'old' and 'new' institutional economics, which may or may not be reconcilable (Rutherford 1989). New institutional conceptions of institutions tend to emphasize 'institutions as constraints' to individual free will and market processes (Williamson 2000). According to 'old' institutionalists, 'new' institutionalist explanations of the existence of institutions are partial as they fail to recognize the enabling and facilitating roles of institutions. Institutions are partly constitutive of individuals and are partly constituted by individuals. For instance, Hodgson (2004, p. 424) describes institutions as: '... durable systems of established and embedded social rules that structure social interactions'.

Definitions of institutions have been subject to increased scrutiny recently, with attempts being made to elaborate upon Veblen's (1969, p. 239) observation that:

> As a matter of course, men order their lives by these principles [of action] and, practically, entertain no question of their stability and finality. That is what is meant by calling them institutions; they are the settled habits of thought of the generality of men. But it would be absentmindedness ... to admit that ... institutions have ... stability [that is] intrinsic to the nature of things.

Examples of institutions include money, marriage, markets, organizations, religions and language. Language is the fundamental institution predicating all other institutions and its recursive and, thus, communicative quality furnishes the key to organizing (Searle 2005; Robichaud et al. 2004). Institutions must be recognized within a community, so cannot be recognized by an individual alone, acting habitually. Recognizing durability in institutions draws attention to the systemic nature of what Veblen terms 'institutional furniture'. In other words, institutions have the potential to be connected one to another, so requiring an assessment of the consequences of connection and disconnection. Institutional furniture is illustrated clearly in Searle's argument that institutions are mediated by language and also given in language.

Institutions exhibit differences in level, scale, scope and durability, and therefore possess multiple roles and meanings for individual actors (Jessop 2000; Parto 2005). Indicating that institutions can constitute boundaries, physically, cognitively and socially, O'Hara (2000, p. 37) writes:

> ... institutions are the durable fabric which structures relations between classes and agents. They provide the social nexus of communication which provides shared symbols, sites of practice, and some degree of certainty which reduces the social cost of human intercourse.

Other definitions of 'the institution' refer to correlated behavioural patterns (Bush 1987), rules, conventions and norms (Hodgson 2004) and mental constructs (Neale 1987). Searle makes no reference to either ethics or values, but it is clear (institutionally) that rules are predicated on norms that reflect particular systems of values and beliefs and so are legitimizing (Avio 2002, 2004). Institutions, when perceived as legitimate and acted upon, correlate behaviour and possess a generic quality in that they can encapsulate norms and conventions as well as formal and legal rules (Hodgson 2004; Scott 1995; Neale 1987; Bush 1987; Dolfsma 2004, chapter 4).

Institutions thus allow individuals to act in ways that enable them to negotiate 'their daily affairs' (Lawson, 1997, p. 187). Yet individuals are situated in a range of positions that each infer roles and status (Searle 1995, 2005), conditioning and moulding their propensities to act in particular ways, affecting distinct individuals differently. Searle (2005, p. 7) emphasizes the capacity of individuals to perform assigned functions requiring collective acceptance. Acting according to an institution may thus be understood in terms of an injunction or disposition that in certain circumstances an individual is expected by others to 'do something' instead of nothing and as an alternative to some other action (Hodgson 2004, p. 14).

Institutions either tacitly or explicitly establish agents' deontic powers, which are in effect rights, obligations, duties, roles and legitimacy (Searle 2005; Avio 2002, 2004). Deontic powers are diffused and accepted within a community by communication. The language used to communicate should be understood in broad terms, and will not only include spoken words. For Searle (1995), individuals' mental representations of institutions are constitutive of institutions since any institution can only exist if people both possess and communicate beliefs and attitudes specifically related to the institution. Agents anticipate actions and communications as and to the extent that – in an ex ante sense – they develop understandings of the institutional furniture of their community (Leydesdorff 2006). If, and only if, they do this, are agents able effectively to express (communicate) 'we-intentions' (Davis 2003). Being able to express we-intentions requires that an agent to some extent – in an ex post sense – shares a worldview in common with other agents (see Jessop 2000).

For Davis (2003, p. 130) and Searle, collective intentionality denotes social relationships between individuals where theories or images of those social relationships are embedded within individuals. Although I neither prioritize the individual nor the social, I do argue that the individual's habits of interpretation and (re-)presentation are guided by social, perhaps codified, means of representation. This, I venture, is a useful way of apprehending Granovetter's (1985) notion of embeddedness. Language plays a pivotal role in distinguishing individual from collective intentionality, between 'I-intentions' and 'we-intentions'. We-intentions, in the absence of fraudulent deceit, infer not only the individual expressing the 'we-term' intent, but also reflect the expresser's belief that other individuals share this intention, and the assumption that other individuals are aware of this shared intention. Unlike 'I-intentions', 'we-intentions' invoke some form of obligation and commitment on the part of the individual that does not exist with the expression of an independent (individual) intention.[4] Institutions imply enforcement properties. Unsuccessful expression of we-intentions, for instance, may trigger the application of legitimate prescriptive sanctions (other connected rules) (Hodgson 2004), but also has the potential to instigate a process of institutional change (Chapter 4).

3.3 Institutional durability and vulnerability

What makes institutions durable? The durability of an institution affects agents' actions and communications, and in turn these may exhibit feedback on institutional durability. I defer the question of what makes institutions vulnerable until Section 3.5 (below) but note here that vulnerability is not necessarily simply the negation of durability as, central to our argument, is the understanding that institutions are always potentially durable and potentially vulnerable. Institutions can be distinguished in part because they have different qualities of durability. Durability does not imply 'no change'; following Veblen (1969) there is no suggestion of institutional 'equilibrium'. Social and communicated, durability in institutions entails reproduction. Instead it begs the question of the ontology and sources of durability. Despite change, institutions may be re-identified through time.

Relations – both hierarchical and non-hierarchical – and roles that define individuals' deontic powers are important sources of institutional durability. Searle (2005, p. 10; emphasis in the original) argues that:

> The essential role of human institutions and the purpose of having institutions is not to constrain people as such, but, rather to create new sorts of power relationships. Human institutions are, above all, *enabling* because they create power ... marked by such terms as: rights, duties, obligations, authorizations, permissions, empowerments, requirements, and certifications. I call all of these *deontic powers*.

In addition to emphasizing language, Searle thus points to the political constellation supported by or expressed through a particular language. Power may be used to prevent changes, but the use of powers by some may also change the system. Power is, of course, a complex, multidimensional and evolving conception and phenomenon, located in an institutionalized system of relationships rather than attributable to people (Foucault 1982; Avio 2004), that may be partly manifest through moral suasion (Hodgson 2003). Lawson also suggests that institutions demonstrate persistence due to the collective, not the individual when he observes (Lawson 1997, p. 163):

> Teachers ... are allowed and expected to follow different practices from students ... employers from employees, men from women ... Rules

> [institutions] as resources are not equally available, or do not apply equally, to each member of the population at large.

The establishment or emergence and subsequent (lack of) change of a particular institution or institutional furniture demonstrate historical and temporal specificities.

In reconstituting Veblen's instinct-psychology, Hodgson (2003, 2004) provides a complementary rationale for institutional persistence. Hodgson (2003, p. 167) argues that all action and deliberation are predicated on prior habits: habit has ontological and temporal primacy over intention and reason. Habits are conceptually and ontologically broader than routines, with which they can nonetheless be closely associated; for example, when functioning as organizational memory (Nelson and Winter 1982), where a routine is, '... a regular course or manner of proceeding or going on, a recurrent performance of particular *acts*' (Lawson, 1997, pp. 159–60, emphasis added). Habits do not necessarily involve acts, but are propensities, dispositions and 'submerged repertoires' of behaviour underpinning particular ways of acting and communicating in specific situations, or as a consequence of particular stimuli (Dewey 1945; Hodgson 2003). Like routines, habits are both acquired through, and necessary for, learning (Dewey 1945). It is through commonly held habits that social systems of rules are manifest. Rules beget habits that beget institutional durability. An implication of this is that habits are not exclusively individualistic, but rather that 'the personal' is social in a kind of highly localized context.

Thus institutional durability is furnished through collective intentionality, the temporal and ontological primacy of habit, and the normative apparatus associated with this. In effect, habits and routines are the conduits of institutional reproduction (Hodgson 2004). The centrality of habit as a partial influence on larger-scale institutional durability is supported by the recursive properties of language (Robichaud et al. 2004). The importance of recursivity resides in pursuing the stable and durable conversational procedures that may embed communication within a broader (or meta) form of communication. The process of embedding also structures discourse (and practice) in particular ways and leads to the persistence of particular organizational forms (Phillips et al. 2004; Maguire and Hardy 2006; Munir and Phillips 2005).

The institutionalist literature appreciates that both feedback from individuals and individual actions have the potential to change institutions (Chapter 4). Rules and norms necessarily require individuals to interpret them. To some extent individuals possess free will in this respect;

they also have recourse to different repertoires of habit and experience (Finch 1997). A classic example of this is provided by Fox (1974) when he alludes to the seemingly simple instruction: 'sweep the floor'. There is an element of individual discretion as to what constitutes the appropriate performance level in discharging even such an apparently routine task. Difference in interpretation can have consequences for action and, more significantly from our perspective, carry potential ramifications for the reproduction of an institution.

In this respect it is essential to appreciate that institutional durability resonates with reproduction as opposed to replication. As a result of the historico-spatial and individual contingency properties of a situation, change – even transformation – is inevitable (O'Hara 2000; Potts 2000, pp. 44–5). Reproduction of institutions, making for durability, is not mechanical. Moreover, the persistence of institutions can obviously be affected by other, wider or more indirectly related and general institutions – environmental or systemic – and historical effects and events. For instance, capitalism is a system of mutually supporting, if occasionally contradictory, institutions (see, for example, Polanyi 1944; Hodgson 2004; Jessop 2001, among others). Even if it were originally crafted on a single exemplary model, the subsequent development of capitalism has diverged significantly.

As noted, institutions (and systems of institutions) clearly possess differing qualities of durability. One of the most enduring institutions in the UK is the monarchy, but here too there has been extensive change in the deontic powers and influence of the individuals placed in the roles defined by this institution. From a position of extensive political power, the monarchy in the UK is presently largely ceremonial. Nevertheless, the influence of such institutions should not be discounted (Veblen 1969).[5]

As O'Hara (2000, p. 39) argues:

> Hence rather than seeing socio-economic reproduction as being purely a process of maintenance, function, and equilibrium, it must be historically situated in a maze of potential dysfunctions, contradictions, and transformations, without, of course, ignoring the historical functions of institutions.

Pace the new institutionalists, it is not efficiency that is the key to durability, but the potential for reproduction:

> '... reproduction implies differentiation; growth, change (continuous or discontinuous). However, there is something that does not change,

> which makes it reproduction. This "something" is the capacity of a system to preserve, for a time, its entirety in relation to its "environment" and to behave as if its aim were to preserve that entirety ... what perhaps best describes social reproduction is ... that this reproduction is a unity of contraries: unity of social contradictions, unity of change and stability, unity of continuity and discontinuity.'
>
> (Barel 1974; cited by O'Hara, 2000, p. 38)

Again the historical durability and autopoiesis of the British monarchy provides an illustrative example of Barel's observations. The monarchy has preserved its identity in the face of considerable environmental change: it pre-dates the emergence of capitalism and democracy, and more recent erosions and recalibrations in class boundaries, as well as the 'loss' of empire. It has successfully adapted to historical change and emergent structures and systems, and broadly maintained identifiable behavioural parameters.

3.4 Vulnerable institutions and boundaries

In seeking to recover the problematic of institutional durability I emphasize institutional vulnerability. Following the lead of systems theorist Niklas Luhmann (1995), I argue that change is instigated when 'information' from outside a system, consisting of institutions, crosses a system's boundaries. The vulnerability of institutions is thus described.

Searle's explanation of the emergence of 'institutional facts' is congruent with Luhmann's explanation of the emergence of 'information (for a social system)'. At first glance, Luhmann (1995) appears to write of social systems while Searle writes of institutions and institutional furniture. Where system and institution both imply the possibilities of durability and vulnerability, Luhmann's explanation of the continuation or 'autopoiesis' (self-reproduction) of a system is nuanced. Communication needs a relatively coherent and homogeneous system, while a system is necessarily distinct from its environment. Communication only makes sense within the terms of a system, but communication that is significant in terms of possibly jeopardizing the vulnerable process of institutional reproduction is communication from outside the system. Significant communication, then, crosses a boundary between the system and its environment. Communication, for Luhmann, occurs in the setting of a social system that necessarily construes itself in interaction with its environment and so also, necessarily, identifies boundaries. Explicitly this provides insights into the dual qualities of institutions as at the same time both durable and vulnerable, or in Luhmann's term 'improbable'. Institutions' vulnerability is largely under-explored among the community of institutional researchers.

As noted, Searle argues that an institutional fact is of subjective ontology because its existence is dependent upon human perception and is held in place through the status function of the form *X* counts as *Y* in *C*. So I first emphasize that an institutional fact is contextual (*C*). The status function is expanded in three directions, that of its necessary social quality, its mutually constitutive expression through language, and its mutually constitutive development of deontic power. An institutional fact is both the achievement and precondition of collective intentions and implies a process by which epistemology may acquire objectivity in its context. The institutional fact is expressed symbolically, as it is not ontologically objective in the sense of being independent of human perception: 'If there are to be these representations, there must be some medium of representation, and that medium is language or symbolism in the broadest sense' (Searle 2005, p. 12).

Luhmann's (1995) discussion of 'communication and action' can be particularly illuminating here because its focus is the emergence of communication, dependent upon the simultaneous emergence of a social system and – crucially – upon that system's seemingly improbable continuation or reproduction. Searle and Luhmann's accounts are congruent in their respective focus on the 'institutional fact' and on 'information, which is for the social system'. However, Luhmann addresses dynamism explicitly because communication bears the weight of a social system's coherence and continuation.

Communication comprises a 'unity of information, utterance and understanding' such that it is difficult to isolate any one component even for analytical purposes. Luhmann argues that communication is the process by which a social system forms in distinction to its environment. Critically, an event to be captured must be new to the social system if it is to have the currency of information. Nevertheless, information is for the system and can only be made sense of in terms generated by the system. Even information from outside of the system is sensible only in terms of the system itself (see DiMaggio and Powell 1983). Communication of information foreign to the system is by means of metaphor such that an event can be carried into a particular social realm. Repeated subsequent communication of the information within a system then tends towards structure, routine and habit so that it eventually loses its informational status. For Luhmann information is necessarily temporal and experimental.

Luhmann argues that social systems are operationally closed so that they may develop through an accumulation of communication, 'autopoietically', but open in the sense that information is a representation of environmental events for the social system. The selection of an event and its representation within the system, and so the rejection of other possible events as noise in the system's environment, is an action according to Luhmann. An actor selecting an event or an observation beyond the boundaries of the system, needs to represent this through the language of the system even if the event is largely foreign to it. An actor making selections of information and utterance can never be sure as to how others understand because, given the social system, that understanding is personal and opaque, yet communication is still made with reference to established rules. Information from outside the system, thus, has the potential to disrupt that system. As communication or action is social, others interpret utterances as a selection and presentation of an event allowing for understanding but also misunderstanding and confusion (Wittgenstein 1954). When in communication, even between actors from the same society, information from outside is introduced, the tuning of interpretations (Wittgenstein) is *not* self-evident. The vulnerability of the institutionalized communication system is perpetual. One needs, however, to acknowledge the role of agents as interpreting beings employing a language that is possibly fraught with ambiguity, certainly when information is introduced from beyond the boundaries of a community or system.

There are three aspects of Luhmann's discussion of communication that can help us draw together an explanation of the vulnerable dimension of institutions. First, communication is dynamic and emerges in a mutually constitutive way with language, supporting a social system's increasing complexity (compare Leydesdorff 2006). Second, social systems come into being and survive through communication. Irrevocably, distinctions emerge between a social system and its environment as the social system necessarily establishes itself and its environment simultaneously. A social system thus entails a boundary. Third, communication is social, placing subjective or personal thinking within a social symbolic system (Chapter 4). The vulnerability or improbability of systems and the institutions that make for a system emphasized by Luhmann thus is intimately related to communication and language. As communication is only meaningful when it crosses system boundaries, it is likely to upset the stability of the receiving system. Communication 'upsetting' the system provokes a response that in turn affects the sending system.

Both Luhmann and Searle analyse social settings, so Searle's collective intentions and Luhmann's communication are similar analytically. However, Luhmann (1995) retains the human individual in the form of a 'psychic' or mentalist system distinct from the social system. Returning to our theme of the personal and the social, for instance as with the I- and we-intentions, and with habits and routines, there is a clear disjunction in Luhmann's argument between an individual's thinking or personal cognition and the social system's communication, which is mediated by the social system's boundary. Agency and (mis-)interpretation, pointing to the vulnerability of institutions and institutional furniture, are thus introduced conceptually.

According to Luhmann social systems distinguish themselves from their environment *by virtue of* communication and so must have boundaries. Searle does argue that institutional structures connect with other structures 'vertically and horizontally' but he does not account for heterogeneity in the social realm. If the existence of separable social systems is not conceptualized, the arguably most important source for institutional change is denied. As Luhmann's systems necessarily exist within environments and thus have boundaries, vulnerability is permitted. Boundaries are simultaneously a signifier of systemic autarky and openness. A system cannot exist without other systems from which it is separated by means of boundaries. Any other system can only be represented in terms of that focal system (Leydesdorff 2006). Actors draw upon language to represent difference, or for that matter to ignore it, consigning it to *environmental* noise. Because communication is, therefore, about information selected for the system (society), by an actor, represented in a language, the communication by which the social system reproduces itself is necessarily always vulnerable as well as temporal and only then is it more or less durable in a way meaningful from the perspective of social science.

3.5 Re-identifying vulnerable institutions through change

O'Hara (2000) rightly emphasizes the incomplete and uncertain nature of the reproduction of institutions. Even when in many cases agents themselves will have no problem recognizing institutions even after spells of incomplete change, conceptually, re-identifying institutions through time and change is problematic. To our knowledge this is an under-represented area in the literature, although Feldman's (2003) studies of changing routines in an administrative setting is an exception. If institutions are durable or persistent, yet subject to change, how can institutions be recognized from one point in (real) time to another? Instructive inferences may be drawn from Davis's (2003) analysis of the conceptualization of the individual in economics. Davis establishes two tests: individuation (can individuals, and by extension in this chapter institutions, be distinguished?), and re-identification (can individuals, and also institutions, be re-identified over time?) It is clearly the re-identification test that is relevant for the purposes of analysing institutional durability.

Davis (2004) notes that in mathematics the mapping of transformations is conducted via fixed-point theorems of the general form such that each point x of a set X to a point $f(x)$ within X has a fixed point x^* that is transformed to itself:

$$f(x^*) = x^*. \tag{3.1}$$

Conceptually, this theorem is closely related to mainstream and game theoretic discourse in economics to demonstrate equilibrium as a particular and very strong form of durability. Furthermore, x^* is characterized reflexively: '... what would be unchanging about individual economic agents amidst change in other characteristics is their being able to take themselves as an object' (Davis, 2004, p. 3). With respect to our analysis of institutions, fixed-point theorems may have a direct bearing as they involve reflexivity on the part of individuals with regard to themselves as well as with regard to the institutions, which they perceive in shaping and facilitating senses (Davis and Klaes 2003; Leydesdorff 2006).

Drawing on Wittingstein's signpost analogy: signposts only guide an individual insofar as there is regular utilization of signposts, and only when others are involved who act upon the signposts as well and share an understanding of them. As Nelson and Winter (1982) suggest, institutions (routines) act as conduits of truce and knowledge. Institutions also provide bases for what may become shared understandings and senses of purpose and meaning (Douglas 1986).

For Searle (2005, p. 14), language provides recognition of institutions: '... a crucial function of language is in the recognition of the institution as such'. In recognition of one's inevitable embeddedness in an institutional and relational sense, taking oneself as an object means understanding institutions, however implicitly, in their general form. Searle (2005) has suggested as a general form for institutions:

$$X \textit{ counts as } Y \textit{ in } C \tag{3.2}$$

Here *X* are certain features of an object, entity, person or state of affairs; *Y* assigns a status function (to *X*) carrying a deontology in context *C* (compare Lawson 1997, p. 162). Crucially, taking oneself to be an object is necessarily reflexive and unequivocally involves the use of language. Language as the fundamental institution furnishes symbolic representation that is essential for institutional recognition and reproduction, and therefore for re-identification of institutions through change. However, the actor understanding an institution, behaving in accordance to it and reproducing it (incompletely) is not a part of Searle's definition. There is, as argued above, inevitably a measure of freedom involved for each individual in interpreting what an institution requires them to do: individual *H* evaluates or judges *X*, *Y* as well as *C*. Some properties of the elements may have changed (somewhat), while other elements, which by achieving stability over time become essential to that overall institution, must have retained their essential identities, at least according to *H* (O'Neill 1998).

For *H* to be able to function properly in a community, *H*'s understanding of *X*, *Y* and *C* must be shared with and by other participants, as individuals are of necessity part of a community (Bush 2007). Individuals' sharing and (thus) reproducing their understanding of an institution is bound up with language; it is a fundamental way of understanding the concept of an institution. A reformulation of Searle's general form can then be proposed:

> *According to H, understood and communicated in language L within a society or system S, X counts as Y in C* (3.3)

This understanding of institutions, importantly, allows one to incorporate a Weberian view of power and state power. (State) power, defined as when a community successfully claims a monopoly of the legitimate use of physical violence, is exerted primarily through a language *L* understood within a community and does not transfer beyond the boundaries of that community *S*. The reason for Weber's argument about power and state power is important is that it points to the need to single out individuals or groups of individuals within a larger community who may be able to exert an influence that others may not. It is important to acknowledge that a community is not a homogeneous grouping, and thus to single out *H* in equation (3.3).

To indicate the vulnerability of institutional reproduction, consider the institution of marriage. As an institution, marriage has been subject to radical change over the past century. People's understanding of the institution has changed dramatically, even when ceremonies demonstrate obvious temporal consistencies. Two people expressing promises to commit themselves to each other in front of an audience of witnesses at the behest of a person of authority, suitably attired, given her/his role, still constitutes a wedding ceremony in most cultures. However, much has changed in the understanding of marriage among people in most communities, even among those who have themselves been married for quite a prolonged period. The obligatory narrative has changed; arguably, especially in the west, the religious element has diminished; women, in general, appear to be less (economically) dependent within such a commitment; divorce is more readily available; co-habitation outwith, but resembling, the structure of marriage is more socially acceptable, and this is increasingly the case with same-sex partnerships.

In terms of Searle's logical sequence, *X*, a woman who is married, attains the status function of a wife, *Y*, but the context, *C*, has changed such that the deontic powers assigned to wives has altered, as a consequence of changing social values and economic conditions, which have changed aspects of the status function, *Y*, at least in legal terms. There is still durability of the institution of marriage, ensuring that it remains recognizable in behavioural propensities that have some coherence through time. There is a need to acknowledge explicitly and conceptually that *X*, *Y* and *C* are to be understood as such in a language *L* by an observer potentially communicating to other members of a community or society *S*. Without observers *H*, including but not limited to scholarly observers, there are no – to use Searle's own term – institutional facts. Perceptions are not integrated into Searle's view of an institution, giving his perspective of language an oddly positivistic flavour.

3.6 Concluding remarks

Institutions stabilize social as well as economic exchange. Searle has argued convincingly that language is the fundamental institution without which there would be no other institutions and without which no understanding of institutions would be possible. Searle does not emphasize the ambiguity in the use of language, however. He appears to assume that meanings do not differ between people and seems to exclude differences in interpretation and perception, especially of information sourced from outside a social system or society. Indeed, to Searle, the social system is conceptualized as one homogeneous system where symbolic boundaries, mediated by language broadly conceived, do not exist. As a result the durability as well as the change of institutions may be ill-understood.

A fruitful understanding of institutional durability and change would draw in part, as I argue, on the work of Luhmann on communication within systems or societies as well as across the boundaries that separate them. Language creates homogeneous groupings, institutionally mediated, separating an inside from an outside by constructing boundaries that may need to be actively maintained. Allowing for institutions to be durable *as well as* vulnerable, one is then obliged to reconsider Searle's generic formula for (re-)identifying them. In order to be able to re-identify institutions over time, his formula must be extended, essentially by contextualizing it.

4

Structure, Agency and the Role of Values in Processes of Institutional Change[1]

Research on institutional change has flourished ever since the debate on agency and structure moved away from the previously uncompromising positions which emphasized *either* agency *or* structure. A conceptual compromise is sought here in a focus on the processes of institutionalization, which enables us to move beyond the idea that institutions are mere mental constructs or the point of view that behaviour is the mere reproduction of institutional patterns. Contributing to an understanding of the processes of institutional change, this chapter analyses institutional change as instigated by tensions triggered by discrepancies perceived by agents between concrete institutional settings and the socio-economic values they are expected to represent. The Social Value Nexus that is presented below introduces an emphasis on the perceived legitimacy of institutions. Describing (types of) tensions between socio-cultural values and institutional settings, the chapter explores the ways in which structure, agency and values interact in processes of institutional change.

The idea that institutions matter has become commonplace. This should not be taken to imply that widespread agreement exists in the social sciences or even within disciplines about the nature and the role of institutions. Following the process of differentiation between the social sciences in the nineteenth century, each discipline has seen its own theoretical development. In turn this has coloured disciplinary perspectives on institutions. Now that the notion of institutions is widely recognized as a foundational concept in social theory, and as an important subject of research in sociology, economics, history, politics, organizational theory and the like, constructing a holistic view proves a difficult task. The fact that, despite renewed attention to the institution concept,

Hodgson (2006) recently published an article with the title 'What are Institutions?' may be a case in point.

One important reason, I believe, for this disarray is the variety of perspectives on the 'polarity between the individual and the social' (Burman 1979, pp. 374–5), or between agency and structure. This issue concerns conflicting views on how social phenomena are to be studied and explained. The agency point of view explains social facts as rooted at the level of the individual, that is, an explanation is to be built from the (given) preferences, expectations and motives or behaviour of rationally acting individuals. It is argued that social phenomena are to be understood as the result of individual actions oriented towards the (expected) actions of others. This point of view was handsomely captured by Elster, when he claimed that 'there are no societies, only individuals who interact with each other' (1989, p. 248). Objecting that social phenomena cannot be reduced to the properties of the individual parts but ought to be studied within the social system in which they occur, adherents of the structural approach emphasize that society is a reality *sui generis*. Individual behaviour, interdependent and interwoven with the behaviour of others, unintentionally gives rise to structured regularities in processes that are relatively autonomous with regard to the intentions and preferences of individuals. As Durkheim observed: 'The first and fundamental rule is: Consider social facts as things' (Durkheim 1947 [1895], p. 14).

This chapter proceeds as follows. The setting for the agency-structure debate is briefly laid out in Section 4.1. There is no attempt here to embark on an exhaustive discussion of the vast literature on this central issue in the social sciences. Section 4.2 elaborates on the ways in which the concept of the institution is implicated in this discussion, introducing the notion of tension that is perceived by actors to exist between institutions and their legitimation in the socio-cultural values subscribed to by a society or community. Given that such tensions need to be activated to induce institutional change, the following section (4.3) argues the importance of the three constituent elements of order and institutions – interests, power and socio-cultural values – in this respect. Taking socio-cultural values and the legitimation these supply for institutional settings as the point of entry for our analysis of institutional change, Sections 4.4 and 4.5 explore the ways in which perceptions of tensions that arise between institutions, concrete practices and behaviour may be seen to produce such change. Section 4.6 discusses three types of tensions, drawing out the conditions for institutional change within our theoretical perspective, while Section 4.7 offers two exemplary cases.

4.1 Agency and structure

Given that opinions in the social sciences range from the view that structures or institutions 'determine' individual behaviour to the idea that social structures or institutions are the unplanned outcome of the interplay of individual behaviour, it is unsurprising that highly divergent explanations of institutions and institutional change abound. Prompted by a growing dissatisfaction with the unrealistic nature of the assumption that economic processes take place within a cognitive, motivational and institutional vacuum, from the 1970s onwards the notion that institutions should be incorporated into economic analysis gained support. With the rise of new institutional economics, built on the same foundations as orthodox economic theory, it is generally assumed that institutions are to be explained as the outcomes of purposeful actions by instrumentally-oriented individuals.

Even though sociologists emphasize that social action has a logic of its own, it would be a misrepresentation to suggest that the differences between economists and sociologists may be cast in terms of agency versus structure. The agency–structure issue also figured as a bone of contention between sociologists Durkheim and Weber. While Durkheim (1947[1895], 1964[1893]) developed a structural (collectivistic) approach and referred to sociology as the theory of institutions, Weber (1964[1922]) adopted an individualistic perspective, arguing that sociology is about meaningful action, and hence individual action, as only individuals can give meaning to action.

The same issue divides old and new institutionalism in economics. New institutional economics sets the stage for analysis by assuming that institutions emerge from the interactions of cost minimizing agents within a set context of institutions designed such that societally optimal outcomes result. Structure and agency thus having been predefined, the emergence of different types of economic institutions is explained in terms of different characteristics of transactions. Notwithstanding the behavioural and situational amendments required to incorporate institutional arrangements into economic analysis, the agency-based neoclassical explanation has remained intact. Presented as solutions to problems of organization, institutions are seen to enhance efficiency, improve predictability and reduce uncertainty, imposing barriers or constraints on behaviour that affect the range of options open to the individual.

Adherents of evolutionary/institutional economics, in which the research programme(s) of institutionalists such as Veblen, Commons, Mitchell and Ayres have been revived, emphasize the role in economic decision-making of pre-existing habits and rules, values and cognitive frames and typically argue that the individual does not take decisions in isolation, but that decisions are pre-defined by the social context in which the agent finds him or herself. Institutions have emergent properties that cannot be explained with reference to individual attributes or motives.

The same difference in explanatory perspective surfaces if views on institutional change are compared. Veblen's account of institutional change as the result of the dynamics of technological change offers an example of a structural approach. An opposite view has been developed by North (1990), who identifies changes in relative prices and changes in preferences as major sources of institutional change driving political or economic entrepreneurs to actions that alter the institutional framework.

In view of this, Hay and Wincott (1998, p. 951) have argued that 'if institutionalism is to develop to its full potential, it must consider the relation between structure and agency'. As long as the structure–agency struggle continues, mainstream economics seems content to await future developments, meanwhile practising an agency-based perspective. Williamson, for instance, has shown in a number of papers (1993, 1998, 2000) his growing awareness of the importance and influence of sociological factors such as values, norms and legal rules on the selection of (governance) structures, but he has assigned the task of analysing and explaining this environment to other social sciences, boldly asserting that the insights from other social sciences may be fitted into his framework.

While mainstream economics seemingly contents itself with an agency-based perspective (compare Davis 2003), the institutional approach has taken up the challenge, tending to a central position between the extremes of either agent or structure, instead emphasizing their interactive relationship. As Lawson (1987, p. 969) put it: 'individual agency and social structure and context are equally relevant for analysis – each presupposes each other. Thus any reductionist account stressing analytical primacy for either individual agents or for social "wholes" must be inadequate.' The same point is made by Hodgson (1988).

4.2 Institutions

This, however, is easier said than done; contributions to the structure–agency debate can often inhibit possibilities of giving substance to the idea of institutional change or the issue can come to resemble a sequence of Russian dolls in the sense that contributions to the theory of institutional change tend to reproduce the agency–structure debate at a different level of aggregation.

To overcome the shortcomings of polar views which take either the individual/agent or society/structure as their point of departure, Giddens developed his critical theory of structuration. Central to structuration theory is the concept of 'duality of structure' or the notion that agency and structure are to be considered as inextricably interwoven. Interacting agents use the rules and resources that make up structures, and in doing so, they produce and reproduce such structures. 'The constitution of agents and structures are not two independently given sets of phenomena, a dualism, but represent a duality ... the structural properties of social systems are both medium and outcome of the practices they recursively organize' (Giddens, 1984, pp. 25–6). Structure, rules, resources and roles only exist in the day to day routines of people (Jackson 2005), while interaction between agents is framed by the rules and resources that make up structures. According to Giddens, these are recurrent social practices where individual and society meet and in which both are constituted.

In Archer's opinion, Giddens fails in his attempt to describe the interactive relationship between agency and structure. In the individualistic perspective, structure is reduced to agency while the structural approach reduces agency to structure. Giddens, in Archer's estimation, fails because structuration theory 'deprives both elements of their relative autonomy, not through reducing one to the other, but by compacting the two together inseparably' (Archer 1988, p. 688). If Archer is right, the problem with Giddens's theory is that, structure and agency being inseparable, one cannot conceptualize institutional change in terms of *interactions* between structure and agency.

Moreover, if not compacted, attempts at bridging agency and structure tend to assume the compatibility of agency and structure. Such compatibility is said to imply that institutions are ontologically indistinct from behaviour in the sense that *institutions are merely mental constructs, which have no ontological status apart from behaviour.*

Thus, for example, Neale (1987, p. 1184) claimed 'An institution is a mental construct ... the components of an institution may be observed, but an institution itself cannot be observed as a whole. Rather, what one can observe are the activities of people in situations.' A similar stance is taken by Sjöstrand (1993, p. 9) who defined an institution as 'a human mental construct for a coherent system of shared (enforced) norms that regulate individual interactions in recurrent situations ... institutions are not objective phenomena but mental constructions of human beings in their (inter)actions' (compare Nelson and Sampat 2001).

A second view suggests that *behaviour is the reproduction of institutional patterns*. For example, in Parsons's structural functionalistic approach, society is taken as an organic whole comprised of interdependent, functional parts, each contributing to the maintenance and integration of society. Stability and cohesion, based on a consensus of values and norms within which individuals are socialized through institutional arrangements, are taken as characteristic of the normal condition of the social system. Reasoning from this social system perspective, Parsons (1951) and Parsons and Shil (1951) argued that human actions are embedded in an institutional system and therefore follow patterns in accordance with norms directed at the preservation of that order. Social order may be said to be secured to the extent that those actions are institutionalized, that is, sanctioned by the social system and internalized by individuals. This institutionalized system of norms is an expression of the consensus about what is just, good and desirable (values). Ultimately in Parsons's conception, it is the common value system, the normative structure of society, that makes social order possible. Parsons's model has been criticized for assuming a common framework of shared values and norms and for its 'oversocialized conception of man' (Wrong 1961).

A third position is one in which *some (sequential) combination of these two possibilities is postulated*. In *The Social Construction of Reality* (1966) Berger and Luckmann, for example, argue that institutions are the product of a dynamic (or dialectic) process in which interactions between actors become habitualized and patterned when expectations and interpretations of behaviour become generalized through negotiations. These evolving patterns in human interactions develop into templates for action and actor which makes it unnecessary to define each situation anew and, in limiting choice, provide stability and predictability. In this process the objectivity of institutional arrangements 'hardens' as individuals internalize these objective social realities, take them for granted and recreate them in their ongoing interactions.

Defining institutions as 'systems of established and prevalent social rules that structure social interactions', Hodgson (2006, p. 2) criticizes attempts to define institutions as mental constructs that have no ontological status separate from behaviour. They are misleading in suggesting 'that institutions no longer existed if their associated behaviours were interrupted' (ibid., p. 3), even though some frequency in behaviour is likely to be required and institutions are only observable through manifest behaviour. Wilson (2006) further explains that the definition of institutions as behaviours is the legacy of the positivist twist in institutionalism to operationalize allegedly unscientific concepts by reducing unobservables such as motives and values into empirically manifest behaviour.

In this chapter, I also draw attention to another line of criticism. The problem with defining institutions in terms of behaviour, I submit, is that it predefines the nature of institutional change. If behaviour is the reproduction of institutions, institutional change takes place at the level of the institution, driven by autonomous or exogenous processes, such as population growth or technological progress, inducing behavioural responses to a changing environment. If, on the other hand, institutions are merely mental constructs, institutional change is seen to result from the changing preferences and/or expectations of individuals. This way the nature of institutional change is conditioned by the concept of institutions and the agency–structure debate is reproduced at a different level of aggregation. Only if institutions are seen as distinct from behaviour, can both structure and agency properly be said to induce change. For the true hallmark of a solution to the structure–agency issue is that '[i]nstitutions mold, and are molded by, human action' (Hodgson 1998, p. 20). Even if it is recognized that a theory of institutional change requires an adequate concept of the individual as well as of an institution, contributions are often seriously unbalanced; some are strong on institutions (as socially-embedded systems of rules) at the same time as they are weak on the concept of the individual (stimulus-response model or habit/instinct psychology).

In our view, thus, institutions are irreducible to behaviour. The irreducibility of both institutions and behaviour to one another implies the possibilities of *tensions*. These tensions are permanently potential as discrepancies between what is prescribed by institutions – possibly in specific situations where a number of institutions come together in a practice[2] – and what individual agents may aspire to. John Rawls's (1955, p. 3) definition of practice is in line with Veblen's (1961, p. 236) concept of institutional furniture and naturally leads one to reject an argument that starts from a purported 'state of nature', that is, an institutional void (Hamilton 1932; compare Hayden 1988). Even though institutions allow for amendments – Hamilton's zone of tolerance – there is likely to be some friction between an institution and its specification or manifestation in a specific practice where agents 'live', as Veblen has it, and can exert an influence.

4.3 Social order and change

The bigger question thus is: what triggers tensions to become manifest and potentially induce institutional change? I submit that institutional change or *transformation*, as distinct from institutional continuity, necessitates some intervening phenomenon, which interferes with what would otherwise be the continuous (and perhaps unintentional) *reproduction* of institutions. In the literature, three models of social order – and, by implication, of disorder – can be distinguished. Each model has its own perspective on what constitutes and changes order and thus represents such a intervening phenomenon.

(1) A *conflict* or *coercion model of society* has developed from Hobbes's argument that given man's egoistic inclinations and struggle for eminence, order is to be maintained by the state's exercise of power. In the elaboration of this model by Marx, Weber and Dahrendorf order is seen as a precarious equilibrium of *relations of power* between status groups.

(2) In the *consensus model*, inspired by Comte and Durkheim, society is taken as an organic whole comprised of interdependent, functional parts, each contributing to the maintenance and integration of society. Stability and cohesion, based on a consensus on values and norms within which individuals are socialized through institutional arrangements, are taken as characteristic of the normal condition of the social system.

(3) The *exchange* or *cooperation model*, which originates in the work of Locke and Smith, understands society as a competitive network of exchange (market) relations between individuals, through which individual interests unintentionally are harmonized with the general interest and order is tentatively and unintentionally brought about. In summary, a number of differences in views on order can be discerned (Table 4.1).

These perspectives may be distinguished according to the primacy of either norms and values, coercion, or interests as the constituent element

Table 4.1 Models of social order

	Model of social order	**Order generating institution**	**Primary bond of social order**	**Source of rules**	**Model of man**
Hobbes	Conflict	State	Political	Power	*Homo lupus*
Smith	Cooperation	Market	Socio-economic	Interests	*Homo economicus*
Comte/ Durkheim	Consensus	Society/ community	Cognitive	Values/ norms	*Homo sociologicus*

of order. Each model, moreover, has developed a compatible model of man and consequently tends to emphasize its conceptual consistency. However, this emphasis on consistency has narrowed down the scope of each model in studying institutional change. As such they present a clear example of the way in which the adequacy of the concepts of structure and agency has been decided on the model's internal consistency rather than on its potency to explain institutional change. However, as Cohen (1968, p. 32) reminds us: 'All social order rests on a combination of coercion, interest and values.'

4.4 The process of institutional change

The irreducibility of institutions and behaviour shows itself in tensions that – in potential – permanently exist between institutions and practices and the behaviour and perceptions of individual agents. I have argued in the previous paragraph that these tensions become manifest when triggered by a change in the constellation of the elements of order: values, interests and power. Here, following Hayden (1982, 1988) in important respects, I will focus on 'socio-cultural values' as potentially intervening phenomena that may expose 'tensions' between institutions and the valuations by specific individuals or players involved in ongoing activity (in a practice), thereby triggering a process of institutional change. To catch this aspect of processes of institutional change, I submit the 'Social Value Nexus' (Figure 4.1).

Following the process of specialization between the social sciences in which the exchange model became the frame of reference, economics has almost exclusively focused attention on the element of interest. In this model of rational choice and (self-)interest, it is assumed that, given alternatives, the economic agent will opt for whichever course

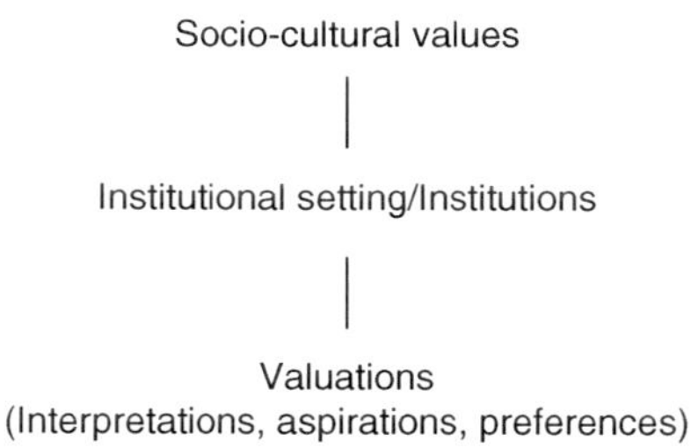

Figure 4.1 The Social Value Nexus
Source: Dolfsma (2004).

of action might be expected best to serve his or her interest, given the agent's preferences and perception of the relevant situational constraints. Institutions and rules within this model are seen as choice-constraining factors. Values, if recognized at all, are seen as embodied in institutional arrangements, and are thus part of the situational constraints. Attention then focuses on the valuations of economic agents aiming to maximize satisfaction; the workings of institutions are only noticeable through demand and supply interactions, and ultimately in prices, thus generating the parameters of choice.

However well suited to explaining market processes, clearly this is a very limited perspective in terms of extending an understanding of institutional change. A more encompassing perspective requires that the examination of processes of change include elements of values and power, or, at least that values and power are not pinned down within parameters of choice, but that it is recognized that they influence and are influenced in these processes (compare Hayden 1982, 1988).

Focusing on the element of values, the first thing to note is that processes of institutional change are conceptually imbued with issues of legitimacy or sense-making and interpretation (compare Berger and Luckman 1966; Scott 1995; Zilber 2004). Besides the question of *how* people behave, the *why*-issue is an essential element of any theory of institutional change (Ullmann-Margalit 1977). Being reflexive, people's perception of their own behaviour is implicated in how they behave.[3] Meanings and actions are mutually constitutive and intimately associated. Institutions build upon socio-cultural values in the sense that such values are 'translated' into or applied to (a constellation of) them. The socio-cultural values are implicitly or explicitly referred to when agents try to understand, act according to, and legitimize institutions. A translation from socio-cultural values to institutions is a tentative process, and instantiation of abstract values to a specific problem situation develops gradually as increasingly standard responses become points of reference in individual decision-making. Institutions emerge or change with reference to socio-cultural values which give them their legitimacy and ensure that they are adhered to by individuals. In trying to make sense of what happens in our surroundings, in attempting to understand why others do certain things, in making decisions about what to do ourselves, I thus invoke what might be called socio-cultural values (Hofstede 1980; Inglehart 1990; Kluckhohn 1962 [1951]). As Rokeach (1979, p. 50) observed '[socio-cultural] values are socially shared cognitive representations of institutional goals and demands'. Socially shared conceptions of 'the desirable' are learned by individuals who are subject to the external and internal 'forces' of socialization on the one hand, and imitation, or the urge to belong to a particular group of people on the other (Rokeach 1979, p. 48). Hayden (1988, p. 416, italics in original) defines values as 'cultural *criteria* or evaluative standards for judgment with regard to what is ideal'.[4] An institutional practice lacking a firm normative foundation in shared socio-cultural values will be perceived as empty and may soon be abandoned. As such, the concept of socio-cultural values is not simply a subjective notion (compare Hitlin and Piliavin 2004). At the same time, however, values do not strictly determine behaviour either (ibid.) The Social Value Nexus shown in Figure 4.1 indicates that people make sense of a constellation of specific institutions (a practice) and the socio-cultural values that provide legitimation for them.

There is considerable confusion concerning the term 'value'. Value is a central notion in ethics; economists equate it with 'price', and some other scientists think of normative science when the word 'value' is used. A distinction between socio-cultural values on the one hand, and *valuations*, on the other, seems necessary. Socio-cultural values denote strong underlying convictions that are held by many people in a group or in society, consciously as well as unconsciously, most of which would be considered to be of an ethical, cultural or philosophical nature. These include matters of justice, beauty, love, freedom of will, autonomy, rightful ways of government and governance, social standing and behaviour and personal identity (see, among others, Campbell 1987; Cowen 1998; Dolfsma 2004, chapter 9). The socio-cultural values that 'live' in a society or community, and are expressed in its institutional settings, may change over time (Inglehart 1990), but are likely to be persistent (Hofstede 1980; Campbell 1987). The socio-cultural values shared in a community point to the kind of things that one can (is socially allowed to) aspire to; they point to widespread preferences and the direction in which society in general moves (Kluckhohn 1951). Valuations, on the other hand, denote the meanings or importance that individuals as individuals ascribe to particular situations, behaviour or goods (Zilber 2004; Dolfsma 2004).

The distinction between socio-cultural values and valuations is rooted in institutional (economic) theory and (economic) sociology. Durkheim, Weber and Parsons, for instance, argued that norms, ideals and ultimate ends should be considered if a social scientist is to understand society and the economy (see Beckert 2002; Davis 2003; Bush 1987; Neale 1987). Valuations, including people's aspirations and preferences, take place in institutional settings or situations that are instantiations of socio-cultural values (Bush 2008; Zelizer 1985, 1979, 1997; Tool 1991). The way in which valuations are expressed differs between different institutional

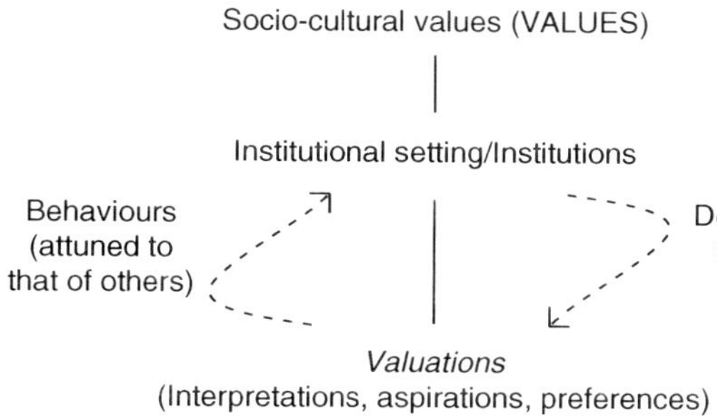

Figure 4.2 The agent in the Social Value Nexus

settings where (possibly) different socio-cultural values are expressed (see, for example, Wildavsky 1987). As much of the actions of agents does not actively question or inadvertently create tensions for existing institutional furniture, research can in many cases focus on the interactions within a given 'actor constellation' or institutional furniture drawing on specific socio-cultural values (Scharpf 1997). Figure 4.2 presents the argument that valuation, aspirations and behaviour need to be understood in the context of locally institutionalized expressions of socio-cultural values deeply rooted in a society or community as understood by agents.

4.5 The agent in institutional change

Many have contributed to the theory of institutional change, although not all of these would acknowledge the role that I suggest here is played by socio-cultural values (Scott 1995; Hodgson 1993; North 1990; Boulding 1956; Wrenn 2006). It would appear that the antecedents and underlying goals of institutional change, rather than the process of institutional change, have most often been emphasized (compare Bush 1987). I submit that analysing the processes of institutional change necessitates an understanding of individuals as agents who interpret and assess their situation, consisting of institutions rooted in socio-cultural values, forming valuations (aspirations, preferences) on which they act. By equating institutions to 'normal behavior', following Neale (1987), Hayden (1988, p. 419) is ill-equipped to focus on (processes of) institutional change or the role of agents. Hayden (ibid., p. 421) emphasizes, for instance, that 'attitudes originate from outside of the individual'. Of an element in his 'Social Fabric Matrix' that could be perceived as pertaining to the agent's beliefs, Hayden (ibid., p. 422) says that they 'are determinants rather than components of attitudes'. In contrast to this, I have argued that agency may be evident in a number of different ways. Agents can exert their autonomy in relation to an existing institutional environment by (1) opting for a particular instantiation of values in one of a number of different specific institutional settings (institutional furniture, practice) – possibly exiting from others, (2) interpreting and seeking the boundaries for acceptable behaviour within an existing institutional setting,[5] or (3) erecting an alternative institutional setting for a given practice, as is typically done by institutional entrepreneurs. Most pertinently, however, agency may be evidenced by (4) changing an *existing* institutional setting.[6] As Hays (1994, p. 69) has argued, however, 'most agency is reproductive of social structure', even when 'reproduction is never automatic' (Sewell 1992, p.19).

Perspectives that emphasize structure typically argue that institutions define the situation to which the individual reacts as well as the appropriate behavioural responses to that situation. Hayden (1982, 1988), while overlapping with the discussion staged here, seems closely aligned with a perspective emphasizing structure. Perspectives departing from agency, on the other hand, tend to emphasize that (institutional) regularities in behaviour develop as a result of people, for pragmatic reasons, tending to attune their behaviour to one another. Both perspectives amount to the same insight if it is assumed that there is a perfect match between people's valuations and the instantiated values incorporated in an institutional setting. Figure 4.2 allows for the possibility that these valuations do not coincide with embodied socio-cultural values and shows how both perspectives are complementary in focusing on the process of institutional change. Such a focus allows for agency not just to exploit the 'zone of tolerance' (Hamilton 1932) or partly open scripts that existing institutions offer, but also to seek to change existing institutions.

Based on socio-cultural values and the institutional setting of a particular practice, people have expectations about the performance of institutional structures. Such a performance is the material outcome of the ways in which socio-cultural values, within a particular constellation of relations of power and interests, are translated into a practice. It is here that the individual becomes aware that tensions exist: the performance of a practice does not live up to expectations because valuations of this material outcome to the individual are felt to be incongruous with (1) the general socio-cultural values or (2) the (change of the) way these socio-cultural values have been instantiated in a practice. The framework presented is not deterministic. Socio-cultural values and the constellation of power and interests within which they function stand in an interactive relationship with the institutional setting they produce. In turn they are themselves affected by the institutional setting. Change can and does go in both directions. The relation between institutions and socio-cultural values may change, questioning the legitimacy of institutions. Implicitly or explicitly, the *perception* by the individual of a *tension* between an institutional setting and the socio-cultural values it refers to triggers a process of institutional change (compare Wildavsky 1987; Dolfsma 2004). To some extent disparities will always occur; in may cases they will result from personal circumstances. If an agent aims at changing an existing institutional setting or practice not only does the agent have (1) to resist the pressure to conform, but also (2) he or she will have to relate to the shared understanding of that setting in order to indicate a tension, as well as (3) persuading others that the setting needs to be changed. An agent will need to act in situations in a way that is recognizable to others. An existing institutional setting allows others to understand divergence from particular institutions. It also allows them to perceive of, understand and conceive new institutions.[7]

4.6 Triggers and tensions: tracking the process of institutional change

Institutions are not mere mental constructs nor is behaviour simply the mindless reproduction of institutional patterns. Such an understanding implies the irreducibility of institutions and behaviour to one or the other. In the previous sections the notion of 'tension' emerged as a possible solution to the understanding of institutional change. From the three order-generating mechanisms of interests, power and socio-cultural values, I place relatively more emphasis on the latter as the Social Value Nexus indicates.

As Figure 4.2 shows, if tensions become manifest, agents come to perceive a disparity between the ways in which institutions define a situation and the behaviour of agents in that practice. Resisting the pressure to conform, agents may attempt to change an existing practice. The concrete form of the process of institutional change may be said to depend on the origin of the tensions involved. Taking these tensions from the perspective of socio-cultural values and valuations as the point of entry for our analysis, I identify three (ideal) types of tensions, each becoming manifest in disparities between instantiated values within an institutional setting or practice and the valuations of individuals. Fully aware that our theoretical account requires further elaboration by including interests and power, I believe that our initial analysis allows us to gain a deeper understanding of the process of institutional change and the way agency and structure interact in this process. These three types of tension are:

A. Value tensions,
B. Institution tensions, and
C. Value-institution tensions.

It is, notably, individuals who perceive the tensions and who can act on them, as the pragmatist philosopher John Dewey (1996 [1916], p. 346, italics in original) also argues:[8]

> Every *new* idea, every conception of things differing from that authorized by current belief, must have its origin in an individual. New ideas are doubtless always sprouting, but a society governed by custom does not encourage their development. On the contrary, it tends to suppress them, just because they are deviations from what is current. The man who looks at things differently from others is in such a community a suspect character ...

Individuals can change institutional settings only when the tension perceived is shared in a community, and an alternative institutional setting proposed is believed sufficiently justified by reference to (some of the) socio-cultural values subscribed to by the community.

Rather than extensively reviewing the literature on institutional change, I thus submit a proposal for understanding institutional change, obviously drawing substantially on institutional economic literature (Bush 1987, 2008; Hodgson 2006; Neale 1987). I will discuss these different tensions, and the types of institutional changes to which they give rise. In Section 4.7 I elaborate on specific examples of institutional change.

(A) Value tensions

At any given moment, socio-cultural values (V) existing in a community associated with differing institutional settings (I) may come into conflict with a different set of socio-cultural values (V′) that (some) members of the community believe should (also) be reflected in the practice. This gives rise to value tensions. If it appears to a community that increasingly conflicting socio-cultural values are alluded to in a practice, V and V′ may be perceived to come into sharp contrast, setting off a process

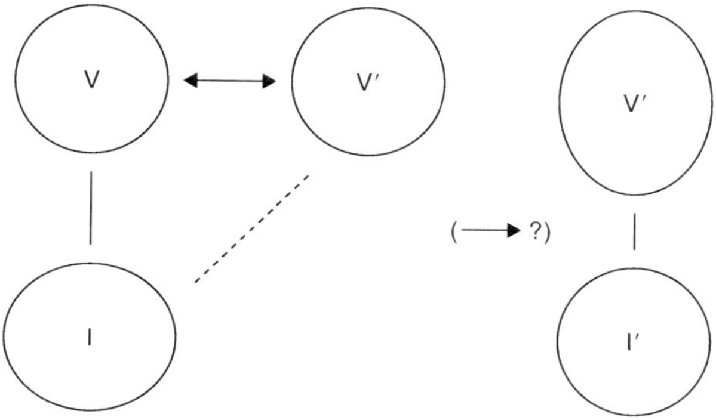

Figure 4.3 Institutional change and type (A) tensions

of institutional change intended to resolve this value tension by forming institutional setting I′ for that particular practice to reflect the new socio-cultural values associated with it. As suggested by Bush's (1987) principle of minimal dislocation, a return to the V – I situation is also possible, while elements from V or from I may be incorporated into a new constellation V′ – I′ as well. Figure 4.3 visualizes this.

(B) Institution tensions

Institution tensions arise when related institutions or institutional settings that build, albeit differently, on the same socio-cultural values come into conflict or such a conflict is perceived to arise, inducing pressure for institutional change. While in this case socio-cultural values are neither at issue nor questioned, a process of institutional change is triggered when the legitimacy of an alternative practice has gained support to the effect that the conventional practice is no longer perceived to be self-evident and is 'reconstructed' to abate tensions – see Figure 4.4. It would seem likely that I′ will supplant I.

(C) Value-institution tensions

An institutional 'furniture' I, originating in a particular (combination of) socio-cultural values V, may drift away in the course of time from these values (V–I to V′–I′; arrow 1 in Figure 4.5). Over time institutions may be adjusted to and come to represent other socio-cultural values. They come to be re-valued (Böröcz 1995). In this case, focusing on a particular practice, tension builds between the original socio-cultural values V, to which some agents immersed in the practice (I) as well as some outsiders

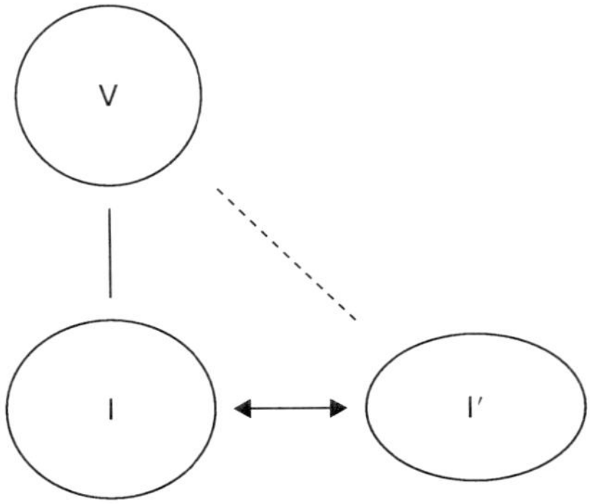

Figure 4.4 Institutional change and type (B) tensions

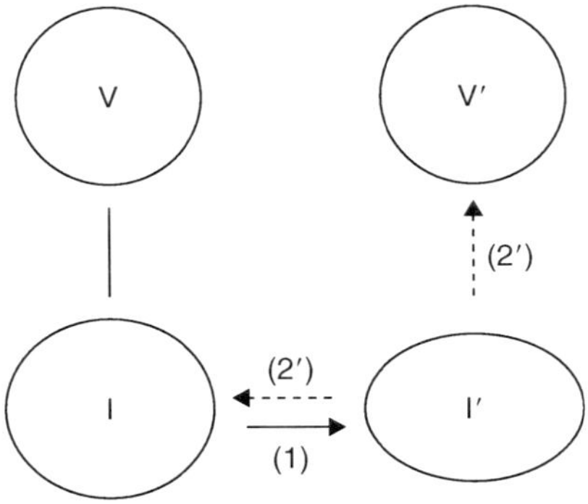

Figure 4.5 Institutional change and type (C) tensions

still refer, and the newly emerged institutional setting I′ building on V′ that others have in mind. Either such tension triggers a change of institutional practice to realign with V (arrow 2′), or a new set of socio-cultural values V′ will be subscribed to (arrow 2′), as indicated in Figure 4.5.

4.7 Two illustrations: rock music and health-care

In empirical research neither the three types of tensions presented above nor the institutional change that they provoke can be particularly easily distinguished. As the following illustrations show, however, identifying and tracking these types of tensions does enable an improvement in the understanding of processes of institutional change.

Rock music

Rock music is associated with highly modernist socio-cultural values such as novelty, speed, autonomy, independence, pleasure, success and youth (Frith 1996; Dolfsma 2004). Such values came to be associated with music in the 1950s. Until then, popular music, mainly big band and crooner music consumed through the radio and the music press, was taken to refer to a different set of socio-cultural values, including aesthetic values, order, authority and hierarchy. From the 1950s onwards tension built between V and V′, ultimately triggering institutional change from I to I′. Conventional values were challenged when selections of music by experts were rejected (authority), definitions of what constitutes 'taste' in music were called into question (aesthetic values) and experts were no longer accepted as representing the knowledgeable outsider standing above rather than being part of the peer group (hierarchy). The pressure involved in these tensions resulted in the rise of the 'chart'. Pirate radio stations, entrepreneurs in the magazine business, and presenters of radio programmes played a role in this, experimenting with different formats for charts. The chart is an example of a new institution that built on the newly emerging values, such as autonomy and novelty, within more democratic processes. In presenting music in the form of chart listings, the institutionalized role of the presenter changed too. The disc jockey (DJ), a peer of the listeners rather than the conventional figure of authority dictating proper tastes (Dolfsma 2004), arrived on the scene. A DJ talks over the intro of a song, he or she should not always talk 'properly' and should understand or use slang.

Charts seem objective rather than endorsing the tastes of a privileged group: music fans can express their agency autonomously, independent of older people or experts who want to teach the 'right' taste and manners. What the majority of people favour, rather than the choice of a single figure of authority, will be played on the radio. Hence, a process of institutional change started to resolve this value tension between V and V′ by forming an institutional setting I′ reflecting the new socio-cultural values associated with rock music.

There was some attempt to minimize institutional dislocation, most notably in the US by the Billboard company, even as institutions were moulded to conform with the socio-cultural values that were associated with rock music (V′). In compiling charts, Billboard pre-structured the information flow they were to receive from record stores on record sales. The 'chart position' set-up, for instance, pigeonholed music into specific categories (Kloosterman and Quispel 1990). It also only allowed record stores to fill in the number of records sold by artists, and only allowed sales figures for songs that Billboard had selected.

Anand and Peterson (2000) analyse the institutional changes introduced by a company called Soundscape, who brought in what they call a 'unit sales' system to compile record sales in the 1990s. The changes only related to the different ways in which charts were being compiled, which means that this is a pure case of institution tension. The socio-cultural values (V′) now related to rock music were uncontested; the conflict was between different ways to institutionalize the chart. Soundscape, aided by new technological developments that made the collection, storage and analysis of digital information easy and inexpensive, pioneered a new institutionalization for the chart. Songs were no longer pigeonholed, and sales figures were no longer collected only for songs from a list of records drafted by Billboard (I). Rather (I′) sales figures for all records on sale were included, and other sales, for example, those from supermarkets, were also taken into account. Socio-cultural values associated with the institution of the chart did not change. In its purity as an institution tension, this is a rare case, but the institutional changes do relate to the earlier attempts by players in the market to gain a measure of control by instituting the chart position set-up after the advent of rock music had seriously shaken the sector.[9] Anand and Peterson show that market institutions are important for participants to make sense of the market, creating a shared focus of attention, a 'market information regime'. The unit sales chart made direct comparisons across genres possible, strengthened the position of the larger record labels/companies (despite fears that their position would be hurt), and created opportunities for marketing departments to take advantage of market segmentation. In addition, country music came to be represented more strongly in the charts, while the charts themselves grew more volatile.

Health-care

Recent developments in European health-care systems present an example of type C tension. Most health-care systems in Europe are built upon the value of solidarity: health-care costs are shared by all in the community, even though there are great differences in the extent to which people make use of health-care services at any given moment in and across time (V). This translates into institutions, for instance, related to how the system of health-care is to be financed (I). Either the system is nationalized and finance is arranged centrally, as in the UK with its NHS (McMaster 2002), or regulation is such that a package of basic care services is available (mandatory) for all citizens at a given rate, as in Germany and the Netherlands (Grit and Dolfsma 2002).

Health-care systems across Europe and elsewhere are, however, under a lot of pressure. As a consequence of both the ongoing process of individualization whereby persons feel less strongly related to and responsible for others (family, neighbourhood, church, society) and a growing emphasis on individual responsibility and reciprocity, the legitimacy of solidarity-based health-care systems has weakened substantially. A different set of socio-cultural values, V′, is seen by a number of players as more attractive. Ever-increasing costs because of the rising number of elderly people among populations, consumerist sentiments expressed by well-informed and assertive clients, growing medical knowledge and expanding technical possibilities have created a widening gap between expectations of and demands on the health-care system and the limited and conditional nature of its supply. As a result of governments' need to control the budget for health-care expenditures, supply of health-care services has lagged behind people's expectations.

These pressures have led policymakers to instigate novel institutional settings. Activities that were formerly a responsibility of the system have been outsourced to the private (market) sphere or redefined as private responsibilities (Grit and Dolfsma 2002, 2007), as governments leave it to market players, such as insurance companies, to rearrange the system of health-care such that a system with 'managed competition' arises (Enthoven 1988; Cutler 2002). Moving the financial responsibility for the use of health-care services to the individual may be needed to prevent free-riding, but it is equally a threat to solidarity as a basis for the system as has existed for decades. By addressing people as 'knaves' one thereby undermines their 'knightly' (intrinsic) motives (Le Grand 2003; Frey 1997).

One example of a new institutional arrangement is the so-called personal care budget, an institutional arrangment (I′) inspired by market-like socio-cultural values (V′). Those with a long-term need for care are given a fixed sum of money each year that they can spend hiring care-givers. The criteria for eligibility for such a budget, the rules on spending it, and the rules on accounting for spending are elaborate (Van den Berg and Hassink 2008). However, 'informal' care-givers, such as grandparents, husbands and so on, see that they may as well be 'hired' to provide the same care that they gave free of charge before, and some make arrangements accordingly. Such individuals do of course sacrifice substantial amounts of time, effort and opportunities forgone by providing care for which others are paid. There is concern among professional care-givers who see this as a potential market that they can move into, and so they argue that the care they give is of better quality. At the same time, there is pressure on quality standards as professional care-givers compete with one another on a cost basis. As a consequence, regulations have been introduced to ensure the maintenance of standards; one result of this is that informal care-givers may have to gain some kind of qualifications in order to provide the care that was once a matter of affection or courtesy.

Still others choose to reduce their supply of informal or home care, believing it is not up to them to suffer the consequences of supplying informal care while the benefits accrue to unknown others in the system who may not be concerned about the public good (compare Le Grand 2003). The resulting scarcity puts strains on solidarity as a principle for structuring health-care. Attempts to save the solidarity-based (V) health-care system from collapse have induced a gradualist policy of downsizing and rationing, trying to minimize the dislocation in line with Bush's (1987) suggestion. Such developments have led to the introduction of new principles of allocation and distribution in health-care systems. This is more akin to I, but traditional boundaries between institutional settings (I as compared to I′) do become blurred. As, increasingly, institutions of type I′, inspired by such socio-cultural values as choice, individual responsibility and financial incentives along the lines of V′ were introduced, people came to feel the tension between the foundational value of solidarity still used to legitimize the health-care system and values embodied in the institutional practice of a market-based system.

The provision of health-care is thus increasingly fragmented into separate institutional furniture – public and private responsibilities, in the latter between different budgets that have their own rationales – each of which draws on different socio-cultural values (as visualized in Figure 4.5). Health-care systems have moved from solidarity-based systems (V–I) towards market-oriented systems based on competition and emphasizing individual interest and responsibility (V′–I′). Socio-cultural values underlying one part of the practice as reflected in the institutions are at odds with those of another part of the practice. Ostensibly, however, the socio-cultural values on which the system is founded are still largely those of solidarity, at least for many participants in the system and not just patients and health-care providers (Grit and Dolfsma 2002). Consequently, the attempts to introduce market institutions have been uneven (Grit and Dolfsma 2007). A shift towards an 'American'[10] system (I′) – with the emphasis placed on choice, freedom and accountability (V′) – at some point will be perceived by individuals to have caused a tension of type C. Either a new ground for legitimating institutions of health-care is sought (in V′), or the institutional setting moves back again from I′ to I. Since health-care is a large sector in the economy and central to society, the actions by players in dealing with these tensions are visible in just about any developed country and too numerous to discuss in full. I do submit, however, that they may be understood in terms of the framework suggested here.

4.8 Agency, institutional structure and the role of values

We proposed here to focus on the *process* of institutional change as a way of avoiding the uncompromising discussion of the structure–agency controversy. Even though individuals cannot escape institutions, behaviour is more than the mere reproduction of institutional patterns; nor are institutions merely mental constructs that change when behaviour changes. Because institutions and behaviour are irreducible to one another, tensions may exist that set off a process of institutional change. Such tensions can be triggered by changes in constellations of interests, power and values. Focusing on the role of (socio-cultural) values in processes of institutional change, I submit that a coherent set of institutions defining a practice or institutional furniture needs to be perceived by members of a community as being legitimate. The Social Value Nexus that I introduced explores the ways in which structure, agency and values interact in processes of institutional change, indicating how (three types of) tensions as perceived by agents in a given practice may arise. In the case of tension between extant institutional furniture and the socio-cultural values referred to for legitimation, individuals can attempt to change an institutional setting.

5
'Silent Trade' and the Supposed Continuum between OIE and NIE[1]

> The Carthaginians say also this that there is a place in Libya, and People living in it, beyond the Pillars of Heracles. When they, the Carthaginians, come there and disembark their cargo, they range it along the seashore and go back again to their boats and light a smoke signal. The natives, as soon as they see the smoke, come down to the shore and then deposit gold to pay for the merchandise and retreat again, away from the goods. The Carthaginians disembark and look; if they think that the price deposited is fair for the merchandise, they take it up and go home again. If not, they go back to their boats and sit there. The natives approach and bring gold in addition to what they have put there already, until such time as the Carthaginians are persuaded to accept what is offered. They say that thus neither party is ill-used; for the Carthaginians do not take the gold until they have the worth of their merchandise, nor do the natives touch the merchandise until the Carthaginians have taken the gold.
>
> (Herodotus 440 BC, book IV, §196)

> [In] the social No-Man's Land between societies, trade in [these] scarcities will often be embedded in ritual and familisticlike institutions.
>
> (Heider 1969, p. 469)

Original institutional economics (OIE) and new institutional economics (NIE) have differing positions on a number of issues. There is an ongoing discussion about the question of whether these categorically different positions (Hodgson 1988) are part of the same continuum (Rutherford

1994, 1995) or may even be reconciled (Groenewegen et al. 1995; Schmid 2004). These discussions tend to focus on methodological points of contention, and often draw heavily on the history of economic thought. I take a slightly different approach by analysing the phenomenon of 'silent trade' (ST).

New institutional economics (NIE) claims that silent trade exists. Indeed, it would constitute the first step 'as trade moves beyond the border of the village' (North 1991, pp. 98–9). In this brief chapter I show both that silent trade – trade between parties who have only the most minimal shared frame of reference without direct contact or form of communication – has never existed and that NIE cannot account for the representational redescription and change in governance structure that it entails. At least then on the issue of language and learning, NIE is categorically different from OIE.

ST is an ephemeral phenomenon that is referred to intermittently in the economic history literature (see Basu et al. 1987). Reference to Karl Polanyi's *Dahomey and the Slave Trade* (1966) is brought in as supportive evidence at times, but he too relies heavily on the Greek chronicler Herodotus. The theoretical possibility of silent trade and its supposed existence seem a central tenet of mainstream economics in general and NIE in particular, as Section 5.2 argues. Section 5.3 reviews the literature on ST and concludes that it has never existed in its pure form. Given that Searle (2005) has argued that language is the fundamental institution, our argument has implications for the way in which economics explains how 'trade moves beyond the border of the village', as well as for the way in which OIE and NIE relate to each other. Communication, thus, is not a fringe phenomenon, but rather a *sine qua non* for trade or exchange (Boulding 1981; McCloskey and Klamer 1995). Section 5.4 presents an empirically sound and theoretically more plausible explanation of how 'trade [did] move[s] beyond the border of the village'. This is the model of gift exchange, common in family and village settings.

5.1 Silent trade and NIE

Douglass North has persistently neglected the stage in economic development between that within a single village and that of a fully fledged economic system: 'gradually, trade expands beyond the village: first to the region, perhaps as a bazaar-like economy; then to longer distances, through particular caravan or shipping routes; and eventually to much of the world ... from local autarky to specialization and division of labor' (North 1991, pp. 98–9; see also North 1955). North denies that these steps are inevitable, or that growth is necessarily entailed; he also bypasses the issue of how these steps might actually have been taken. One of the early steps in the sequence will in this view have been ST. The possibility and effectiveness of ST is assumed, not only for expositional convenience, but also as a matter of theoretical consistency (compare Ankerloo and Palermo 2004; Williamson et al. 2007). In line with good NIE practice, Basu et al. (1987, p. 11) explicitly state that ST in its pure form existed, claiming it as socially optimal.

Silent trade is trade between two parties 'without the help of middlemen but also without speaking to one another, or coming face to face or even within sight of each other' (De Moraes Farias 1974, p. 9). Only a bare minimum of what Denzau and North (1994) call 'reasonably convergent (shared) mental models' between the trading partners from different societies exists. There is no prior intensive or mediated contact at hand.[2] The trade, as described most famously by Herodotus, takes place in the course of gradual adjustments of quantities arrived at through a sequence of alternating moves by the trading parties. At every alternate move the goods have to be left unguarded in a place accessible to the other party. The exchange is performed without immediate interaction by means of language or gesticulation. There is only signalling of the offering of exchange goods. Herodotus writes about the use of smoke and De Moraes Farias (1974, p. 11) and Bovill (1929, p. 29) about traders beating drums to inform locals that they have arrived to exchange.

In a potlatch among America's West Coast Indians, a major concern was to avoid being given a gift one could never reciprocate. Reciprocation was so important that to fail in it was, in effect, to be excommunicated from society (Mauss 2000 [1954]). Veblen (1899) would liken such behaviour to conspicuous consumption. Indeed, potlatch has been banned for some time as a wasteful activity.

NIE holds, of course, that the prices of goods and services are the result of impersonal forces of supply and demand, in a setting where agency does not play a role. In a competitive market structure prices are parameters. Competitive pressure will force individual players to hold similar beliefs and respond similarly to changing circumstances. Communication does not play any role: the responses are immediate (North 1996). Hence Williamson's dictum: 'in the beginning there were markets' (Williamson 1975, p. 20; Williamson 1985, p. 87). In this version of events, the commodities exchanged in silent trade were search goods whose characteristics were readily visible, whose use did not require an idiosyncratic investment by either party, and which did not involve future markets. The homogeneous good should be traded anonymously under classical contract law (Williamson 1985). No barter or even communication is needed. NIE can thus presume that ST is, at least theoretically, possible, and even likely to exist pervasively, its origins 'reach[ing] far back in history', as Karl Polanyi (1966) has it.

Yet, the strangers involved in ST have no prior knowledge of each other. As 'the threat of violence is a continuous force' in the 'absence of a state that enforces contracts' (North 1991, p. 99), so that 'safety of life and limb as well as property' (Polanyi 1966) cannot be assumed, how can they trade? The game is not obviously repeated and reputation effects are absent. Indeed, the parties involved are unknown to each other in a pure case of ST. Kin or armed forces for contract negotiation and enforcement, or for the development of standards (contra North 1991) do not enter the picture.

5.2 Searching for silent trade

The first account of the practice known as silent trade or silent barter comes from the works of Herodotus, who mentioned the trade between the Carthaginians and peoples of the west coast of Africa [Libya], beyond the Pillars of Heracles (Herodotus 440 BC: IV, §196).

Since Herodotus, quite a few accounts of silent trade have been published. Hamilton-Grierson (1904) collected reports of silent trade from ancient and modern writers in order to determine its existence. He drew on second- and third-hand reports of incidences of silent trade, but did not systematically analyse their accuracy, which would be required, however, if the existence of silent trade were to be proved (compare Herskovits 1940, p. 162).

Cosmas Indicopleustes (*c*. AD 550 [1897], pp. 52–4), the first merchant-writer (Laiou 2002, p. 694), gives the sole Byzantine account of ST, based on his own observations in combination with hearsay from other traders. Cosmas' (pp. 52–3) account deviates from that of Herodotus in that he reports a degree of face–to-face contact:

> the traders make a halt at a certain spot and form an encampment, which they fence round with a great hedge of thorns. Within this they live, and having slaughtered the oxen, cut them in pieces, and lay the pieces on the top of the thorns, along with the lumps of salt and the iron. Then come the natives bringing gold in nuggets like peas [. . .] and lay one or two or more of these upon what pleases them – the pieces of flesh or the salt or the iron, and then they retire to some distance off. Then the owner of the meat approaches, and if he is satisfied he takes the gold away, and upon seeing this, its owner comes and takes the flesh or the salt or the iron.

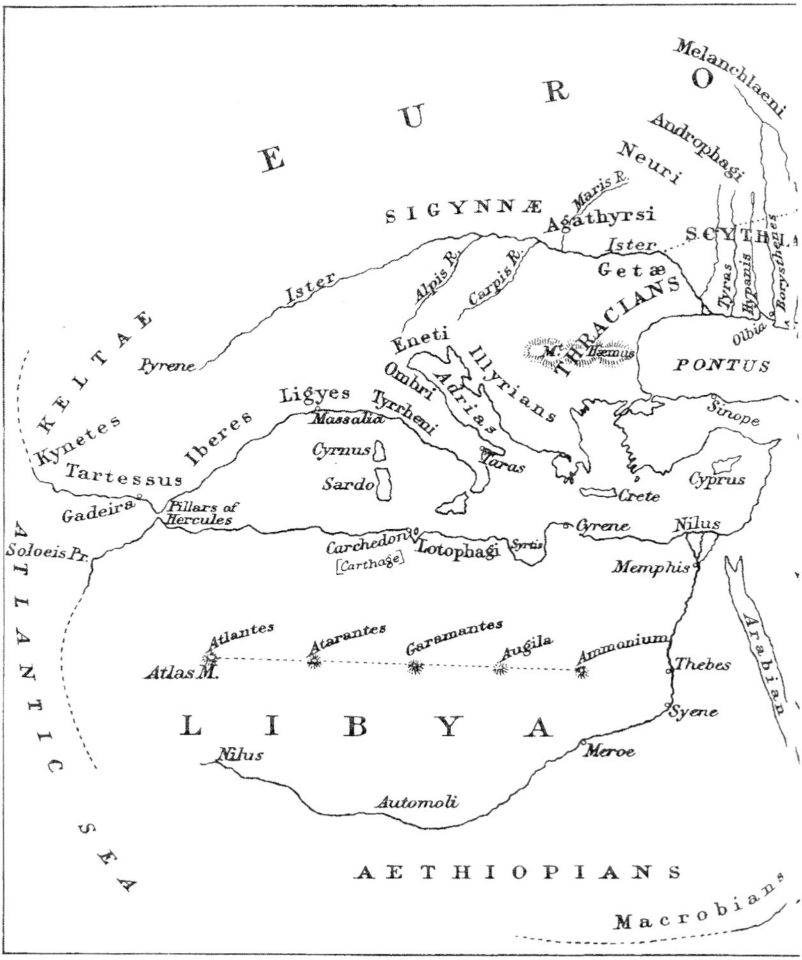

Figure 5.1 The world according to Herodotus, 440 BC
Source: Herodotus (pp. 294–5).

Cosmas and Herodotus are both vague about exact places, times and processes of bargaining.

Sundström (1965) analysed a number of (mainly) European accounts of trade without immediate intercourse. He finds that the romantic appeal of Herodotus' account has contributed to the perpetuation of the story. All accounts of silent trade analysed by Sundström are largely based on hearsay and are not ST in a genuine sense.

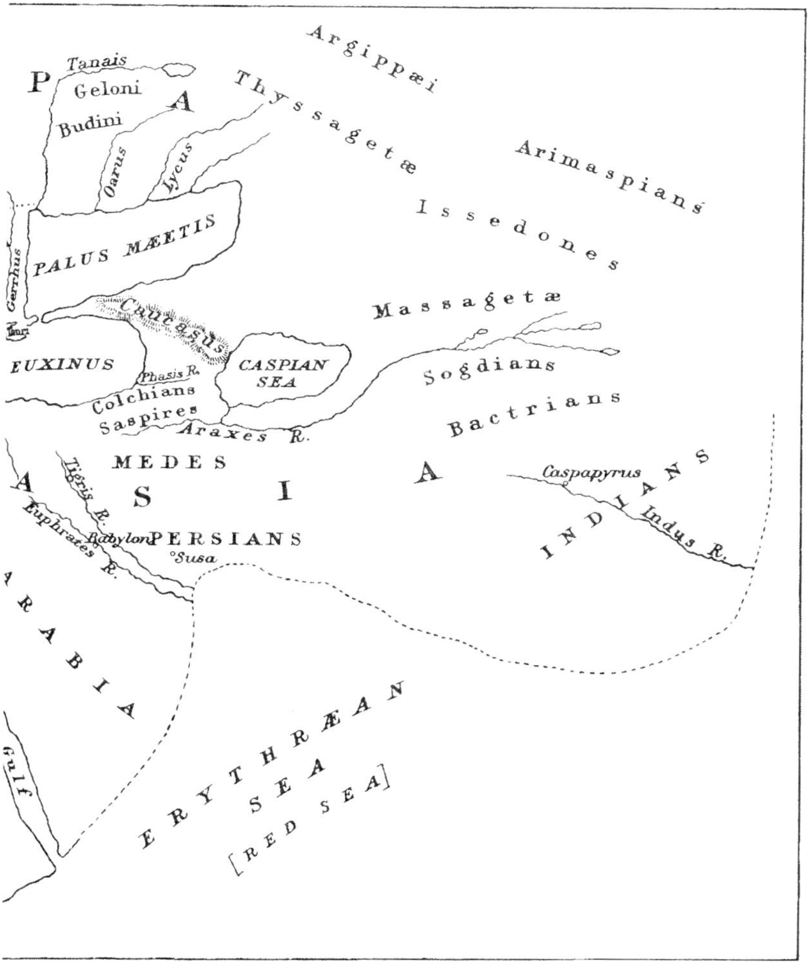

De Moraes Farias (1974) also examined the phenomenon of silent trade, closely studying available material, much of which was of Arab origin. His critique of those who believe that the phenomenon has indeed existed is sharp: 'accounts of silent trade in west Africa are a misleading combination of a mythical stereotype with concrete evidence about the traditional African trade-through-broker pattern of exchange' (De Moraes Farias 1974, p. 10; see also Harper 2004, p. 57). Many incidences of trade are described wrongly as silent trade. For example, the thirteenth-century account of Yāqūt, often portrayed as silent trade, is analysed in depth by De Moraes Farias who finds that the trade is not silent, but involves third-party mediation. The quality of the merchandise is determined by outsiders to the trade. Yāqūt's account does not fit the definition of ST: rather a broker-system is superimposed on its reality.[3] Even the closely analysed and fairly detailed narrative of the expeditions of Alvise Cadamosto in 1455–56, supposedly engaging in ST, remains vague in relation to geographical locations and times of presumed ST (De Moraes Farias 1974, p. 13). De Moraes Farias suggests that the evidence for the existence of silent trade is even weaker than Sundström had realized. Indeed, Garrard (1982) is adamant – after carefully weighing the evidence and giving the truth of Herodotus' story every possible opportunity – in his conclusion that the Carthaginians did not trade gold with peoples on Africa's west coast and that there was no trans-Saharan gold trade (Swanson 1975).

There is no proof for the existence of silent trade. Herodotus' account is unconfirmed and highly implausible. No first-hand report of *trade* between two parties that do not know each other, do not communicate meaningfully, have only the barest of shared institutions and only use a minimum of signals to attract each others' attention – pure ST – has ever been published. Silent trade may be dismissed as a real existent phenomenon.[4] However, to dismiss it theoretically as well, an additional argument is needed, one that would allow an explanation of what happens 'as trade moves beyond the border of the village'.

5.3 Trade, language and learning

Can there conceivably be trade without communication in a broad sense of the term? The existence of only minimal communicative common ground need not of course stand in the way of fruitful communication (compare Jordan and Fuller 1975), yet it would seem that 'as trade moves beyond the border of the village' people with fundamentally differing frames of reference will be obliged to relate to each other in such as way as to successfully interact. Not surprisingly, Harper (2004, p. 9) documents a number of attempts at ST that were unsuccessful. As language is the constitutional institution for all other institutions, including economic ones (Searle 2005, p. 12), interaction must draw on common understandings that can also change because of and through the use of language.

What does NIE have to say about language and learning? Denzau and North (1994) have taken up the issue of language and its implications for learning and institutional change. Their account is oddly split between sticking to the notions of equilibrium and information and learning of the Bayesian kind on the one hand, and on the other hand an acknowledgement that people will need to interpret their environments and that such interpretation can but need not be shared. Ideologies do diverge, as 'information feedback from [individuals'] choices is not sufficient to lead to convergence of competing interpretations of reality' (Denzau and North 1994, p. 4). Multiple equilibria are likely to result. Individuals' interpretation of their environment reflects their learning (p. 3) as well as the feedback they receive 'from the physical environment and those from the socio-linguistic environment' (p. 13), as each acquires a mental model over time (p. 11); equilibria, or 'reasonably convergent mental models', thus emerge. Language is seen as the means by which individuals achieve this convergence (p. 20), although the process by which this happens is left unspecified. Learning is inductive (p. 11), is perceived as irreversible (p. 8), but 'sudden shifts in viewpoint' (p. 14) are possible. Their degree of departure from the Bayesian idea of learning and information common in economics (compare Dolfsma 2008a) is difficult to ascertain.[5] Language, encoding and decoding, thus occurs in a social setting that individuals both need to understand and to be able successfully to relate to others about, and 'may be noisy and imperfect' (Denzau and North 1994, p. 19). These authors, however, do not pursue this issue but rather qualify it as a 'purely technical problem', suggesting that it relates to the 'patterns of activation in neural cells' (p. 19). Thus, while the potential for 'representational redescription' (p. 23) is acknowledged possibly to emerge 'endogenously' as a result of a 'lack of logical consistency' or a 'discovery of a new set of implications' (ibid., p. 25), Denzau and North do not see fit to investigate this further.

Is the frame of a market the most likely frame that people who are involved in ST will adopt? Why should observed trading behaviour be seen as haggling in a market? People will behave differently within the decision frame of a market from the way they would behave had they framed the situation in another way (Bowles 2007). Why would the 'common features' in the 'mental models' of 'the speaker and a listener' (Denzau and North 1994, p. 20) be that of a market? Exchange can be perceived in other than market terms. When trade expands beyond the village and it is not perceived as market exchange from the start, at some point 'representational redescription' occurs that will need to be explained in a way that gives an important role to language and learning at the level of social entities. NIE has not accomplished this.

5.4 Trading with family

What institutions may be drawn on in cases where strangers meet to exchange goods, what 'neutrality devices' may be found (Polanyi 1963)? As Alchian (1977, p. 133) argued, in the case of 'ignorance of availability of goods and their terms of trade and attributes ... several institutions have evolved to reduce costs of reducing that ignorance'. Money is one such institution, specialist middlemen constitute another, so, in Alchian's view, do unemployment and specialized marketplaces. All of these cannot be involved in what Polanyi (1966) calls 'dumb trade' – indeed, in a way, money is also a semantic system, similar to speech and writing, as Polanyi argues, requiring mutual recognition of a shared institutional furniture; its use also requires trust. What if there is no social structure that the use of money can solidify (Polanyi 1963)? What if Denzau and North's 'reasonably convergent (shared) mental models' have not yet emerged?

In such circumstances 'beyond and between social networks', as anthropologists and economic historians have suggested, the one institution 'between societies' is that of the family (Heider 1969; Herskovits 1940). Exchange then is not constructed as a quid pro quo market exchange, but as gift exchange (Hamilton-Grierson 1904; Heider 1969; Polanyi 1963; Boulding 1981): 'A primitive hunter evolves the idea that a man of another tribe has desirable things that may be more easily or simply obtained by peaceful than by violent methods; and as one good turn deserves another, the hunter places something tempting where the other man will find it, in the hope that it will be accepted *as a gift* and that the stranger will leave something of value in exchange' (Hamilton-Grierson 1904, p. 711, emphasis added).

According to Mauss (2000 [1954]), one needs to give, receive and reciprocate if one is to be and remain a member of society or if one is to establish new relations. Motives for the exchange of gifts are primarily social, where altruism may play a role; but self-interest, and a search for status and power are also involved in gift exchange (Mauss 2000 [1954]; Malinowski 1922). Gift exchange is ritualized such that the value of a gift is not articulated, but at the same time that the scales are not too far out of balance or for too long (Van der Eijk et al. 2009; Dolfsma 2008a). Failure to reciprocate a gift will reflect badly on a recipient, in effect excommunicating him. There is thus an obligation to return a gift, but it is not formally enforceable: 'Custom demands that the return gift both be preferably superior to the initial gift and commensurate with the social status of the giver' (Sunström 1965, p. 2). Initiating a relation requires that one starts a gift exchange sequence. Refusing a gift is seen as a hostile act, but one can avoid being offered one.

Gift exchange is not absent from modern economies (Boulding 1981; Van der Eijk et al. 2009; Dolfsma 2008a): similar processes can be found among mature industries where commodities are traded (Darr 2003) and in trade in highly complex, risky and volatile surroundings (Ferrary 2003).

5.5 Conclusions

Information on how trade gradually 'expands beyond the village' is scarce. New institutional economics assumes that silent trade is an early step in the process. However, the little information that there is indicates that trade without any communication whatsoever is impossible: ST has never existed. The gap created by NIE's inability, so far, to offer a theoretical explanation of the kind of 'representational redescription' that would have to occur for this initial expansion of trade has been plugged by the notion of silent trade. Relying on ST entails that NIE provides a static approach to the choice of contracts, incentives and governance structures, assuming pure theoretical market conditions. Language and learning are nevertheless largely exogenous to NIE. The possibility of ST and thus the place of language in economic theory constitutes a theoretical and methodological watershed between NIE and OIE. From an evolutionary perspective, however, market exchange can be seen to have developed from gift exchange. In the beginning there was gift exchange under familistic-like conditions.

6
Knowledge Coordination and Development via Market, Hierarchy and Gift Exchange[1]

From hunter-gatherer societies onwards people living in communities have understood the need to cooperate. This need, wherein individuals become dependent on one another, has grown over time as a result of continually increasing division of labour and growing specialization. Indeed, as Adam Smith (1981 [1776]) claims, division of labour and specialization have been important drivers of economic development. As individuals are no longer able to master the totality of available knowledge and skills so the need for exchange of resources and cooperation has increased. This is broadly acknowledged in economics (Hayek 1945; Schumpeter 1978 [1934]; Nahapiet and Ghosal 1998), but remains ill-understood (Lopes and Caldas 2008). As individuals have only partially overlapping goals and interests, exchange and cooperation needs coordination of some sort (Barnard 1968). By necessity, coordination of cooperation – be it through the market or a hierarchy or by some other means – requires that not only self-interest is relied on, but that shared goals and moral convictions are assumed to exist and to play a role (Akerlof 1982; Dolfsma 1998; Le Grand 2003; Lopes and Caldas 2008).

In a world characterized by emerging knowledge economies, intangible assets such as knowledge and information have become increasingly important for economic dynamics (OECD 2001). The conceptualization of the coordination of economic activities is problematic even in the case of tangibles, in the discussion of knowledge creation and diffusion the problem is greater still. Knowledge has specific properties as a commodity that need to be taken into account when discussing coordination in this context.

This chapter will discuss the three different mechanisms of coordination between actors that have been acknowledged in the literature.

A first coordination mechanism is market exchange. Well known among economists, market exchange can be defined as voluntary agreement involving the offer of any sort of present, continuing or future utility in exchange for utilities of any sort offered in return (Weber 1978). Second, hierarchies or bureaucracies have been well established as a coordination mechanism at least since Williamson's (1975) exposé. Here the significant attribute is authority, derived from an individual's position in an organization. A third coordination mechanism is less well established and the literature employs different terms: social relations (Adler and Kwon, 2002), communities (Adler, 2001; Bowles and Gintis, 1998), clans (Ouchi, 1979, 1980), (social) networks (Powell, 1990; Miles and Snow, 1986; Thorelli, 1986). However, despite the different terms and descriptions the majority of these concepts describe situations where the coordination between individuals is based on socio-cultural mechanisms instead of those of the market or hierarchies.

A considerable literature has examined the merits of the market and of hierarchies as means of coordination, but not in the context of knowledge development and diffusion. Given the relevance of innovation in the current economic context, this is a major concern. Social economics is well positioned to address this issue, as it is able not only to analyse the two most-frequently studied coordination mechanisms – market and hierarchies – but it is also able conceptually to seize the middle ground where social relations and social values play a role. Notwithstanding the ideal typical approach that a conceptual discussion takes almost by default, these exchange mechanisms may not necessarily be alternatives but can be complements (Akerlof 1982; Bradach and Eccles 1989).

6.1 Ways of coordinating

In market exchange the presumption is that economic order will emerge from independent, egoistic acts of autonomous individuals in pursuit of their own gain. Hierarchy assumes that the best economic outcome will result from standardization and following the chain of command. A third way, one I shall describe as gift exchange, generally refers to a type of exchange conducted between parties who are characterized by social properties and particularistic ties the nature of which influences the exchange. In a world with zero transaction costs one may argue that markets as a way of coordinating behaviour might be preferable (Coase 1937; Williamson 1975). When transaction costs are present, hierarchy might work better (Hennart 1993; Kreps 1990; Williamson 1975). The literature that has developed to understand hierarchy from an economic perspective may be able to deal conceptually with situations where individuals are boundedly rational, have only partially overlapping goals, and are opportunistic (Williamson 1975). However, when discussing knowledge development, and diffusion, trust and social norms may also play a role. To arrive at an understanding of this role it might be necessary to look for ways of coordination utilized where parties involved are not legally obliged to behave in a certain way because a labour contract specifies it, nor are they involved in a quid pro quo where all relevant goods traded are specified. I will briefly present the different ways of coordinating – markets (A), hierarchies (B) and social relations or gift exchange (C) – and discuss the extent to which they help us to understand the process of knowledge development and diffusion.

A. Markets

For economists, a perfect market is not an empirical reality but, rather, a set of assumptions: a large number of firms compete in a market for homogeneous commodities to cater to the demand of a large number of consumers. No producing firm or consumer is able to influence the price; all parties have complete knowledge (Stigler 1968). Markets are where demand and supply meet to set an equilibrium price; all necessary information is summarized in the prices quoted in a market. Modern economics views the market as a price-setting mechanism and has left its workings implied rather than explicitly discussed (see Barber 1977; Coase 1988 [1937]; Rangan 2000; Stigler 1968). Cooperation between actors can take place anonymously; the rules of the game are clear to all participants. As Hayek (1945) puts it 'The marvel of the economic system is that prices serve as sufficient statistics, thereby economizing on bounded rationality.' In this ideal type of market exchange, the exchange that takes place is de-socialized in nature, it is not 'embedded' in a larger social context (Granovetter 1985). In addition it is assumed that exchanges are freely consented to by opportunistic economic actors (Williamson 1975), exchange takes place within the context of complete contracts, marginal pricing assures optimized production and allocation, and lastly that property rights are protected by the state and the appropriate legal institutions. A Pareto-efficient situation will result from free and unfettered working of the market; exchange in a competitive market assures that the exchange is equitable.

In the 'pure' market model it is assumed that risk but no fundamental uncertainty is present. If not all possible future states of the world and the likelihood of their occurrence are known, there is a situation of fundamental uncertainty. Certainly in such a situation complete contracting is impossible. Prices are likely not to reflect the true value of the commodity exchanged and/or prices do not contain all relevant information (Hennart 1993). One may characterize such situations as market failure, and economists do so. The term implies that markets may be made to work in these situations. One may also claim that a different mechanism is at work.

Knowledge and the market

Many firms make use of the market mechanism to develop and procure relevant knowledge. In the year 2000 $142 billion was paid internationally by users to parties that owned intellectual property rights (IPRs) in order to make use of knowledge that was legally protected under IPR law (Dolfsma 2008a).[2] The IPR system thus allows for a market that coordinates the exchange of knowledge. Knowledge as a commodity to be exchanged on the market is no ordinary good. It is non-rivalrous: that is, knowledge is not consumed by its use (Adler 2001; Arrow, 1984), and non-exclusive: consumption or use by non-payers cannot be excluded. Knowledge is a (quasi) public good – reliance on the market creates a trade-off between production and allocation. The market may not stimulate the creation of new knowledge in amounts that are beneficial for society (Adler 2001; Stiglitz 1994; Nelson 1959; Romer 2002). If knowledge is available in an explicit form, and possibly digitized too, it can be very easily copied by others (Soete and ter Weel 2005; Cowan et al. 2000).

Knowledge development is cumulative, though the extent to which this is true differs across fields. New knowledge is for the most part based on (related) work done by others (in the past): we stand on the shoulders of giants (and dwarfs). Thus, one of the conditions conducive to scientific progress is 'open research' or the full and free dissemination of research results (Nelson 1959). However, from the perspective of the party that invested in the generation of new knowledge, the notion of 'open research' may be less appealing since it increases the risk of failing to recoup initial investment.

Furthermore, Grant (1996) points out that for knowledge creation, but less so for knowledge diffusion, due to the far-reaching extent of specialization, the coordinated effort of many individual specialists and organizations of different kinds is needed. Markets are at a significant disadvantage when it comes to performing this coordinating role. Because they address actors as motivated by extrinsic benefits, markets may actually increase the risk of opportunistic behaviour (Le Grand 2003; Grant 1996). Thus, while markets as a means of coordinating behaviour for knowledge development and diffusion are not to be dismissed, neither are they to be relied on exclusively.

B. Hierarchy

Transaction cost theory (Coase 1937; Williamson 1975) stresses that to make a transaction involves actors in costs – transaction costs – other than those needed for the good or service exchanged. These transaction costs are costs of coordination, and include costs of contract drafting and contract enforcement. According to transaction cost theory, transactions may take place in one of two alternative places, in the market or in a hierarchy (firm, organization). Transaction costs will differ according to the type of transaction (for instance its frequency, investments required, number of competitors faced, duration of the contract) and the characteristics of the good involved (Hennart 1993; Kreps 1990; Williamson 1975).

By seeking to explain what type of activities need to be left to the market and which need to be brought within the domain of the firm, transaction cost theory endogenizes the boundaries of the firm. Hierarchies coordinate the activities of individuals through the use of authority (legitimate power) aiming at some organizational goal (Williamson 1975; Ouchi 1979, 1980; Adler 2001; Adler and Kwon 2002). This authority is used to set rules and issue directives with regard to processes completed or standards of output or quality (Grant 1996; Ouchi 1979). Members must abide by the rules and directives. Surveillance and direction of subordinates are used by the hierarchy to ensure that rules are followed, which itself involves a cost (Hennart 1993; Ouchi 1980). A perception of equity around the coordination in a hierarchy is the result of social agreement that the hierarchy has the ability and the right to value each contribution and reward it fairly (Ouchi 1980). Hierarchies can be efficient, especially in a complex situation where the activities of multiple specialized units and large numbers of people need to be coordinated (Grant 1996; Jacques 1990; Romme 1996).

Hierarchies' costs are associated with measuring performance. When 'tasks become highly unique, completely integrated or ambiguous for other reasons' performance may be impossible to measure (Ouchi 1980, p. 134; compare Adler 2001). Certainly when the counterfactual – the outcome that could have resulted had someone acted in line with the interests of the hierarchy rather than in their own interests – is impossible to determine, performance of hierarchy members cannot be measured. This is obviously the case when new knowledge is (not) created or diffused. Hierarchies may offset performance measurement problems when an incomplete employment contract allows for providing directions on a day-to-day basis and almost casual monitoring as a by-product.

As Homans (1950) has argued, however, when people work closely together within a organization an atmosphere of trust and goal congruence results. Opportunistic behaviour and therefore the need for monitoring are reduced. Hierarchies can create an atmosphere of trust since they can not only provide the stability of long-term cooperative relationships but also employ socialization to create goal congruence and a sense of shared destiny and belonging (Ouchi 1979; Adler 2001; Grant 1996). Thus, hierarchies permit parties to deal with uncertainty or complexity in an adaptive sequential fashion. While it may be granted that an atmosphere of trust may be more likely to grow within a hierarchy than in the market, trust may be established between parties in the market as well (Van der Eijk et al. 2009). What is more important to observe, conceptually, is that the emergence of trust within a hierarchy is not taken into account in transaction cost theory.

Knowledge and hierarchy

Hierarchies coordinate through the creation of horizontally and vertically differentiated units of labour. Such organizational structuring might be especially efficient when performing routine tasks but might encounter difficulty in the case of creation of new knowledge (for example, Mintzberg 1979; Scott 1992; Adler 2001). Hierarchies also coordinate by centralizing information. However, centralizing information functions effectively only if information is characterized by a substantial degree of confirmation and negligible novelty (compare Romme 1996) and is not tacit in nature (Grant 1996). Managers may not be able to coordinate and absorb the knowledge their experts have mastered. Knowledge also gives rise to performance measurement difficulties (Adler 2001). According to Adler (2001) vertical differentiation performs well in facilitating downward communication of explicit knowledge and commands, but is less effective in facilitating upward communication of new ideas and knowledge. Hierarchy might thus be an obstacle to learning that would benefit from team-like, non-hierarchical structures (Iannello 1992; Levinthal and March 1993; Peters 1987; Senge 1990; Romme 1996). As Powell et al. (1996, p. 116) point out 'Knowledge creation occurs in the context of a community, one that is fluid and evolving rather than tightly bound or static. The canonical formal organization, with its bureaucratic rigidities, is a poor vehicle for learning.'

Direct horizontal communication between the relevant experts in different units might compensate for the difficulty within a hierarchy of facilitating upward communication of new ideas and knowledge needed for coordination. However, horizontal differentiation within hierarchies makes cooperation with regard to knowledge creation between units difficult, because units often have different goals, priorities, working procedures or even locations, depending on their own needs and circumstances, which make direct, horizontal (informal) contact between experts difficult. What is more, even though formal structures are able to stimulate knowledge development and diffusion, imposing directives on creativity is not likely to work well. Coordination of knowledge development activities often requires a more 'personal' kind of interaction between experts rather than managers than can be achieved by means of rules and directives (Galbraith 1973; Grant 1996; Hansen 1999; Kogut and Zander 1992).

Galbraith (1973) points out that information processing within a hierarchy often occurs via informal horizontal linkages as well as through the formal vertical linkages. In this connection, Romme (1996) points towards the importance of teams for knowledge production. Brown and Duguid (1991) emphasize that knowledge creation takes place within the context of an informal community that generally spans departmental and even organizational boundaries. Given the informal nature of many of these horizontal linkages and exchanges, the effectiveness of authority as a hierarchy's central coordination mechanism is weakened. This, however, does not prevent horizontal knowledge exchanges from taking place. In the absence of hierarchy (and the market mechanism), whose rigidities are considered a poor vehicle for learning, who coordinates these exchanges?

C. Social relations: gifts

A number of scholars have proposed alternative ways of coordinating the behaviour of actors. Sometimes these are presented as lying between markets and hierarchies and to be analysed in similar terms, sometimes they are posed as alternatives in their own right. Terms such as social relations (Adler and Kwon 2002), communities (Adler 2001; Bowles and Gintis 1998), clans (Ouchi 1980) and networks (Powell 1990; Miles and Snow 1986; Thorelli 1986) have been introduced. Most of these conceptions share the aim of coordinating by curbing the effects of opportunism and goal incongruence using social and/or cultural mechanisms such as trust (Adler 2001; Bradach and Eccles 1989; Nooteboom 2002), common values and beliefs (Ouchi 1980; Granovetter 1985) or network and reputation effects (Powell 1990; Nooteboom 2002).

Coordination through both hierarchy and the market can fail, especially, as I have argued, in the context of knowledge development and diffusion (innovation). However, coordination does not need to be formal either in terms of (labour) contracts or directives (Ouchi 1980; Scott 1992), as informal mechanisms of coordination can provide an alternative. Trust, the expectation that the exchange partner will act honestly and in good faith (Ring and Van de Ven 1992), can alleviate fears of opportunistic behaviour and as such has been described as a lubricant to both social and economic activity (Arrow 1974). Economic transactions that might otherwise prove extremely costly and time consuming to arrange, or that involve extensive use of bureaucratic procedures to supervise are undertaken in informal settings. Values and beliefs held in common by a community – a 'culture' in the anthropological sense of the term – will allow for and support such informal dealings. A national context, social stratification as well as a group or organizational culture can be involved, even when each could prevent trust emerging in the informal setting. Common values and beliefs become internalized via socialization and habituation partly in the form of tacit knowledge (Hofstede 1991; Schein 1992; Rousseau 1990) and are associated with shared representation and systems of meaning between parties (Cicourel 1973; Rousseau 1990; Schein 1992; Allaire and Firsiroty 1984). Common agreement between individuals about what constitutes proper behaviour and a sense of solidarity or common destiny reduces goal incongruence. While usually not explicitly employed for that purpose,[3] the tendency for opportunistic behaviour and thus the need for monitoring are thereby reduced, sometimes significantly so. While Ouchi (1980) emphasizes the ability of the organization to employ common values and beliefs as a result of socialization, coordination on the basis of informal and sociocultural mechanisms can also take place across organizational borders (for example, Allen 1977; Kreiner and Schultz 1993; Von Hippel 1987; Agrawal et al. 2003).

Social relations and gift exchange as a third coordination mechanism beside market or hierarchy have been little explored, though some useful contributions have been made to this debate (Ouchi 1980; Powell 1990; Van der Eijk et al. 2009). Table 6.1 summarizes some of the main features of each of these three coordination mechanisms. I will elaborate on this somewhat below in the context of knowledge development and diffusion. What needs to be acknowledged, however, are the interconnections and interactions between mechanisms discussed here as ideal types (Williams 1988; Nooteboom 2000, 2002; Parsons 1951; Shapiro 1987).

Table 6.1 Coordination mechanisms

Dimension	**Coordination mechanism**		
	Market	**Hierarchy**	**Social relations/ gift exchange**
What is exchanged?	Goods and services for money or barter	Obedience to authority for material and spiritual security Time in return for some type of monetary compensation	Favours/gifts: tangible (goods/money) and intangible (information/ services/love/status) (Foa and Foa 1980)
Specific or (deliberately) unclear terms of exchange	Specific	Unspecified, open (employee will follow directives within general limits of law and of morality)	Deliberately unclear (a gift/favour creates an obligation to reciprocate, however, the value, form and timing of the counter-gift is left open to discretion (Van der Eijk et al. 2009)
Expected individual orientation	Self-interest	Subordination to directives and rules	Reciprocity, social obligations (vertical and horizontal)
System regulation	Self-regulation; contract law, property rights	Organizational procedures; third-party arbiters; labour law.	Reputation effect; benefits of continued cooperation; hostages; moral norm of reciprocity; norms and social solidarity; network closure

Sources: Adapted from Adler and Kwon (2002), Biggart and Delbridge (2004), Bugental (2000), Fiske (1992), Ouchi (1980) and Powell (1990).

Thus, individuals may be motivated by, or addressed as having, egoistic or other-oriented considerations. Other-oriented considerations might be altruistic, but need not be solely directed at the well-being of others. Similarly, coordination of the actions of individuals might be through particular individuals or might take a more impersonal character, through explicit directives and rules. Coordination through both the market and through hierarchies has generally been conceptualized as involving egoistically motivated actors where coordination takes the route of impersonal interaction. In Table 6.2, both market and hierarchy are to be found in Cell I only. It should, however, be noted that social

Table 6.2 Coordination dissected

Motivation	**Sources**	
	Impersonal	**Personal**
Egoistic	I Sanctions imposed by authority; contractual obligation	II Calculative self-interest; benefits of continued cooperation (Abreu 1988; Telser 1980; Axelrod 1984; Hill 1990; Heide and Miner 1992; Parkhe 1993); reputation (Weigelt and Camerer 1988; Kreps 1990; Coleman 1994); hostages (Williamson 1985)
Other-oriented	III Norms, value and belief systems, ethics (Porter and Sensenbrenner 1998; Nye 1979; Hofstede 1991; Schein 1992)	IV Relations of affect; routines, habituation; empathy

Sources: Adapted from Willliams (1988) and Nooteboom (2000).

and personal interaction can also be egoistically motivated. As has been argued by social scientists since classical anthropologists Mauss and Malinowsky, social interaction and gift exchange involves egoism and power struggles as well as altruism (see also Bugental 2000; Williams 1988; Sherry 1983; Komter 1996; Vandevelde 2000);[4] such acts can be highly personal, involving strong ties, but they can also be impersonal, for example, where immediate personal relations are absent and actors address (unknown) others. Social relations and gift exchange thus encompass Cells II through IV. Thus, coordination through gift exchange can complement the market and hierarchy as a means of coordination. For instance, in a context where the value and belief system emphasizes the moral significance of reciprocity, gift exchange may need to depend less on calculative self-interest to coordinate.

Gift exchange is known for its role in establishing social ties and maintaining relationships (Cheal 1986; Darr 2003; Mauss 2000 [1954]; Gouldner 1960; Larsen and Watson 2001; Belk 1979; van der Eijk et al. 2009),[5] despite the possibility of ulterior motives (Sherry 1983). As the exchange continues, positive emotions are generated and uncertainty is reduced which, in turn, generates cohesion and commitment to exchange relations (Lawler et al. 2000; Homans 1958). As both Granovetter (1985) and Homans (1950) argue, what may have started out as a purely goal-oriented interaction tends to become embedded over time in social trust relations. These relations of affect can act as a source of cooperation and exchange (Coleman 1988; Ingram and Roberts 2000). Altruistic behaviour can result from routines and habituation, as can be argued even from a psychological, behaviourist point of view. Operant conditioning in exchange, that is, behaviours that are reinforced by rewards, are more likely to be repeated over time (Homans 1958, 1974). Behaviour that becomes routine, or non-reflective and tacit in nature, can continue even when the behaviour is no longer reinforced by (immediate) rewards (Homans 1958, 1974).

Some social mechanisms, such as the expected benefits of continued future cooperation, hostage and reputation effects, emphasize the egoistic element of social interaction by focusing on the incentive structure that participants face when deciding to honour their obligations. Reputation effects are among the less egoistic mechanisms, and may occupy the boundary between self-interest and other-orientation, indicating the difficulty of distinguishing these social mechanisms conceptually or empirically. In a situation where the focal actor and the recipient are part of a tryad[6] (Simmel 1964), given that the reputation[7] effect is sufficiently strong, the incentive structure can be constructed in such a way that calculative self-interest makes honouring debts rational (Kreps 1990; Ostrom and Ahn, 2003; Coleman 1988; Sherry 1983; Ferrary 2003; Gouldner 1960). As Williamson (1975, p. 107) formulates it in a rare instance where he acknowledges the social in the economic realm: 'Individual aggressiveness is curbed by the prospect of ostracism among peers, in both trade and social circumstances.' By the same token, an individual who has a reputation for generously compensating those who have helped him or her will be likely to induce others to reciprocate with favours (Barney and Hansen 1994, see Rose-Ackerman, 1998). In the literature on gifts, this is known as the 'Matthew Effect': to those who have shall be given. This may lead to a situation where those who do not have are excommunicated. Nevertheless, as the value of a gift is defined within a specific context, the deleterious effects may be more limited than in cases where action is coordinated by the market or by hierarchy. The Matthew Effect is also well-documented in literature on the development of science (Merton 1968).

6.2 Knowledge and gift exchange

I submit that exchange outside the market and hierarchies is predicated on gift exchange (for example, Akerlof 1982; Blau 1964; Boulding

1981; Heath 1976; Homans 1974; Mauss 2000 [1954]; Sherry 1983) and involves actors, resources and structures (Molm 2003). Gift exchange is omnipresent and not just limited to charitable ('altruistic') gifts. It is a significant economic phenomenon (*The Economist*, 2006). Gift exchange allows for the exchange of both tangible and intangible goods.

Gift exchange has a number of properties that differentiate it from other forms of coordination. First, according to the norm of reciprocity[8] an individual is obliged to give, to receive[9] and to reciprocate. The imperative nature of this three-fold obligation derives from its cultural embeddedness (Sherry 1983). Gift exchange is carried out without a legal contract, even in business settings (Darr 2003; Ferrary 2003), but does create strong obligations to reciprocate (Gouldner 1960; Levi-Strauss 1996; Malinowski 1996; Mauss 2000 [1954]; Sahlins 1996; Schwartz 1996; Simmel 1996). Those who cannot or will not reciprocate do not remain part of the community or are subordinated. Gift exchange gives rise to a psychological contract between the giver and recipient (Schein 1965). Acceptance of the gift is, to a certain extent, acceptance of the giver and the relationship between the parties (Larsen and Watson 2001; Carrier 1991). Gifts valued most highly tend to be those that involve a personal element. It is for this reason that the material value of a gift is often hidden from direct view, though it is not unappreciated, especially between actors who know each other and are close. By the same token refusal of a gift marks the refusal to initiate the dynamic of exchange, thus to refuse a gift is to refuse a relationship (Ferrary 2003; Mauss 2000 [1954]).

Second, the nature of the reciprocal gift is not specified beforehand; reciprocity is open to discretion as to value, form and timing (Bourdieu 1977; Gouldner 1960; Mauss 2000 [1954]; Deckop et al. 2003). Schwartz (1996) states that an equal-return 'payment' (homeomorphic reciprocity) in gift exchange is prohibited, since this is tantamount to returning the offered gift to the donor (in the context of knowledge development returning the same good makes no sense as knowledge has public goods characteristics; at the same time paying for a gift of knowledge in a social context of trust negates the personal element and symbolically ends the relationship). Many scholars emphasize that the return gift should ultimately, over the longer term, be of roughly equal value, even when equivalence is context-dependent and defined by the actors involved (Gouldner 1960).

Third, the diachronous nature of the exchange means that the gift is not immediately reciprocated, but instead is compensated by a deferred form of return (Mauss 2000 [1954]; Bourdieu 1977; Ferrary 2003; Deckop et al. 2003). A deferred return obligates one individual to another, and thus creates a social debt. As a coordination mechanism it operates through time, making it particularly useful for knowledge development and the circumstances in which it flourishes.

Coordination by gift exchange works through interlocking personal and impersonal sources of coordination based on both egoistic and altruistic motivation, enabling exchange in circumstances where the market and hierarchy cannot (Ferrary 2003; Smart 1993). Some have argued that gift exchange may be the only type of exchange to develop specific commercial products – open source software being a case in point (Zeitlyn 2003). The literature generally stresses that there is a propensity to give, yet there also is a need for equity (Adams 1965; Deckop et al. 2003; Gouldner 1960; Maitland 2002; Walster et al. 1973). Reciprocity is essential to this conceptualization, since an initial gift creates an informal obligation to reciprocate in due time or when needed (Gouldner 1960; Levi-Strauss 1996; Malinowski 1996; Mauss 2000 [1954]; Sahlins 1996; Schwartz 1996; Simmel 1996) and has been characterized as short-term altruism for long-term self-interest (Putnam 2000, p. 134). Much of the effectiveness of gift exchange hinges on the force of the felt need to reciprocate, whether internalized or socially imposed, in which the value, form and moment of the reciprocal gift is not specified beforehand.

It has been argued that intellectual objects are more often the result of cooperation than are physical objects (Bowles and Gintis 1998; Dolfsma 2008). Some consider knowledge creation as equivalent to combination, exchange and recombination of existing knowledge (Schumpeter 1978 [1934]). In that sense knowledge development is a cumulative process (Nelson 1959, 2004) in which scientists necessarily draw on the work of others. Moreover it often requires the integration of the specialized knowledge of multiple individuals (Grant 1996) and collaborative teamwork, cooperation and knowledge sharing become essential components (Adler 2001; Moran and Ghosal 1996; Nahapiet and Ghosal 1998; Tsai and Ghosal 1998). At the same time, coordination via the market and hierarchy has been shown to be difficult when dealing with knowledge. Partly because the outcome of the innovation process is fundamentally uncertain, the viability of the use of contracts is limited: detailed rights and obligations for all possible future scenarios is prohibitively difficult and thus extremely costly (Nooteboom 2002). Even when drafting elaborate contracts is still just feasible technically, such contracts will tend to undermine the trust necessary for knowledge development (Klein Wolthuis et al. 2005). Monitoring activities during the process of knowledge development may be difficult too; indeed, establishing the quality of the knowledge developed after it has been created may be difficult, even ex post. The linear model of developing knowledge, where a separate group of individuals is to develop knowledge and then pass it on for design of a product that will be sold in the market, is obsolete. Knowledge development is a perpetual process, and the market does not offer definitive tests, ex post, of the usefulness of what is developed. There is far more involved than a situation of asymmetric information and a problem of determining the individual contribution to a group outcome.

For anything more than the very minor adaptations of existing goods and processes, actors will resort to an alternative coordination mechanism, at least to some degree. The generation and diffusion of knowledge depends to a very large extent upon 'communities' (Brown and Duguid 1991; Cohendet et al. 2004). These communities are often made up of informal networks and ties (Freeman 1991; Cross et al. 2002; Madhaven and Grover 1998). Gift exchange provides an alternative perspective on such coordination.

A number of features of gift exchange are especially relevant when dealing with and engaging in the exchange of knowledge-based assets: decentralization of monitoring, provision of incentives for knowledge sharing at an individual level, and guiding knowledge exchange within and across organizational boundaries.

Monitoring

One of the striking features of gift exchange is the occurrence within it of coordination in the absence of a centralized structure capable of making decisions binding on its members. When 'tasks become exceedingly unique, fully integrated, or ambiguous for other reasons, then even bureaucratic mechanisms fail' Ouchi (1980, p. 134). However, performance ambiguity on an organizational level does not necessarily equate to performance ambiguity on an individual level. As coordination via gift exchange generally takes place on an individual level, the need to monitor is effectively decentralized to that individual level. Given that actors are usually fully capable of monitoring and valuing one another's performance, gift exchange can coordinate in the face of extensive performance measurement difficulties.

Motivation

For coordination of behaviour to be effective, the willingness of the actors involved to engage is required. This is especially relevant within the context of innovation since knowledge sharing cannot be forced; people will only share knowledge if there is a *personal* reason for it (Huysman and de Wit 2004). For effective coordination between individuals in the context of innovation there must thus be an intent or willingness in addition to the ability to share relevant knowledge (Hansen 1999). The willingness issue is especially relevant, though infrequently analysed, considering the costs and uncertainty associated with sharing knowledge in terms of time, energy and vulnerability on the part of the donor (Reagans and McEvily, 2003). The actor's position is vulnerable as redundancy increases, competition from the recipient may result and a reciprocal gift may not materialize (Davenport 1997; Reagans and McEvily 2003).

Yet, despite the possible costs from the donor's perspective, knowledge continues to be shared (for example, Wenger and Snyder 2000; Wenger 1998; Brown and Duguid 1991, 2001). Why do individuals, in the absence of clearly defined, formal, enforceable obligations or contracts, continue to provide recipients with knowledge? Gift exchange provides the parties involved with a context for the exchange of resources, as well as a socially embedded informal sanctioning or enforcement mechanism. Gift exchange incorporates altruistic as well as more self-interested motives, of which the latter are generally emphasized. The act of giving creates obligations on which the giver can draw in the future (Coleman 1988; Mauss 2000 [1954]; Bourdieu 1977). The recipient owes the giver, at some point in the future, something of similar value, depending on the rituals for giving within the relevant group (Avner 1997; Blau 1964; Bourdieu 1977, 1986; Humphrey and Hugh-Jones 1992; Darr 2003). At the same time, through giving, a reputation can be established and grow, providing prestige and status as well as facilitating access to resources held by others. A reputation for generosity or trustworthiness can be a valuable asset (Bourdieu 1977).

Access to knowledge within and between organizations

Horizontal differentiation or departmentalization within hierarchies makes cooperation with regard to knowledge creation between units difficult, firstly because units have different knowledge bases and secondly, because units often have different priorities (Adler 2001). Cooperation aimed at knowledge development requires the participation of specialists, not only because of the tacit nature of much knowledge (Burt 2004; Grant 1996; Hansen 1999; Kogut and Zander, 1992). The coordination of tasks related to knowledge development requires a more 'personal' interaction than can be achieved by means of rules and directives (Galbraith

1973), though the formalized interaction should not be underestimated (Aalbers et al. 2006). Galbraith (1973) argues that information processing within the hierarchy often bypasses vertical linkages, taking place via informal (horizontal) ties. Romme (1996) points to teams for knowledge production. Brown and Duguid (1991) emphasize that knowledge creation takes place within (informal) communities of practice which may span departmental and even organizational boundaries. The informal nature of many of these linkages weakens the use of authority as the central coordination mechanism within a hierarchy.

Gift exchange can facilitate knowledge exchange in circumstances where the market and hierarchy are inappropriate mechanisms (Ferrary 2003; Smart 1993). It allows actors to forge and personalize relationships and to develop personal ties that can act as a 'guarantee' that the initial gift will not be abused and will also be reciprocated (Zucker 1986; Shapiro 1987). Given sufficient trust, knowledge and favours that are classified and highly sensitive may be exchanged between individuals from different firms, on the understanding that whereas abuse of the process could jeopardize both giver and firm, effective gift exchange could benefit giver, recipient and their organizations (Bouty 2000). The risks and costs of knowledge development and diffusion can be considerably reduced when gift exchange is used as a coordination mechanism. Knowledge is thus exchanged via informal routes and personal networks, possibly transcending organizational borders (Allen 1977; Kreiner and Schultz 1993; Von Hippel 1987) as communities of practice may extend beyond them (Wenger and Snyder 2000; Wenger 1998; Brown and Duguid 1991, 2001). Gift exchange both relies on and establishes a shared frame of reference that allows the parties involved to determine what the risks and costs are of using this mechanism rather than another (compare Van Eijk et al. 2009). Gift exchange allows people to establish and maintain social relations[10] that can help actors gain access to relevant individuals and communities while allowing at the same time some 'guarantee' to prevent abuse.

6.3 Conclusion

In addition to markets and hierarchies there is a third coordination mechanism, one that is not much discussed: gift exchange in social relations. Some have argued that gift exchange is conceptually of the same order as market or hierarchy; I argue that it is of a different order and that additional concepts are necessary to understand it (Biggart and Delbridge 2004). In this chapter I argue that in the context of knowledge development and diffusion gift exchange has often been the preferred alternative. I discuss this coordination mechanism conceptually, especially focusing on the context of knowledge development. Depending on the circumstances, one mechanism may be better suited to provide coordination than another; in some situations coordination mechanisms work in tandem (Adler 2001; Bradach and Eccles 1989). Gift exchange offers an understanding of the development and maintenance of the social relations that allow for the trust that is necessary under the circumstances of uncertainty that characterize knowledge development.

Gift exchange allows actors to forge and personalize relationships and to develop guarantees through personal bonding (Zucker 1986; Shapiro 1987). As anthropologists have argued, in line with Mauss: there is a need to give, and to receive, and to reciprocate. If one does not adhere to this, one may be excommunicated and barred from exchanges that are both socially and economically meaningful. This certainly holds for non-standard situations where technological and market uncertainty and the possibility of opportunism are high, such as for venture capital provision in Silicon Valley (Ferrary 2003) and in markets that are mature (Darr 2003). Contrary to the dictum of the new institutional (neoclassical) economics that 'in the beginning there were markets', Boulding (1981) has even claimed that gift exchange is the quintessential kind of exchange. In the context of knowledge development he is certainly correct.

7
Making Knowledge Work: Intra-firm Networks, Gifts and Innovation

Knowledge exchange between individuals working in a firm, across and even within divisions, does not occur automatically (Szulanski 1996). It is not obvious that people exchange ideas, point one another towards useful information or give feedback, even in the absence of any motives for not cooperating in such a manner. However, as a firm's competitive advantage is closely related to its innovative capacity, which is largely based on how it uses knowledge that is already available, the questions that arise are: how does knowledge flow within a firm? What can be done to stimulate or re-direct knowledge flow within a firm?

In recent years, increasing attention has been given by scholars in social sciences in general and in management in particular to the networks of relations between individuals within firms involved in knowledge transfer and development. Consultancies too are scrambling to set up units that can analyse these networks for firms. In addition to the structural issue of who relates to whom and how, I will argue that there is a need to look at *why* relations are established and maintained. This chapter thus discusses insights from both the literature on social networks and the anthropological literature on gift and favour exchange. Bringing together all these insights, the *how* and the *why* of knowledge transfer may become clearer.

7.1 Knowledge flows

It is possible to distinguish different, possibly partly overlapping formal and informal organizational networks. Informal contacts are believed to stimulate knowledge flow in particular (Cross et al. 2002; Stevenson and Gilly 1991). Figure 7.1 presents the informal network of people (the dots or 'nodes') working in the daughter company of a large European

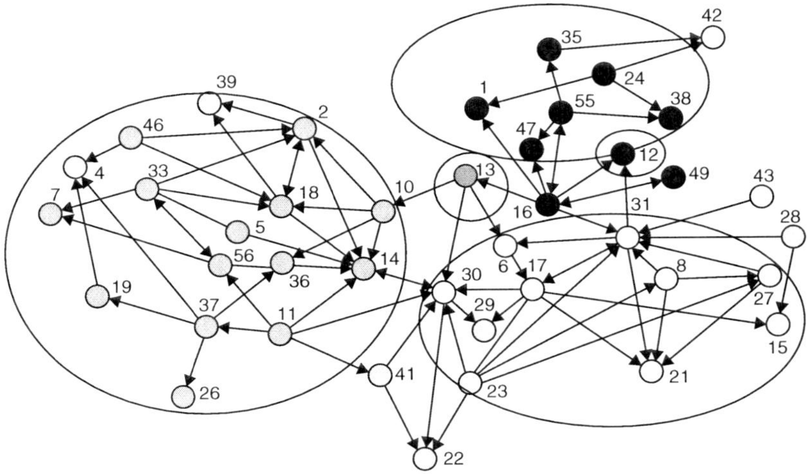

Figure 7.1 Informal network
Source: Aalbers et al. (2006).

multinational firm in the field of electronics and electrical engineering.[1] A similar picture could be shown for the formal network. This company, in reformulating its corporate strategy, emphasizes cooperation between the different divisions to stimulate innovation. Dots are individuals, and the shading of the dots indicates the divisions in which the individuals are based; the circles do so as well. Figure 7.1 is typical in the sense that a few individuals bear the brunt of the entire communication flow, within but especially between units.

A visual representation of the network is illuminating, but network data can also be statistically analysed. However, even before doing statistical analysis, it is obvious that there are a surprisingly small number of individuals involved in knowledge exchange across division boundaries. Only a few people constitute the linking pins or structural holes between divisions (Burt 1992). This visualization came as something of a shock to senior management in the company represented. It became clear that for better or for worse, these few individuals are in a position to have a considerable influence on the flow of communication. In addition, Burt (2004) has claimed that such individuals can come up with new ideas themselves, combining ideas from two or more separated fields.

In addition to such an immediate, in-your-face finding, statistical analyses can bring out other insights and address further questions. Such analyses can be done at the level of the network or at the level of individuals. One example of the former approach might be to pose the question of whether the knowledge transferred within the company is primarily exchanged through formal or informal routes? I have found (Aalbers et al. 2006) that both these networks contribute, but that the formal network might even contribute more than the informal one. Formal contacts within an organization that go beyond the organizational chart do affect knowledge flow and thus a firm's innovative capacity. An example of the latter approach, focusing on individuals within the network, could be to tackle the questions: does the centrality of an individual matter for knowledge exchange? Are individuals who have many connections, or who connect otherwise disconnected cliques able to tap into separated but complementary sources of knowledge, or are they only distracted by too frequent interactions and meetings? Could substantial work developing specialized new knowledge be hampered by the number of relations maintained or because of the translations that have to be made between fields? I have found that people centrally located in the formal structures of an organization seem to be better positioned to transfer knowledge between units, while people centrally located in informal interactions are better placed to transfer knowledge within units (Aalbers et al. 2006). Given that where knowledge from diverse sources comes together new knowledge is more likely to be developed (Burt 2004), formal networks set up by management are relevant for innovation. This goes against some of the intuitions common in the field of organization studies and knowledge management (Granovetter 1973; Hansen 1999; Reagans and McEvily 2003).

There is thus a growing recognition that certain features of a network might suit some purposes, while other goals are best attained if the network has different characteristics (Reagans and McEvily 2003; Schulz 2003; Stevenson and Gilly 1991; Kilduff and Brass 2001). For instance, if individuals working in a firm are in need of much and diverse information, a few close relations will not do. Employees in such a company will need many weaker ties (Granovetter 1973) rather than trying to maintain an inevitably limited number of strong ties. If a firm is dependent on employees working on a (technologically) complex issue, at the frontier of a scientific field, there is likely to be much tacit (taken-for-granted, unarticulated) knowledge involved. Strong ties where people have learned to understand each other without much ado are required (Hansen 1999).

Especially in recent years, then, social network analysis has offered a wide range of important insights into the workings of organizations, not least concerning the ways in which people in organizations cooperate, transfer knowledge and thus how organizations innovate.

7.2 Action problem

Will the knowledge that is exchanged through the network actually be used? Will the knowledge exchanged set in motion a sustained wave of interaction, perhaps over time involving more people who would benefit from the exchange, or who might contribute to it? Network analysis has looked primarily at the structure of exchange. Recently the ability to exchange has also been discussed at length (Hansen 1999), for instance, in terms of the strength of ties. However, the *willingness* to exchange or motives for exchange are ignored: network analysis is confronted with an *action problem* (Obstfeld 2005). When will people draw in (rather than exclude) others? The structure of the network does not compel action, but innovation requires that dispersed individuals and knowledge are actively brought together.

One is inclined to relate this to the way in which people are motivated: intrinsically or extrinsically. Even though I know that the two types of motives are possibly contradictory, and that emphasizing one of them might offend or put off those who are motivated by the other (Le Grand 2003), in many cases people have more than one motive to act in a certain way. Certainly in the case referred to above no relation could be established between knowledge transfer and the motives of people involved. This leaves us with some nagging doubts: what does resolve the action problem? When will knowledge flow within a firm be put to work?

7.3 Gift exchange

When cooperating in an innovation project, the outcome is uncertain, the relation between one's input and the innovative output is highly obscure, and the incentive to shirk is consequently strong. No (labour) contract will be able to cover every possible contingency. When people are called upon to be creative, the usual command and control measures within a firm are of limited use (Hodgson 2005).

In Chapter 6 I drew on the anthropological literature on gift exchange to tackle the action problem. I argue, with Marcel Mauss in his 1954 book, *The Gift*, that there is a strong obligation for people to give, accept and reciprocate. Those unwilling or unable to do so will not be allowed to become a member of a community or will be excommunicated. Objects of material value may be given, but so may compliments, hints and tips, pieces of information, feedback on another person's plans even if they are still in an early stage of development. People will not give, or will not give something of value to someone who is not part of their group. A group may, but need not, equate to a division; there can obviously be social boundaries within a division. For example, giving an improper (for example, sexist) gift can create a schism between groups (men and women).

Ferrary (2003) reports on Silicon Valley venture capitalists and the gifts they exchange. They are in a situation of great uncertainty – information about the options they face, the likely outcomes of these and their chances of occurrence is absent. These players will have to rely on the soft information they receive from people in their network. The information given can be crucial, but its value can only be established with hindsight.

A Stanford professor giving information about former supervision students to a venture capitalist who is about to invest in the firm that they are setting up signals that the professor values the relationship with both the VC and the former students. He may expect something in return too, at a later date. Accepting a gift – in this case information about the former students when deciding to invest in their venture – entails accepting the perspective of the giver; an improper first gift might alienate a potential business partner in a deal between venture capitalists in much the same way as it might sabotage a romantic relationship. A gift not given can alienate too. The core group of venture capitalists in Silicon Valley will not accept the offer of a newly established VC firm to participate in a deal (Ferrary 2003). One might find this irrational, as business is forgone, but it might also be interpreted as a rational concern for their reputation that pays off in the long run (Dolfsma 2006). Where uncertainties abound, yet where being perceived as a reliable partner is of profound importance, it pays not to do business with newly established undertakings that might not be sufficiently embedded to be able to obtain the necessary information (Podolny 1993).

However, if players view each other as members of the same group, a company failing to involve another venture capitalist in a deal, perhaps because it can handle the business itself and does not want to share the prospective profits, will alienate others. The first firm might be kept out of the loop for future deals by the other firms, even if there is a cost involved in so doing. Relations between firms may be rational, but they are established and maintained by individuals (Child and Faulkner 1998). Rational considerations and personal relations thus both play important roles. Rational calculation must however remain unspoken in gift exchange.

In gift exchange, it is essential that the return gift is not immediate. Having given in the past means that you have credit outstanding, but this cannot be called on at will. A gift may never be returned – if that is the case, the relationship will surely suffer.

7.4 Gift exchange and knowledge transfer between scientists

Reciprocal gift exchange establishes a transactional relationship between individuals (Sherry 1983) and allows actors to forge and personalize relationships and to develop guarantees of personal bonding (Zucker 1986; Shapiro 1987). As these relationships develop and the exchange interactions progress actors learn to cooperate with these particular others (Starpoli 1998; Gulati 1995) and establish a common frame of reference allowing them to incorporate new (tacit) knowledge (Hansen 1999; Kogut and Zander 1992; Von Hippel 1994).

In every empirical piece of research on gift giving, in whatever context, the Matthew Effect is found to be true: to those who have shall be given. This may hold in particular when the individuals who exchange are involved in the uncertain business of knowledge development (compare Merton 1968). Those in a powerful position thus receive more than others. They also give more than many others, if only because their networks tend to be more elaborate. What constitutes an appropriate gift or what is the appropriate value of a gift then depends on the understanding of the position of giver, recipient and their mutual relationship.

In studies looking at what determines the success or lack of success among corporate scientists, some noteworthy findings emerge. Those who actively engage in the publication of papers, giving to the scientific community at large, are more successful than those who don't. This is, obviously, partly due to the fact that this is a means for them to be up to speed with the most recent developments in their fields, keeping their own and their organization's absorptive capacity high (Cohen and Levinthal, 1990). However, these scientists themselves claim that they also receive more from others working outside their own organization, formally and informally, in the form of access to scientists in other organizations and to unpublished tacit knowledge (Furukawa and Goto 2006; Hicks 1995). Most of the knowledge at the frontier of advanced research may be tacit (Hicks 1995); such knowledge is likely to be shared with researchers with whom one has established a longer-term relationship of trust and understanding, a relationship of strong ties

(Hansen 1999). This active (publishing) behaviour of some scientists in an organization also boosts their effectiveness within their own organizations. The resulting flow of knowledge encourages innovation in the tasks in which they and their co-workers are involved, thereby benefiting the organization as whole (Furukawa and Goto, 2006). Corporate scientists, creating goodwill and establishing obligations 'by building a relationship of give and take with the scientific community' (Hicks 1995), can act as technological gatekeepers and serve as a bridge between external sources of knowledge and their co-workers.

The story of successful corporate scientists cooperating informally through gift exchange continues. Bouty (2000) has shown that they are involved in relations with scientists they know in other, sometimes competing, organizations, helping each other out in ways that may counter explicit organizational regulations, and which, if taken advantage of, could seriously hurt the organization. Nonetheless, laboratory test results, feedback, hints and the like are exchanged with specific others. The gift element is clear: if a person is not known, no gifts are exchanged; if a person is not known well, gifts of low value such as commonly available knowledge are exchanged; if a person is known well and the relationship is long term, very valuable knowledge can be exchanged. In each of these cases, of course, there is no guarantee of a reciprocal gift of equal value. Opportunism is always a possibility, but one that would lead to excommunication and a loss of reputation. The existence of such relations between corporate scientists within and between firms is not a new observation (see Allen 1977; Kreiner and Schultz 1993; Von Hippel 1987; or the communities of practice literature, Wenger and Snyder 2000; Wenger 1998; Brown and Duguid 1991, 2001), but it tends not to be conceptualized in terms of gift exchange.

Even in markets where standard products are exchanged, however, gift giving is commonplace. One well-researched example is that of electronic parts (Darr 2003). Sellers' representatives try to build a relationship with buyers not just because it is satisfying on a personal level, but also to stabilize sales and to further increase sales volumes. Buyers in such a relationship hope to be kept more fully up to date about developments than might otherwise be the case (as this is not stipulated in any contract) and hope to be given special consideration should unforeseen circumstances occur. Sudden additional supplies may not be available (at attractive conditions) when buyers have had a tendency to buy 'on the street'.

Gift exchange is risky, can backfire easily, but at the same time, cannot be avoided and is a prerequisite for innovation in modern organizations.

7.5 Some implications for management

While much of the academic work on networks is both highly theoretical and employs complex statistical tools for network analysis, there is an inescapably mundane element to it as well. Pictures such as that represented in Figure 7.1 never fail to amaze even those who have worked at the relevant firm for many years. 'Does communication within my firm really depend on so few individuals? What happens when they leave? Do these few individuals have the company goals in mind all the time? Are the few linking pins sufficiently recognized, let alone rewarded?'

What should be a relief to managers is that formal networks within their organization *do* play an important role in knowledge exchange and *will* contribute to innovation. Setting up teams is one way to promote this. Network analysis also allows one to pinpoint the weaknesses in the communication structure of a firm: which individuals are important for the flow of knowledge? Are these recognized and rewarded sufficiently, or are they disgruntled? Are certain divisions cut off from others? Is there enough redundancy in the networks so dependence on a single person is reduced? The communication profiles of people in the organization are not necessarily those one would expect given their position. Is the staff organization that should be stimulating innovation and exchange between divisions – represented by node 13 in Figure 7.1 – doing a proper job? Do some people under-communicate, can their communication be redirected in a way that is more beneficial to the company? Perhaps informal relations can be built on to develop formal relations.

The evolution of the networks over time can also be scrutinized: are more links emerging? Is there too much communication going on, particularly across division boundaries after the early phases of an innovation project have been concluded and when there should be a focus on the development of the product (Ancona and Caldwell 1992)?

But will the knowledge exchange that the presence of networks would lead one to expect actually take place? Do the employees of a firm contribute to knowledge transfer to the extent that might be expected of them, including division heads and members of staff departments? Will the 'action problem' be overcome in a firm? The exchanges in a firm relating to innovation and knowledge development are best understood as a gift exchange. Gifts of ideas, tips, feedback and the like are typically exchanged between people in an organization. These create bonds, trust and mutual obligations. However, putting too much explicit emphasis on the need to exchange, on the instrumental value of gift exchange, is counter-productive. What is 'too much' in one context or for one person can be acceptable in other circumstances. Management, finding command and control instruments of decreasing use when it comes to persuading people to be creatively involved, must be sensitive to the possibility of divergent meanings attached by persons to contexts and signals.

From a gift exchange perspective, the skewed nature of the knowledge exchanged in networks is not surprising and not necessarily problematic. That those in central positions are given much more than those at the periphery is to be expected. But a lack of reciprocity in knowledge exchange leaves the firm vulnerable too. Is a bias in the pattern of knowledge transfer introduced because some individuals are more involved than others? Are there people who might have important knowledge to offer who are out of the loop because they have not been allowed or able to enter a group? These are questions that managers may want to address, and that they can only answer in the context of their own organization. People on both sides of the divide may fail to recognize what the peripheries have to offer. Stimulating informal contacts can help, but so can making sure that procedures for establishing the value of proposals are formalized so that peripherals will bring new ideas and proposals to the table as well.

Formal measures and structures seem to contribute more to knowledge exchange than informal arrangements. Formal opportunities can be created for exchanges where people might otherwise forgo these. Formal meetings might even be occasions on which informal relations between people might start to develop (Aalbers et al. 2006). Gift exchange does not stop when the formal department meeting starts: there is gift exchange in formal settings too (compare Ferrary 2003). And gift exchange can continue after the meetings if the circumstances are conducive to it. Individuals who do not or cannot contribute to knowledge exchange, even in formal settings, may however hurt the firm. Was an initial meeting frustrated because gift exchange has gone bad?

Thinking this over in general terms is all well and good, but high-flown theory is easily forgotten when you are standing with your feet in the mud. Giving problems a real-life feel can, for instance, be done by using a case study where a stylized real-life description is given. Fortunately, there are increasing numbers of such case studies.[2]

8

Path Dependence, Initial Conditions and Routines in Organizations: the Toyota Production System Re-examined[1]

The notion of path dependence was first explicitly used to explain prevailing technical standards (David 1985; Arthur 1989). It has also been discussed in recent decades as a useful way of analysing the development of a range of other subjects, including national innovation systems (Iammarino 2005), industrial districts (Kenney and von Burg 1999) and politics (Pierson 2004). For a long time, at the micro-level of individual organizations a much less elaborate use of the concept has been made (with the notable exception of David 1994) and it is only recently that interest in this field of application has expanded further (for example, Sydow et al. 2005). I argue that using path dependence for the historical analysis of organizational change can be very fruitful. To do so, however, the key elements of path dependence – sensitivity to initial conditions and lock-in mechanisms – need to be conceptualized more precisely and linked to one another.

We show this by empirically re-examining the Toyota Production System (TPS). This is a subject that has been studied before (Cusumano 1985; Fujimoto 1999; Coriat 2000), but in this chapter I draw on a wide range of relevant empirical literature, including (recent) accounts that have not previously been used, and analyse the case from a more elaborate path dependence perspective than in earlier publications on TPS. This, I argue, sheds new light on both this important empirical case and on the conceptualization of path dependence. Our empirical analysis includes comparisons with Toyota's main Japanese rival, Nissan; a comparison that is quite frequently made in the literature.

8.1 Path dependence and routines

While in fields that have a more extensive history in using the concept of path dependence the precise understanding of this concept is certainly not uncontested (see, for example, Schwartz 2004; Beyer 2005), a study of organizational change in these terms implies specific problems. This reflects the complex, multifaceted nature of organizations in comparison to technical artefacts. At an abstract level, a path dependence interpretation can be reasonably straightforward. Path dependence consists of two separate elements. To explain an extant phenomenon, one must first identify a moment in its history to stand as a starting point (determined by what is referred to as initial conditions) at which it emerged in its basic form. Second, it is necessary to determine which distinct lock-in mechanisms have kept the phenomenon on track.

In this common interpretation, sensitivity to initial conditions is defined as separate from lock-in mechanisms. The latter are usually explicitly defined in the path dependence literature, albeit suggesting different degrees of determinacy. Beyer (2005), for instance, prefers to reserve the term 'lock-in' for the complete absence of change of the phenomenon as initially envisaged. He distinguishes several mechanisms creating continuity: increasing returns, sequences of events, functionality, complementarity, power, legitimacy and conformity. In vain, however, does one search for a theoretical elaboration on the nature of initial conditions other than that they form a 'critical juncture' (Mahoney 2000). In the strategy field, studies using the term 'initial conditions' provide us with something to hold on to, by either understanding them as (mainly) internal to the firm (Porter 1991; Doz 1996; Dahlquist et al. 2000) or as external (Swaminathan 1996). In the path dependence literature, specific (sequences of) events are often regarded as playing a vital role during the selection of a starting point, but there is no clear consensus as to whether they are part of initial conditions or not. Goldstone (1998a, p. 834) explicitly notes that: 'a system that exhibits path dependency is one in which ... the particular outcome ... depends on the choices or outcomes of *intermediate events* between the initial conditions and the outcome' (italics added). This statement seems in line with the prevailing view that path dependence implies that the path taken is not determined by initial conditions; in this sense extreme sensitivity to initial conditions is a misplaced description of path dependence (Page 2006). Nevertheless, Goldstone's analysis of the British Industrial Revolution as a path dependent phenomenon (Goldstone 1998b) suggests that he understands initial conditions as the prevailing 'social formation' at a certain point of time. This is hard to equate with a common path dependence interpretation that initial conditions themselves are very sensitive to 'small influences' (Dopfer 1991, p. 545) or 'small events' (Pierson 2004, p. 251), or in other words, are 'chance-like' (Howlett and Rayner 2006, p. 5).[2]

The critical period involved, prevailing circumstances, events, characteristics of the phenomenon to be explained itself and the way it is selected are all too often (implicitly) amalgamated in one diffuse category of 'initial conditions'. This is a serious shortcoming of the literature and one that I aim to address, since identifying initial conditions should be an important part of the research to be carried out under the banner of path dependence (Goldstone 1998a, p. 841). In fact, as I argue here and show below for Toyota, which conditions are salient is neither self-evident to the actors themselves nor to the scholars studying their behaviour. In particular, selection mechanisms as part of the initial conditions need to be more clearly conceptualized, since the initial direction a path takes is not as indeterminate as is customarily assumed in the path dependence literature (for example, Arthur 1989; Dopfer 1991; Mahoney 2000; Bassanini and Dosi 2001). I agree with Sydow et al. (2005, p. 28) who point out that the stage before a path starts 'is not dominated by undirected search and random selection'. Unlike these and other authors (Marquis 2003), however, I thus consider 'imprinting' by a general societal structure during the time of founding of organizations (Stinchcombe 1965) part and parcel of a path dependent process.

To substantiate this claim, I draw on the concept of routines in order to be more specific about the way in which the initial selecting comes about. Organizations may fruitfully be seen as collections of routines held in common, where routines have been alternatively defined in a behavioural sense as recurrent interaction patterns or cognitively as rules (Becker 2004). Several kinds of routines can be distinguished, for instance, operational characteristics, investment rules and higher order routines (Nelson and Winter 1982, pp. 16–17). In studying path dependence, higher order routines are of special interest, since they both modify existing routines and guide the search for and the selection of new routines (Nelson and Winter 1982, p. 18). For convenience I denote these higher order routines as 'meta-routines'. These routines need not be formalized, and I would like to avoid exclusive connotations of the term 'meta-routines' with formal procedures for standardized problem-solving as has been done by Adler et al. (1999), or with very specific phenomena such as production lines (Szulanski and Jensen 2004).[3] Below I will argue that a meta-routine of 'self-testing and adaptation' played a central role in the adoption and further development of the Toyota Production System. Following a suggestion by Becker (2004, p. 664), in linking behavioural and cognitive interpretations of routines I primarily understand meta-routines as a propensity to select particular solutions for certain types of problems. They make the adoption of certain routines much more likely than others: 'A firm's search policy will be characterized as determining the probability distribution of what will be found through search ...' (Nelson and Winter 1982, p. 18), thus following a non-deterministic line of reasoning that is analogous to Greif's analysis of institutions whereby 'beliefs, norms, and organizations inherited from the past influence subsequent institutions by constituting the default in new situations ... are part of the initial conditions in the processes that influence selection among alternative new institutions' (Greif 2006, pp. 187–8; see also Chapter 4 above).

Meta-routines can thus be a part of the initial conditions. They may be rather general in nature, may not be so explicit in what salient solution is to be opted for, and may be unarticulated. Like other initial conditions, meta-routines can be both external and internal to the firm. Some of these routines prevail in the industry as a whole or even in the economy at large, some emerge within the organization itself and thus are firm-specific. Industry or economy-wide routines can be held responsible for the time-sensitive social 'imprinting' (Stinchcombe 1965; Marquis 2003). Alternatively, as firm-specific meta-routines are not so easily imitated by others, imprinting will often occur at the mundane level only, and thus contribute to variety in choices of firms that are confronted with more or less similar external conditions. The term imprinting should not be taken too literally, as interpretation and conscious action by agents is also always involved (Johnson 2007; Foray 1997; Djelic and Quack 2007). Arrow (1974, p. 63) suggests that a 'code' (for which one can read 'routine') 'is determined in accordance with the best *expectations* at the time of the firm's creation' (italics added). Along these lines, Porter (1991) argues that (internal) initial conditions partly result from earlier managerial choices, in their turn reflecting a then current environment. Boeker (1988, p. 35) connects internal and external elements of initial conditions through the figure of the founder of a firm, who acts as 'a primary conduit by which larger social conditions become incorporated into organizational strategy and structure'. The plural is vital here, since imprinting of organizations by initial conditions is never predetermined, if only because several factors are influencing organizations at the same time. Slightly reframing a categorization made by Kriauciunas and Kale (2006), the initial conditions potentially having an imprinting effect can be grouped in three categories: environmental requirements, resources and values or philosophies. Unlike Kriauciunas and Kale (2006), I consider not only resources, but also values or philosophies as potentially both internal and external to the firm (and thus do not limit this category to the founder's general orientation). Philosophies are likely to express themselves through meta-routines. Routines as an analytical instrument bridge initial conditions and lock-in mechanisms.

Two reasons can be given for qualifying the strict separation of initial conditions and lock-in mechanisms. First, initial conditions are a combination of elements, and gradual changes in one or more of these elements can create a context that differs from the initial conditions, but that is still related to them. Second, organizational features such as a company's production system are manifold phenomena that are not created or selected in their entirety at a certain distinct point of time (compare Thelen 2004); the phenomenon under study itself is dynamic. Regarding the first consideration, as Schwartz (2004) argues, initial conditions partly act as 'constant causes' (see Stinchcombe 1968). This, however, undermines the idea of path dependence as consisting of the separate mechanisms of 'production' and 'reproduction' (Schwartz 2004). The second consideration implies that more than one path should be investigated, which is not incompatible with at least some interpretations of path dependence (for example, Mahoney 2000; Djelic and Quack 2007), but nevertheless casts doubts on a straightforward application of the concept. Still, I think using the concept of routines can bridge the current gap between sensitivity to initial conditions and lock-in mechanisms, without losing the analytical advantages of – at least to some extent – separating the two elements in a path dependent analysis. Meta-routines may develop over time, and exert a lasting influence on later developments. They thus conceptually provide the dynamic link between initial conditions and lock-in. Understanding meta-routines as mechanisms that modify existing routines and guide the search for and selection of new routines implies that I understand lock-in not as rigidity, but as a dynamic element creating continuity. This implies that not only the selection mechanism, but *what* is selected should be conceptualized as routines. In other words, I should study path dependence of routines (Becker 2004) as a corollary to routines creating path dependence.

We thus argue that until now initial conditions have been underspecified in the path dependence literature. The distinction between external and internal conditions and the role of selection mechanisms in the shape of meta-routines have not been sufficiently acknowledged. There is also no consensus on the exact conceptual status of (sequences of) events, which is disturbing since they also figure as lock-in mechanisms. This lack of clarity has meant that the use of the concept of path dependence in a context of organizational change has not been exploited to its full potential. As organizational phenomena are – unlike technical artefacts – multi-faceted, it is essential to provide conceptual clarity and acknowledge that distinguishing initial conditions and lock-in mechanisms may be problematic. The constitutive elements of path dependence, in particular initial conditions, must be unpacked, and the interrelations between them further analysed and conceptualized. I have argued that in particular the concept of meta-routines will allow one to do this. These theoretical considerations lead to pressing questions for empirical research. Which initial conditions can be specified? Do meta-routines meaningfully relate sensitivity to initial conditions on the one hand and lock-in mechanisms on the other? How do these routines interact with specific circumstances and (sequences of) events in selecting and locking-in certain choices?

The origin and development of the often-studied Toyota Production System (TPS) seems an appropriate case for such an empirical application. Fujimoto (1999) stresses 'multi-path system emergence' and the difference between the logic of the first adoption of several elements of TPS on the one hand and their subsequent diffusion through the company on the other. Likewise, Coriat (2000, p. 218) holds 'a variety of "small" events and macro conditions…' responsible for the emergence of just-in-time (JIT) or more general 'auto-activation' at Toyota Motor shortly after the Second World War. These studies, and also that by Cusumano (1985), take an implicit path dependence perspective and so cannot fully exploit the concept as developed here. I show that one of the elements hinted at by these studies, a firm-specific meta-routine, rooted in the prehistory of the Toyota Motor Company, rather than general circumstances, was predominant. This routine adopted by Toyota was not only part of the initial conditions, but has shaped the development of the company ever since. Meta-routines created a dynamic lock-in guiding the development of TPS, in interaction with certain events, in particular during the crucial 1949–50 period. I am thus trying to steer a middle road between overly deterministic and overly voluntaristic interpretations of change in organizations (Beyer 2005).

8.2 Methodology and data

Our case study is a combination of a within-case analysis of TPS and, to a lesser degree, a cross-case analysis of the Toyota and Nissan production systems (George and Bennett 2005).The case analysis is based on secondary literature. For this, I traced around eighty journal articles, books and book chapters, primarily on the evolution of Toyota, but also on Nissan and the Japanese car industry as a whole, through searching electronic databases and checking references. This collection includes a few journalistic accounts and several biographies and autobiographies of Toyota and its leaders. Popular accounts of the Toyota system, sometimes containing hagiographic descriptions, and manuals on how to implement the system were largely ignored. I also consulted some selected historical publications on leading US car manufacturers' production systems and a few general works on the development of the Japanese economy. All publications used are written in English, including translations from the Japanese. To the best of our knowledge, some major publications, including recent ones (for example, Wada and Yui 2000; Hino 2006), have not previously been used in scientific analyses of the evolution of the Toyota Production System published in English. Our analysis here thus builds on the broadest possible collection of internationally available material.

We focused on identifying the long-term historical influence of certain circumstances and events, both internal and external to the company, on the evolution of Toyota's production system. 'Process tracing' (George and Bennett 2005) was applied to identify in particular the causal mechanisms through which meta-routines tended to select and lock-in certain features of the Toyota Production System. I concentrated, however, on the development of the internal side of Toyota's production system since relations with the preceding activities of Toyota's managers were more salient in this regard than the company's famous multi-tiered supplier system. Some caution was needed when using the descriptions and analyses published by Toyota's former leaders themselves or the official Toyota history. Where appropriate, I have put these expositions into perspective. When the sources contain contradictory information on certain important facts, I have indicated this in the text or in footnotes. I dealt with differences in interpretations in the literature by carefully weighing their plausibility and empirical base, in particular in regards to the supposed temporal order of 'cause' and 'effect' at vital 'turning points in the causal chain' (George and Bennett 2005, p. 92).

8.3 Toyota and the development of the Japanese car industry

A number of Japanese firms started to produce cars on a small scale from around 1900, but with the exception of one of the forerunners of Nissan from 1911 without much enduring success (Odaka et al. 1988, pp. 21–7). After the Kanto earthquake in 1923, demand for buses and trucks boomed, and the leading US car makers Ford (in 1925) and GM (Chevrolet in 1927) opened so-called knock-down plants on Japanese soil, driving the domestic producers from the market (Odaka et al. 1988, p. 27). In May 1936, however, several years after Japan had occupied Manchuria and under the circumstances of a war economy, a new military law increased import duties, making production within Japan by foreign companies virtually impossible (for a timetable of crucial changes external and internal to Toyota between 1931 and 1955, see Table 8.1). Ford and GM finally ended their activities in Japan completely in 1939 and left the market to domestic producers recognized by the Japanese

Table 8.1 Important events external and internal to Toyota, 1931–55

Date	Environment	Toyota
September 1931	Japan invades Manchuria	
May 1936	Japan virtually prohibits imports of cars	
1937		Founding of Toyota Motor Company
1938		JIT production at Koromo plant
1939	Ford and GM discontinue car production in Japan	
July 1941	Full US-British-Dutch embargo on Japanese imports	
August 1945	Japan surrenders to Allied powers	
c. 1947		Starts multi-machine handling in machine shop
c. 1948		Starts JIT in machine shop
April 1949	Anti-inflation measures (Dodge Line)	
October 1949	Ban on producing private cars lifted	
End 1949		Toyota faces bankruptcy
April 1950		Split between Toyota Motor and sales
June 1950	Start of Korean War; US places mass orders for trucks	Lay-offs of *c*. 2000 workers; Kiichiro Toyoda resigns
1955		Toyota issues first passenger car to be produced on a substantial scale

government: these were Nissan, Toyota and United Motors (later called Isuzu) which was formed from the merger of three other firms in 1939. Nissan pioneered large-scale domestic production of private cars in Japan from 1935. Kiichiro Toyoda was working towards the same end under the roof of a textile machinery factory, Toyoda Automatic Loom Works from 1930. The Toyota Motor Company was founded in 1937. By this time, the government was obliging motor manufacturers to focus on military trucks, and in 1939 passenger car production was virtually outlawed. This ban was finally removed in October 1949, more than four years after Japan's defeat in World War II. After Toyota was almost bankrupted as the result of a shortage of capital, the Korean War saved the Japanese auto industry from extinction: US forces placed massive orders for military trucks from June 1950. Like Nissan, Toyota developed into a mass producer of automobiles and after 1965 it produced more passenger cars than trucks.

Toyota became famous for the Toyota Production System. Its two closely related main elements are (1) 'lean production', of which small lot production using a just-in-time system – which implies that parts are only made or delivered when needed at the next stage in the production process, thus minimizing intermediate stocks – is the best-known element, and (2) the use of a flexible and integrated multi-layered network of suppliers. I focus on the first element of lean production. The gradual extension of lean production, pioneered by Toyota from 1938, reflects, as I will argue, Toyota's routine of 'self-testing and adaptation'. After seeing the successes of the system (Womack et al. 1990) other car makers, both in and outside Japan, have tried to emulate Toyota's approach, but have certainly not completely succeeded in this. Toyota has been considered the best organized and most productive car maker in the world for decades and is currently at the point of taking over the number one global position from ailing General Motors.

8.4 Assessing the initial conditions for lean production

Opening the black box of initial conditions implies precise separation of the individual causes of the emergence of the phenomenon under study. I have structured the discussion on the emergence of lean production at Toyota presented below accordingly. The initial conditions to be considered are grouped within the three categories mentioned above: requirements (demand), resources (material, financial and labour) and philosophies (meta-routines). This strategy illustrates what I see as the way forward for path dependence approaches to understanding organizational change, specifying the complex nature of initial conditions, in terms both of content and timing.

Dating the initial conditions

A first major analytical problem is dating the start of a phenomenon, and thus defining the initial conditions. Toyota Motor Company's founder, Kiichiro Toyoda, introduced the concept of JIT a few months before the official opening of the Koromo factory in September 1938 (Wada and Yui 2002, pp. 278–9). He actually installed a JIT system in this Toyota factory, the first new one built for automobile production (*Toyota* 1988, pp. 70–3). In May 1939, Kiichiro ordered coordination of the work in all shops and, interestingly, gave the factory workers freedom to leave for home when they had achieved their target production for the day, even if this was before the end of their official working hours (Wada and Yui 2002, pp. 288–9). This enabled him to detect bottlenecks in other parts of the company, a significant advantage of JIT production. However, in September 1939, Toyota's inventory of parts and materials could still have produced more than half of its annual vehicle output (Wada and Yui 2002, p. 290). Thus, even before the war made application of this philosophy increasingly difficult, Toyota was still far from the ideal of minimizing intermediate stocks (*Toyota* 1988, p. 142). The individual often considered to be the founding father of TPS, engineer Taiichi Ohno (1912–90), reintroduced lean production practices at Toyota in the years 1947–49.[4] In hindsight, it can been seen that this was the start of a diffusion of lean production across Toyota's factories and those of its external suppliers. The best choice for dating the initial conditions is thus most probably the years 1947–49, but they were preceded by events that foreshadowed the phenomenon.

Nature of demand

Dating the initial conditions is highly relevant, since it determines our conclusions on the relevance of particular circumstances influencing the adoption and diffusion of lean production at Toyota. A peculiar combination of scarce resources and low, fragmented demand (Odaka et al. 1988, p. 39) could have instigated innovation in the organization of car production in Japan, and some leading studies on the Japanese auto industry indeed more or less suggest that this was the case (Cusumano 1985; Fujimoto 1999). Low levels of demand prevailed even before the war. The early car market in Japan was affected by 'small land space, bad road conditions, and low income levels', all of which increased demand for small cars rather than large ones (Shimokawa 1994, p. 226). Initially, however, Toyota, was not particularly responsive to these market conditions. In the 1930s Kiichiro Toyoda, driven by his ambition to compete head-on with US car makers, unlike Nissan opted for a 3000cc 'people's car' – which had to be large enough to cater to the US market – instead of a small car (Wada and Yui 2002, pp. 239–41). His first prototype automobile was based on American models (Odaka et al. 1988, p. 125; Wada and Yui 2002, p. 247) and only once car production was re-established after the war did Kiichiro define the production of a small car, of between 1000 and 1500cc, as an aim for his company (*Toyota* 1988, pp. 100–1). Ohno is emphatic that the post-war fragmented demand for many product varieties required JIT production (Ohno 1988, p. xiii). However, in the first years following the defeat of Japan, Japanese car makers mainly produced trucks for civilian purposes and demand for private cars remained low. The Japanese government was subject to the authority of the US Supreme Commander of Allied Powers (SCAP) or General Headquarters (GHQ) between 1945 and 1952. In a continuation of wartime policy, scarce resources were to be directed to necessary goods, in particular toward the revitalization of heavy industry. GHQ moderated the ban on domestic production of passenger cars in June 1947 (raising allowable production slightly to a maximum of 300 cars per year) and lifted the ban altogether only in October 1949. Moreover, Japanese car makers were not protected against imports of US cars that were far superior in quality (Cusumano 1985, p. 7). Post-war demand was thus indeed initially low, but it was not particularly diverse. Toyota produced some 20,000 trucks and buses and a few hundred passenger cars between 1947 and 1949 (*Toyota* 1988, p. 461); overall, production consisted mainly of one type of truck for the depressed civilian market (Cusumano 1985, p. 266). Thus the combination of both low and fragmented demand to imprint Toyota's lean production between 1947 and 1949 did not exist, an argument reinforced by the fact that Toyota's first application of JIT by Kiichiro Toyoda was not to diverse vehicle production but was almost exclusively concerned with manufacturing standard military trucks.

Availability of material and financial resources

The same qualification applies to a frequent suggestion in the literature that an initial scarcity of material resources imprinted on the Toyota Production System. For instance, a group of Toyota officials has labelled the lack of natural resources as 'the most distinctive feature of Japan' (Sugimori et al. 1977, p. 553) and claimed that this focused Japanese industries – more closely than industries in other countries – on minimizing costs while still maintaining the production of high quality goods.

More specifically, Coriat (2000, p. 218) identifies the lack of raw materials as a circumstance peculiar to the early post-war years, stimulating Japanese companies to search for material-saving working methods. In fact, scarcity of raw materials plagued the Japanese economy, including Toyota (*Toyota* 1988, pp. 75–6 and 99–100), from 1941, when the allied forces blocked shipments to Japan, through the initial post-war years when the victors put the Japanese economy on short rations (Cohen 1949). Nonetheless, the literature does not contain any references to specific empirical data indicating that scarcity of raw materials actually stimulated or even necessitated the (re)introduction of JIT production at Toyota in the first post-war years. Around 1948, when Ohno was beginning his experiments, Toyota often had to wait for parts from its suppliers until the middle of the month, forcing it to realize its planned monthly production in just two weeks (Cusumano 1985, p. 278). Shortage of materials thus *prevented* JIT-production, as Kiichiro Toyoda had experienced in 1939. Cusumano (1985, p. 264) offers a more plausible version of an explanation in terms of material resources: 'The Japanese, reacting originally to *shortages of space* and low production volume, developed the practice of consolidating various shops under one roof rather than building separate facilities for casting, body stamping, final assembly, or other distinct operations' (italics added). Still, consolidation does not necessary imply JIT production. A lean production system characterized by multi-purpose equipment, low intermediate inventories and a minimum of warehouse space, makes at least as much sense from a perspective of limiting investments as of minimizing the use of materials. More relevant therefore were perhaps the limited financial means available to Toyota that – like Nissan – had great difficulty during this period in remaining in business (Fujimoto 1999; Cusumano 1985).

Availability of labour resources

Characteristically, Ohno himself stressed the importance of JIT for the identification and avoidance of 'waste' – in the shape of idle *labour* rather than of raw materials (Ohno 1988, p. 13; Shingo 1989; Williams et al. 1994). This despite the abundance of labour in the first post-war years, when production for the military had stopped and many skilled workers were on the labour market (Gordon 1985, pp. 334 and 346). It should be noted that, on the other hand, the auto workers' position was strengthened considerably by the democratization policy of GHQ in the first post-war years. Japanese union membership grew from negligible roots to more than 6.5 million in June 1948 (Okayama 1987, p. 171) and an industry-wide car workers' union was formed in 1947. In the same year, Ohno introduced the practice of workers handling more than one machine each in the so-called L-layout in Toyota's machine-shop (Ohno 1988, p. 11). Multi-machine handling, a prime example of what was later denoted by the company as 'autonomation' ('automation with a human face'), became a central element in Toyota's lean production system. To save labour, Toyota increasingly used multi-functional workers, restructuring jobs so that operations became more versatile, but also demanded less skill than before. The craft element of production that had prevailed in Japanese car production until then was abandoned (Daito 2000, pp. 147–9; Okayama 1987, pp. 178–9; Fujimoto, 1999, p. 64). Toyota's first post-war application of lean production thus owed more to a strategic decision to reduce dependence on skilled labour than to any 'imprinting' by the external condition of scarcity in material resources.

8.5 Meta-routines as selection mechanism

The common focus on specific external economic initial conditions as the main imprinting factor on the emergence of lean production at Toyota does not pass the empirical test. The adoption of JIT has also been related, however, to an economy-wide 'wartime passion for avoiding the waste of resources [which] laid the foundations of one of post-war Japan's most successful managerial techniques: the famous "just-in-time" system' (Morris-Suzuki 1994, p. 155). In addition to such an explanation being rather unspecific, it does not explain the differences between Japanese car manufacturers. The fact that Toyota and Nissan reacted differently to largely identical external initial circumstances – Nissan did not try early on to develop a JIT system and related elements whereas Toyota did – suggests instead that different mechanisms were at work in the two companies.

The different approaches of Toyota and Nissan from the start of car production have been widely noted in the literature (Cusumano 1985; Daito 2000; Fujimoto 1999). Nissan was the abbreviation that came into use in 1928 to denote the Nippon Sangyo holding firms created by Yoshisuke Aikawa, an engineer who had been active as an entrepreneur in Japan since 1911 (on Nissan, see Cusumano 1985 and Odaka et al. 1988). Nissan comprised a range of firms engaged in the production of metal parts, machinery and chemicals, including the well known Hitachi company. Through a complicated series of mergers and restructurings, Nissan became involved in the production of Datsun cars in 1933. Aikawa admired US big business and had worked in the United States between 1905 and 1907. He had also spent several months there buying machines in 1908 and 1909 (Cusumano 1985, p. 30). Although he started his working life on the shop-floor (Odaka et al. 1988, p. 93), Aikawa has been described as someone '... who was more interested in building empires than cars...' (Cusumano 1985, p. 52). From 1935, Nissan produced Datsun cars and parts for US car plants in Japan under the guidance of American engineers, which was in fact a continuation of the cooperation between Aikawa and William R. Gorham and other US engineers dating back to 1920 (Odaka et al. 1988, p. 95–6). When after a few years Nissan shifted its focus to truck production in response to demand from the military, Aikawa '... hired American engineers and imported designs and an entire truck factory from the United States – creating a bias in Nissan toward American automated equipment and mass-production techniques that continued through the 1980s' (Cusumano 1985, p. 27).

Toyota's general orientation can be described differently: 'Kiichiro Toyoda made every effort to develop an indigenous product and a production system compatible with local conditions' (Daito 2000, p. 141). This typical Toyota approach can be traced back to the activities of Sakichi Toyoda (1867–1930), the father of Toyota's founder (Mass and Robertson 1996; Wada 2006). Sakichi was a famous Japanese inventor, active in the textile machinery business. Sakichi learned the carpenter's craft from his father, but he became obsessed with improving the hand looms that he saw his mother and other women using in the textile cottage industry in the Aichi region. Sakichi specialized in developing and improving looms and gained his first patent in 1891. In 1924 his achievements culminated in the famous type-G loom of 1924 – the first automated loom with a non-stop automated shuttle change. Sakichi's concerns throughout his career were securing sufficient funds to finance his inventions and improvements of textile machines, and creating opportunities to test them in practice. He founded, owned, restructured and/or managed a range of firms in the textile and textile machinery business between 1895 and 1933. The poor performance of his first power loom in comparison with the British Platt Bros looms in a year-long mill experiment conducted by the Kanegafuchi Cotton Spinning Co around 1907 (Wada and Yui 2002, pp. 26–7) taught Sakichi to develop and test his innovations under (his own) mill conditions (Mass and Robertson 1996, p. 6; *Toyota* 1988, p. 30). This provided the germ of what Fear (2001, p. 172) calls 'tinkering', or the 'self-testing and adaptation' meta-routine of Toyota.

While Sakichi was self-educated, his son Kiichiro (1894–1952) went to Tokyo University at the instigation of his uncle Heikichi who persuaded Sakichi to let Kiichiro graduate as a mechanical engineer in 1920 (Eiji

Toyoda 1987, p. 22). Similarly, Heikichi's son, Eiji Toyoda, eighteen years younger than Kiichiro, also went to the university and graduated as an engineer in 1936. From 1921, Kiichiro was mainly responsible for technical improvements in his father's businesses (Mass and Robertson, 1996, p. 25). Toyoda Automatic Loom acted as the seedbed of Toyota automotive production (Mass and Robertson, 1996, p. 33). With the income from these textile activities, Toyoda Automatic Loom Works financed Kiichiro's experimenting on car production from 1930 onwards. In 1933 an automobile department was set up (Wada and Yui 2002, p. 235). When Toyota Motor Co. was founded in 1937, Sakichi's son-in-law Risaburo – who had also been adopted by him – became president, but Kiichiro, formally vice-president, ran the company. Unlike Nissan, which relied heavily on US engineers, Kiichiro and his collaborators – supported by university people – tried to master the production of parts themselves through various and lengthy experiments during the first years of the company's existence (Odaka et al. 1988, pp. 125–30). Between September 1933 and May 1935 not a single car was actually produced – which indicates both the care that Kiichiro took to master production processes and the considerable problems involved.

The adoption of Toyota's lean production system should be seen against the background of the meta-routine of 'self-testing and adaptation'. Kiichiro Toyoda's early attempt to use a JIT system at the Koromo plant as a device to identify bottlenecks in production was in line with this general focus on continuous testing and adaptation. Similarly, it fitted well with Ohno's permanent obsession with removing 'waste'. For routines to exert an influence over long periods of time, 'transmission mechanisms' are needed that should be identified by process tracing. Toyota's policy of transferring knowledge through the circulation of personnel and the extensive recording of experience were vital for the enduring effect of the meta-routine. Kiichiro became famous for his habit of writing down very detailed reports of his experiments and manuals for production and organization (Wada and Yui 2002). Such a formalization by the president himself was highly unusual among Japanese companies (Hino 2006, p. 10) and was vital for the transfer of experience on all kinds of practices to other (later) Toyota managers and workers (Hino 2006; Eiji Toyoda 1987). In the case of Toyota, the transmission by personal interaction was probably at least equally important (Hino 2006, pp. 28–9). Both Kiichiro and Eiji were stimulated to keep in touch with shop-floor practices and insights – in line with Sakichi's philosophy of 'actually trying comes first' (Wada and Yui 2002, p. 130; see also *Toyota* 1988, p.38). Ohno, the architect of Toyota's production system who started to work at Toyoda Spinning and Weaving in 1933, also came to adhere to this conviction. Characteristically, after an extensive study of textbooks and articles on the latest American management methods in 1937–38, he decided that 'the best way to improve the Toyoda factory was to put the textbooks aside, go to the shop floor, and study the plant and workers in operation' (Cusumano 1985, p. 272). Later, Toyota's top management consistently supported Ohno in his innovations. As we have seen, path dependence in the development of organizations is a multi-faceted phenomenon in which several interacting paths may be identified. Evidently, Kiichiro's early experiments with JIT production directly inspired Ohno's post-war approach. The latter's experiences at Toyoda Spinning and Weaving were crucial for his shaping of the production system after he moved to Toyota in 1943. In this regard, there is at least one intriguing example of a creative replication of a template that can be considered as an earlier, idiosyncratic outcome of the application of the routine of 'self-testing and adaptation'. Multi-machine operating (see above) had been common at Toyoda Weaving and Spinning before it was applied at Toyota in around 1947. It required that machines automatically stop in case of trouble or at the end of the production process and 'Ohno got part of the idea for this system from the device Sakichi Toyoda had invented many years earlier, where a loom would stop automatically when a thread broke' (*Toyota* 1988, p. 142). There may be some romanticization in this, but the connection is striking nonetheless. It should be stressed that the empiricist meta-routine adopted by Toyota's key managers also implied that they were receptive to American management methods.[5] Like Sakichi, Kiichiro visited the United States and Great Britain, in 1921 and 1929–30, studying operations in textile and machinery firms. He urged his collaborators to read Henry Ford's *My Life and Work* (*Toyota* 1988, p. 42). For his part, Ohno was a great admirer of both Ford and Frederick Taylor; in his obsession to reduce 'waste', he made extensive use of time-and-motion studies (Ohno 1988). Ohno (1988) also emphasizes the model of the (American) supermarket, where supplies were replenished according to actual purchases by customers, as a source of inspiration for the JIT approach.

8.6 Identifying lock-in mechanisms

The Toyota case illustrates that making a distinction between first selection under initial conditions and subsequent lock-in in practice is arbitrary. Toyota's meta-routine had an enduring effect long after the emergence of the first lean-production applications at the firm by acting as a 'constant cause', rather than only having a 'one shot' impact during a critical juncture (initial conditions), as I will show in the last part of this section. As 'lock-in' was expressed at Toyota in a steadily wider application and improvement of lean production, I should consider it a dynamic phenomenon. Next to a meta-routine, specific circumstances arising after the initial adoption of a form of lean production – undertaken in a comparatively short period of time between 1949 and 1950 – locked-in Toyota to the system. These vital circumstances were related to the initial conditions identified above, but were heavily coloured by a sequence of specific events. This latter, typical path dependent element, makes a strict analytical separation of individual causes even more difficult than is the case in regard to initial conditions – for convenience, I have combined several factors under one subheading.

Shifts in demands, shortage of capital and lay-offs

Shortly after Toyota's first post-war experiments with lean production, a sequence of events committed the company more firmly to the path of small lot and JIT production. An acute shortage of capital for Toyota at the end of 1949 was crucial. After the government presented a five-year plan in August and October 1948, setting a national production target of 120,000 vehicles per year by 1953, Japanese auto makers sharply increased their output (*Toyota* 1988, pp. 92 and 104–5). Toyota aimed at producing 15,840 units in 1949, compared to 3900 in 1947. However, the anti-inflation measures implemented by GHQ in April 1949 depressed business conditions and, as the number of unsold cars rose sharply, brought Toyota to the verge of bankruptcy by the end of 1949 (*Toyota* 1988, p. 105). This episode proved to be a turning point in Toyota's history (Coriat 2000). The banks were only prepared to save Toyota if it split sales and marketing into separate companies. Thus, in April 1950, Toyota Motor Sales (TMS) Company was founded, headed by a separate management. TMS would act as a customer of Toyota Motor Company. Through this separation, which was discontinued only in 1982, the banks sought to prevent overproduction in the future. This dramatic episode made Toyota's leaders acutely aware of the importance of balancing production and sales (Fujimoto 1999, pp. 60–1). However, it appeared that extending Ohno's infant JIT system in the machine shop to Toyota's production as a whole was particularly suited to meeting the banks' demands (Togo and Wartman 1993, p. 103). Application of a JIT system was appropriate to the still low-volume, but increasingly diverse demand for cars that developed in Japan in the 1950s (Cusumano 1985,

p. 266), that is, after the period that I have defined as constituting the initial conditions.

After Toyota's near-bankruptcy, monthly production declined sharply, from more than 1000 vehicles at the beginning of 1950 to slightly more than 300 vehicles in May that year (*Toyota* 1988, p. 109). The banks pressed Toyota – belatedly following the example of Nissan – to undertake mass lay-offs, despite an earlier promise to the unions not to do this. After prolonged disputes with the union and a lengthy strike, in the summer of 1950 Toyota-founder Kiichiro resigned from his post and around 2000 workers (one-third of the workforce) lost their jobs (Cusumano 1985, p. 147; Okayama 1987, p. 175; *Toyota* 1988, pp. 106–10).[6] At precisely the same time, an exogenous event in the shape of the Korean War saved the Japanese car industry from extinction, as US forces started placing large orders for military trucks from June 1950. Toyota now had to expand production with a reduced workforce, which invited an intensive search for rationalization, for instance by increasing the number of machines per operator (*Toyota* 1988, pp. 110–11) along the lines already pioneered by Ohno.

This episode also contributed to breaking the power of the industry-wide union of auto workers. A new industry-wide strike in 1953 ended with a settlement at Toyota and Isuzu within two months, but culminated in a long and bitter power struggle at Nissan, which finally led to the collapse of the industry union (Okayama 1987, p. 176–7; Cusumano 1985, pp. 149–54). In the end, this left Toyota with a more cooperative company union than Nissan (for details, see Saga and Hanada 1999; Cusumano 1985, pp. 180–3, 309; Halberstam 1986; Grønning 1997). This was vital, since Ohno – perhaps exaggerating his own performance – stressed the strenuous resistance of both the workers and lower-level managers that he encountered in applying his lean production approach (Ohno, 1988).

The enduring relevance of the meta-routine

Ironically in the light of dominant interpretations in the literature, if one looks for major tangible time-specific influences creating path dependence, it was thus a sequence of events between 1949 and 1950 put in motion by an overstocking crisis rather than enduring post-war scarcity in materials that locked-in Toyota to the JIT system. Pioneered by Ohno in the machine-shop, it was implemented at an ever-wider scale within Toyota and eventually also at the company's suppliers. The diffusion of JIT throughout Toyota closely followed Ohno's career from management positions (among other appointments) in the machine shop

(1948), the manufacturing department for engines, transmissions, and vehicle assembly (1953), and the Motomachi factory (1960). Only in 1962 was JIT put into operation in all Toyota plants.

The prevailing meta-routine made Toyota much more receptive to such an approach than Nissan, which still largely faced the same external circumstances as Toyota. After years of high turnover in top management, Genshichi Asahara, an academically trained chemist, resumed Nissan's presidency in 1951. Like Aikawa, with whom he had collaborated until 1944, Asahara considered technology as something you bought (Cusumano 1985, p. 90). In line with this, in 1952 Nissan picked up the thread of its pre-war policy by forging an alliance with British car manufacturer Austin, whose blueprints for production were followed as far as possible to the letter (Cusumano 1985, p. 100). Despite the fact that the Japanese government stimulated cooperation with foreign car manufacturers, Toyota was the only Japanese car maker that did not forge a tie-up. In its official history, Toyota suggests that it did not need this because it had started making prototypes of private cars even before the prohibition on producing passenger cars was lifted. These and other preparations for mass production of private cars culminated in the introduction of the first Crown model in January 1955 (*Toyota* 1988, p. 134; see also Kamiya 1976, pp. 60–3). Still, as noted, Ohno's thinking was heavily influenced by both Taylor and Ford, and he also visited US and British automotive companies after the war (Toyoda 1987). In 1939 and after the war, Kiichiro Toyoda actually favoured cooperation with Ford (Wada and Yui 2002, pp. 292–4). Two plans for a tie-up with Ford were cancelled at the last moment, the first early in 1939 and the second in June 1950 by the intervention of the Japanese and the US governments respectively (Kamiya 1976, pp. 71–2; *Toyota* 1988, p. 113; Fruin 1992, p. 296). There is more reason to qualify the tie-ups as distinguishing the other car makers from Toyota, as – in line with Japanese government policy – complete 'domestication' of production by Nissan, Isuzu and Hino was reached by 1958 (Odaka et al. 1988, p. 45). On the other hand, Toyota, too, adopted American-made specialized tools from the 1950s onwards (Okayama 1987, p. 178; Daito 2000), but much more selectively than Nissan and while maintaining its older, multi-purpose equipment alongside them (Cusumano 1985, p. 275). Here again the Sakichi-loom functioned as a template: 'Ohno found that it was possible to make older machinery, with different functions and capacities, perform repetitive operations almost automatically by adding feeding devices, limit switches, timers and other attachments, on the principle of the Toyoda automatic loom' (Cusumano 1985, p. 275).

In the 1960s, Japanese car production, protected from foreign competition by the Japanese government, boomed. Toyota's production of passenger cars surpassed that of trucks by around 1965 and its total vehicle production expanded massively from 150,000 to 1.6 million between 1960 and 1970. Despite its development into a mass producer of cars, Toyota only selectively utilized the typical US practice of long production runs of single components or cars (Cusumano 1985, p. 280; Togo and Wartman 1993, p. 173). By means of technical adjustments of existing machinery, Ohno and colleagues succeeded in reducing set-up times for stamping dies, from two to three hours before 1955, to no more than three minutes by 1971 (Cusumano 1985, p. 284). This enabled 'mixed production' of short production runs, which kept inventories low and made Toyota relatively flexible in dealing with the trend among car manufacturers to increase the number of models and with the slump in demand in the 1970s, when Toyota quickly made an end to exceptions to the company policy of producing more than one type of car per factory (Togo and Wartman 1993, p. 189; *Toyota* 1988, pp. 326–7). Above I have suggested that among the initial conditions a lack of financial means was possibly the most constraining resource. Remaining faithful to the doctrine of lean production was certainly not the result of any lack of financial resources: the company accumulated sufficient capital to finance expensive specialized machinery and large buffer stocks and – by 1977 no longer dependent on borrowing (Cusumano 1985, p. 76) – even became known as the 'Bank of Toyota'.

Nissan too began trying to reduce its inventory levels and to synchronize operations with suppliers from the mid-1950s, with considerable success, but its reliance on computers instead of *kanban* – the 'low-tech', self-developed technique typically preferred by Toyota – tended to give its production system more of a push than a pull character (Cusumano 1985, pp. 307–19). Nissan proved to be less competitive than Toyota: the latter was more productive and profitable from as early as 1951 (Cusumano 1985, pp. 396–7; Odaka et al. 1988, pp. 91, 108–9). In 1955 Toyota took over Nissan's no. 1 position in overall Japanese vehicle production (Cusumano 1985, p. 392) and in 1963 it took the top spot in passenger car production (Shimokawa 1987, p. 229). This of course does not necessarily prove the superiority of Toyota's production system: its distribution and marketing approach shaped by Shotaro Kamiya, first appointed at Toyoda Automatic Loom in 1935, is also to be credited (Kamiya 1976; *Toyota* 1988, pp. 62, 99; Kawahara 1997; Williams et al. 1994, pp. 117–19). It was the 1973 oil crisis and the subsequent worldwide depression that put Toyota's production system (including its multi-tiered supplier network) in the international spotlight, making it the model to be emulated by both domestic and foreign car makers (Womack et al. 1990).

To reiterate, lock-in by meta-routines does not mean that a rigid or static organizational system ensues: 'efforts of definitively nailing down the TPS are constantly stymied by Toyota's annoying habit of ceaselessly developing and improving its own practice' (New 2007, p. 3547). For instance, Fujimoto (1999) considers Toyota's export success, based on a production model aimed at the domestic market, as an example of its superior evolutionary capability to learn from unforeseen opportunities. This author further emphasizes consensus-building at Toyota with and on the shop-floor. He argues that this has been an important element, as the 'core group of shop floor leaders function as an informal intra-organizational mechanism for pre-screening the routines...' (Fujimoto 1999, p. 275)[7] and an effective convergence system could 'quickly convert a variety of organizational elements into a coherent system' (Fujimoto 1999, p. 264). These learning mechanisms observed by Fujimoto are aligned with Toyota's meta-routine of self-testing and adaptation. Similarly, the rule that workers could stop the lines when JIT production became in danger or when other problems occurred, which was introduced in the engine shop in 1950 (Cusumano 1985, p. 280), can be considered to have helped to sustain the application of Toyota's routine of self-testing and adaptation.

The meta-routine of Toyota originating from Sakichi Toyoda is still identifiable. Two authors claim that four rules form the 'DNA' of TPS; they all prescribe that 'activities, connections and flow paths have built-in tests to signal problems automatically' (Spear and Bowen 1999, p. 98). Stated otherwise, this DNA implies 'integration of problem identification and problem solving procedures into the actual work processes' (Towill 2007, p. 3620). As late as the mid-1980s, Toyota's efforts in continuously improving operations were still more oriented to the organization of processes than Nissan's stronger focus on machines and equipment (Totsuka 1995; Nohara 1999, p. 38; Fujimoto 1999, p. 69). Typically, after a 'high-tech solution' implemented in its Tahara plant in 1991 resulted in only marginal savings in labour, Toyota decided to use relatively simple machinery again in its green-field Kyushi plant from 1992 (Benders and Morita 2004, pp. 435, 438). Toyota's experiment with high-tech followed a change of circumstances during the 1980s. Mounting criticism of the demanding nature of working under lean production conditions, shortage of workers and technical difficulties in production (Nohara 1999, p. 39) forced Toyota to reconsider its production system (Benders and Morita 2004; Hampson 1999; Nohara 1999). This implied that in some factories, Toyota explicitly began to accept the necessity of buffer stocks, not such a revolutionary change as it might seem since 'zero-inventories' have never been a core element of TPS (see also Pil and Fujimoto 2007).

8.7 Discussion

The re-examination of such an extensively researched subject as the development of the Toyota Production System shows how difficult it can be to pinpoint initial conditions and assess their individual influence. In an organizational context this is further complicated by the difficulty of separating initial conditions and lock-in mechanisms. A production system such as TPS does not fall like manna from the heavens, but is as complex a creation as organizations are multi-faceted. Initial conditions are complex and interlocking, not only in regard to their contents, but also in their timing. Factors that have frequently been seen as the major initial conditions – low and fragmented demand, scarcity of raw materials, and/or a general fashion of avoiding waste originating from the Japanese wartime economy – upon closer examination do not significantly explain the emergence of TPS right after the Second World War. From among the three elements to be theoretically distinguished as initial conditions for paths of organization change – environmental requirements, resources and value or philosophies – while the first two undoubtedly constrained choice, it is arguable that Toyota's specific philosophy was the major imprinting force.

This indicates that the initial conditions as assessed at a certain point of time may themselves have a history that is relevant for a proper path dependence perspective. Our analysis shows how the philosophy expressed in a meta-routine of 'self-testing and adaptation' at Toyota Motor Company emerged before the firm itself had been set up. The meta-routine at Toyota itself resulted from a path dependent process related to the idiosyncratic experiences and approaches developed by the first generations of (family) managers. It has had a profound and lasting influence on its production system. I argue in this chapter that meta routines both initially select phenomena and exert a 'lock-in' influence thereafter by ascertaining diffusion of the chosen form and by steering search and selection processes that determine how solutions to occurring problems are developed and implemented. Toyota's meta-routine did not make the development of TPS inevitable, only a much more salient choice. The meta-routine has inspired the development and use of more mundane routines, such as multi-machine operating. In addition, the typical path dependence element of a specific sequence of events, put in motion by a overstocking and liquidity crisis in 1949, was important for locking-in Toyota to the path it had entered only shortly before. A combination of a separation of production and sales activities into two distinct firms, reducing the labour force and a sudden boom in demand resonated with a still infant system suited to lean, demand-induced production.

The Toyota meta-routine was perpetuated in particular through the extensive and systematic use of formal documentation of factory experiences introduced by founder Kiichiro Toyoda and the consistent support by Toyota top management of the innovations of Taiichi Ohno. Other car makers, both domestic and foreign, could imitate Toyota's systematic reliance on testing as well as specific JIT elements, but could match less well the underlying commitment and rigour in implementation: 'What Toyota could do better than its rivals seems to be not so much rational calculations before the trials as systematization and institutionalization *after* the trials' (Fujimoto 1995, p. 212, italics in original). Toyota's meta-routine was important in continuing its dedication to a production system characterized by small lot sizes and multi-purpose machines, despite the disappearance of financial bottlenecks in the 1960s (Grønning 1997, p. 428). Some even sense an ideology at work: 'The insistence of the Japanese assemblers on the reproduction of the just-in-time system worked against profits in the short run, since it made the expense of international expansion ever so much greater' (Schwartz and Fish 1998, p. 66). It is interesting to contrast this with the large Detroit car makers, who abandoned an early JIT type of production system from the late 1930s since they no longer considered it the best cost-reducing device (Schwartz and Fish 1998, p. 66).

This explanation – heavily reliant as it is on a firm-specific meta-routine interacting with sequences of events – has its limitations. The effects of meta-routines on factory practices cannot be directly observed in a study based on secondary sources. I focused on the most salient meta-routine identifiable in the secondary literature. The development of TPS was influenced from many different directions (Fujimoto 1999), and I have not focused on other possibly relevant meta-routines, either specific to Toyota or more widespread in Japanese business. What is more, the self-testing and adaptation orientation did not prevent Toyota from prematurely introducing defective models on the market up to the early 1960s, in particular several versions of the Corona (Togo and Wartman 1993).

Nonetheless, dedication to its meta-routine differentiated Toyota from its main domestic competitor, Nissan, not only in regards to the internal development of production. A concise analysis of the second pillar of

TPS, a reliance on a flexible and integrated multi-tiered supplier system (Dyer and Nobeoka 2000; Ueda 1997; Shiomi 1995), reveals striking similarities with our path dependence account of the genesis and development of lean production. A dearth of material resources during the war and immediately following it is unlikely to have been decisive in imprinting Toyota's outsourcing policy. In fact, from 1939 Toyota reoriented itself toward more in-house production, in particular because suppliers could not offer the quality demanded (Wada and Yui 2002, pp. 282-6). Similarly to Morris-Suzuki's interpretation of the historical foundations of JIT, the Japanese wartime economy between 1931 and 1945 is considered to have left 'a range of institutional prototypes on which the post-war evolution of Japanese subcontracting is based' (Nishiguchi 1994, p. 31). However, the quoted study does not specify what precisely these institutional prototypes were and how they shaped post-war developments. Toyota's approach, adopted early on, of making long-term commitments with suppliers (*Toyota* 1988, p. 76), irrespective of the immediate payoff, can be better considered an outflow of its typical meta-routine. Kiichiro's drive to gain detailed knowledge of major processes in car production led him to follow the example his father had set at Toyoda Automatic Loom:

> Kiichiro began by setting up departments or factories to specialize in particular products or functions such as steel, electrical components, machine tools or body stamping. Later, he incorporated these factories as nonconsolidated subsidiaries, since this format offered greater possibilities for expansion and fund-raising than maintaining them as in-house departments.
>
> (Cusumano, 1985, p. 248)

Thus, as we have seen before, the meta-routine of self-testing and adaptation was effective in combination with a more specific template originating from Sakichi Toyoda's entrepreneurial activities – developing first and then spinning-off for strategic and financial reasons. In addition, and again similarly to the internal development of TPS, the 1949 financial crisis was a major *event* that contributed to locking-in Toyota to its developing supplier system, since it forced Toyota to spin-off, among other things, its main ancillary company Nippondenso (Fruin 1992, pp. 365–6; Fujimoto 1999). In all, this early history of outsourcing clearly had a path dependent effect: all but one of Toyota's main subsidiaries as they existed in the mid-1980s were founded by Kiichiro

(Cusumano 1985), a fact that is not fully recognized in one of the latest historical studies of this subject (Sako 2004).

More recently, Toyota has begun shifting towards a more arm's length approach in dealing with suppliers (Ahmadjian and Lincoln 2001). This would bring Toyota closer to Nissan's position in outsourcing. The move is in line with a more 'aggressive' policy adopted by Toyota top management in 1995, when Hiroshi Okuda became CEO. This policy change was partly contested by members of the Toyoda family (Hino 2006). It shows that Toyota's meta-routine is not immune from erosion: philosophies at the top are starting to change, weakening one of the existing meta-routines and possibly replacing it with another. The current CEO, Katsuaki Watanabe, has spoken about a '*kakushin*' (revolution) needed at Toyota, as opposed to the traditional '*kaizen*' approach of incremental improvement (Stewart and Raman 2007). There is reason for concern, since, at the point of becoming the largest car producer in the world, Toyota is dealing with serious quality problems in car production (*The Economist*, 2007).

8.8 Conclusion

This chapter has re-examined the Toyota Production System from the perspective of the rapidly developing literature on organizational change as a path dependence phenomenon. I have argued for the necessity of opening the black box of initial conditions as part of a path dependence analysis, and relating them to mechanisms creating lock-in. The two elements, largely discussed in the literature as strictly separate, are in fact intricately related conceptually and empirically. Using the concept of path dependence forces scholars to specify the nature of the historical explanation of change of organizations. A careful assessment of the exact timing and plausible effect of the (supposed) initial conditions helps us to understand whether and how they shaped the phenomenon under study. Meta-routines are of particular relevance both in imprinting organizational features during initial conditions and in creating dynamic lock-in, interacting with specific sequences of events. Although competitors have imitated many features of the Toyota Production System, the continuous application of an underlying meta-routine has given Toyota's way of producing a special dynamic nature.

9
Paradoxes of Modernist Consumption: Reading Fashions

It is often lamented by academics and others that contemporary patterns of consumption are 'post-modern' (see, for example, Van Raaij 1993). Some perceive of consumption in general as post-modern (Jameson 1988). Its volatility and fickleness is such that it is beyond understanding. I argue that the characterization of contemporary consumption patterns as post-modern is based on an incorrect understanding of these consumption patterns, as well as an incorrect understanding of the term post-modernity. Underlying present-day consumption patterns are broadly supported socio-cultural values that – so the literature on modernism and post-modernism indicates – are thoroughly modernist in nature. Modernist values such as autonomy, novelty, speed, success and uniqueness underlie consumption patterns. In their consumption, people want to express such values. The volatility and fickleness of consumption patterns is, as I will argue in this short chapter, to be explained by reference to the modernist values involved, and in relation to the fact that these modernist values often contradict one another, particularly when expressed in the consumption of concrete objects. The paradoxes that are inherent in modern consumption, particularly as consumption patterns are institutionalized to allow for communication, give rise to the kind of patterns we see today.

Underlying post-modern accounts of consumer culture is the 'loss of the real' (Slater 1997, p. 198), and an idea that such culture cannot be understood. Contemporary consumption patterns are, however, not beyond understanding. And they are certainly not post-modern, as the short first section argues. There is a need explicitly to incorporate into the analysis the concept of (socio-cultural) values, and the expression of these in institutions. In Section 9.2, I elaborate on this point and discuss the Social Value Nexus I have introduced elsewhere (Dolfsma 2004;

Chapter 4 above). Section 9.3 discusses and analyses fashion from this perspective, drawing on secondary sources. This consumption practice, believed to be quintessentially post-modern, is best understood from the social and institutional economic framework presented in Section 9.2. Final remarks follow in Section 9.4.

9.1 Modernism, post-modernism and consumption

The view expounded by scholars of the Frankfurt school, such as Adorno (for example, Adorno 1941), of consumers as mindless creatures that can be manipulated at will into buying goods, has long been influential. Not only scholars inspired by the work of Marx, on the left, but also scholars on the right, who are perhaps more inclined to the rational choice school of thought in sociology and the neoclassical school in economics have thus given the phenomenon of consumption short shrift. Despite, as Adam Smith so famously observed, consumption being the sole end of production, only marketing scholars have given it significant attention. Corralled in business schools, their contributions are not always trusted as genuine scientific studies. More recently, consumption in general, and fashion in particular, have been described as 'post-modern'. Indeed 'contemporary postmodern society is best defined as a "consumer society"' (Firat and Venkatesh 1993, p. 228), and 'hype' (or fashion) the quintessential form of consumption (ibid., p. 230).

Consumption is not merely the act of purchase, but involves much more, including on the part of the consuming individual (Miller 1995). It is true that an increasingly large number of products are being offered on the market – a larger number than in previous eras. The life and times of many products seem entirely incomprehensible: why some succeed incredibly well and others fail miserably is often difficult to comprehend. The regularity and predictability that science looks for seem to be lost and the scientific task of looking for patterns and explanations in consumption behaviour becomes (much) more difficult – some might even suggest insurmountably so (Venkatesh 1999); to the point of giving up hope, it would seem, of trying to understand the patterns other than as 'post-modern'. In fact, however, post-modernism signifies ambiguity, compelling people to be reflexive and to engage in continuous reassessment of meanings and positions (Kaiser et al. 1991).

Conceiving of contemporary consumption as incomprehensible and (thus) post-modern is based on two related misunderstandings. The first concerns the terms 'modernity' and 'post-modernity'. Modernity is often regarded as ordered, whereas post-modernism is seen as the opposite: chaos (for example, Sherry 1991). Modernism and post-modernism are, of course, not to be perceived as historic periods, but as characterizations of society, or better still as characterizations of world-views (ideologies). Post-modernism is defined in negative terms: it is not ordered but fragmented, hyper-real, it de-centres the subject, and it involves paradoxical juxtapositions (van Raaij 1993; Firat and Schultz 1997). The very modernist nature of such an opposition often fails to transpire. Post-modernism, it is claimed, should be understood differently. Second, the misunderstanding of post-modernism leads scholars to disqualify present-day consumption patterns all too quickly. These patterns purportedly remain inexplicable. Now the debate about modernism and post-modernism is of course contested and a matter of heated argument. My point here is that whatever the merits or demerits of post-modernist/modernist philosophical perspectives, the phenomenon of present-day consumption of fashionable items is best understood as modernist.

Modernism is, of course, a rationalistic view of the world, where knowledge is relentlessly accumulated and progress inevitable. The world outside is contrasted with the representation that the individual has of it in his or her own mind. Such a representation, trying to find a central meaning, is necessarily reductionist and formal, often based on axioms only (Klamer 1995; Firat and Venkatesh 1993). A fundamental, invariant structure that underlies appearance is hypothesized, and so the thinking in terms of universals and unity can be observed. The world is perceived as working towards completion, equilibrium. Machines and mechanistic processes are the preferred metaphors. The world out there is ephemeral, however, and representation is problematic. Some, then, equate reality with the individual's representation of it. However one may think about this issue, it is true that it is the individual who represents the world and not some larger social entity, even were one to believe, as is the position here, that the former is influenced by the latter (Dolfsma 2004). The natural sciences, specifically before the development of quantum mechanics, are exemplary (Mirowski 1989). The individual stands at the centre in the modernist project (Slater 1997).[1] The individual makes her or his own choices – the individual is sovereign. The idea that individuals might not be fully in control of their own actions tends towards anathema in a modernist perspective, but is not necessarily alien to it. Considering individuals, and consumers particularly, as socially connected (Belk 1995) does not entail taking a position that should be characterized as post-modern, even when accepting the description of post-modern consumption provided by its proponents (Venkatesh 1999).

However, modernism is not single-minded, homogeneous and without contradictions (Lefebre 1995). Different societal and theoretical developments can lead to fragmentation, a fragmentation that is acknowledged by 'modernist' scholars such as Jürgen Habermas and Max Weber. In relation to this, Lichtblau (1999) argues that modernist society has a 'fundamentally dynamic character', consisting of various 'subsystems', that modernity itself is 'internally split' and 'self-differentiating'. What he calls 'the socio-structural core of modernity' is by no means ordered and continuous.

9.2 Paradoxical, modernist consumption

There is no sea-change in consumption patterns that justifies calling the more recent period a post-modern era.[2] Changes in consumption patterns may have speeded up and led to fragmentation – but the point made in this chapter is that this does not mean a different process is now at work. Present-day consumption patterns are predicated on the same modernist values as before. The internal paradoxes of these values, however, have become more pronounced, causing new dynamics to arise. Social influences, manifesting themselves indirectly and not necessarily directly through the observable actions of groups or organizations play an important part in this. Scholars such as Mary Douglas (1986) have convincingly argued this point.

It is modernist ideas – or socio-cultural values – in society that persuade the individual to pursue the virtues of autonomy, material success and individuality that in turn create the dynamics of consumption. These socio-cultural values need to be expressed in a way that makes them understandable for others (Cosgel 1997). Hence the observation made by Simmel (1957 [1904], p. 546) with regard to fashion that there is a simultaneous 'need of union on the one hand and the need of isolation on the other'.[3] The argument that socio-cultural values and the institutionalized way of expressing these are related is depicted in Figure 9.1 (see also Chapter 4). In previous chapters as well as in Dolfsma (2004) the theoretical argument is developed further. The relation between values and institutions is not a straightforward one: it runs both ways although institutions tend to change faster than socio-cultural values. In the case of symbolic goods – which are important in establishing an identity and thus need to signal clearly – enough (relevant) others should understand the signal emanating from their consumption, but not too many, for then the message itself is undermined.

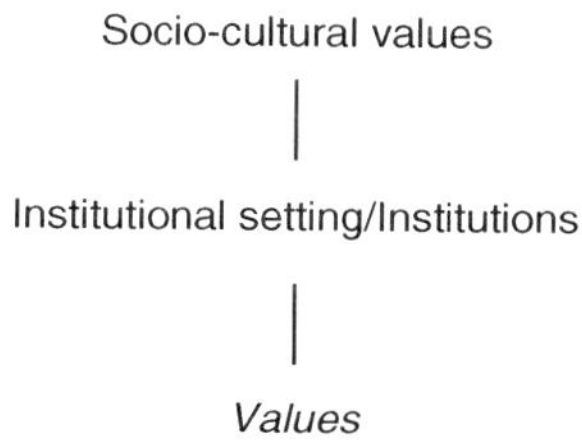

Figure 9.1 The Social Value Nexus
Source: Dolfsma (2004).

Socio-cultural values denote strong underlying convictions held by many people in a group or in society, consciously as well as unconsciously, most of which would be considered of an ethical or philosophical nature. They include matters of justice, beauty, love, freedom of will, rightful ways of government and governance, social standing and behaviour and personal identity. When people consume conspicuously they express shared socio-cultural values.[4] Institutionalized or ritualized (Rook 1999) consumption in large part creates identity through reference to these socio-cultural values. Some goods, however, incorporate more powerful symbolic meanings than others. Music and dress are among these, but food, art, culture and sports are others. They offer a way of communicating to the relevant 'audience' (compare Coşgel 1992, 1994; Douglas and Isherwood 1979; Crane 2000; Dolfsma 2004), they enable individuals to make and maintain social relations (Douglas and Isherwood 1979; Miller 1995). The socio-cultural values that 'live' in a society or community, and are expressed in its institutional settings, may change over time, but are likely to be persistent. *Values*, on the other hand, are the terms of trade or exchange established in society for specific goods or services. In this chapter, the focus is on the relation between socio-cultural values and institutions. The distinction between socio-cultural values and values is not meant to be exhaustive, but does help to clarify the discussion. The way in which *values* are expressed – prices are one example, but there are others – varies between institutional settings where different socio-cultural values are expressed. The distinction between socio-cultural values on the one hand and *values* on the other is rooted firmly in institutional and social economics as well as in sociology (Beckert 2002; Bush 1987; Davis 2003; Wildavsky 1987). Socio-cultural values do not determine exactly which institutions emerge – indeed, scholars who claim that present-day consumption patterns, and fashion in particular, are post-modern have rightly pointed to the tenuousness of the relation between observable, institutionalized patterns of behaviour and underlying values. Change can and does go in both directions. Socio-cultural values, however, change much less quickly than institutions. Changes in the former may take decades or even centuries to materialize (compare Campbell 1987; Inglehart 1990; Hofstede 1980), although institutional change can also be very long term; for one thing, because institutions are interrelated.[5] The socio-cultural values referred to in a particular domain, such as dress or music, can change, of course (see Dolfsma 2002, 2004 for a fuller discussion). Although reference to socio-cultural values in analysing the phenomenon of fashion and its dynamics is rare, some scholars have preceded me in pursuing this route (Ryan 1966; Back 1986). The frequency with which, for instance, the modernist term 'new' is used hints at this, and it should be surprising that this surprises 'marketers' (Lovelock 1984).

9.3 Fashion

Fashion in particular, but consumption in general, is, because of its associations with emotions, irrationality and non-productivity, seldom analysed in the social sciences. To some observers, the fickleness of fashion – clothes and other means of decorating the body – means that it represents *the* quintessential post-modern practice (Firat and Venkatesh 1993).[6] Some point to the production side of the story to explain the dynamics of this practice (Crane 1997; *The Economist* 2002, 2004). This element is also picked up by an economist looking at fashion (Pesendorfer 1995). Although this is undeniably an important aspect, it is not the dominant one.

Fashion is not simply 'high fashion', but can describe all clothing and the like used to cover and decorate one's body (Steele 1997). Crane (2000) has argued that in the 1960s there was a shift from a single fashion – *haute couture* – to a more fragmented situation comprising, at least, luxury fashion, industrial fashion and street style. However, there is a symbiotic relation between *high fashion* or luxury fashion and everyday clothing (Steele 1997; Sproles and Burns 1994), a symbiosis that is reflected in high fashion's dynamics, as Simmel (1957 [1904]) pointed out. The desire to belong to a certain higher (elite), possibly imaginary group and the simultaneous desire to distinguish oneself from other, lower groups is manifest in fashion (Thompson and Haytko 1995; Karni and Schmeidler 1990). The history of fashion, and of music, shows a continuously changing scene of styles, emphasizing what I describe as different socio-cultural values in a different way (Thompson and Haytko 1995). An emphasis on functionality, freedom, progress and simplicity in one style of clothing is followed by another on speed, uniqueness, frivolousness and authenticity (Lewenhaupt and Lewenhaupt 1989). At any one time, besides the fashion mainstream are co-existent 'anti-fashions' (Steele 1997). Some styles present themselves as fashion, others do not, or they may claim an oppositional standpoint such as the 'Anti-Fashion' from the 1970s. As Crane (2000, p. 167) argues, the sources of fashion have diversified.

Ireland (1987) shows how often and to what extent new fashions build on previous ones at the micro level of institutions in design and design process. Even avant-garde designers of fashion use elements from previous fashions when creating a new design, in fact they are referring to the same values. The institutionalized communication about the new designs, in the media and during fashion parades, also refers to such values. Thus the signal displayed by consumers of fashion is likely to be comprehensible to others; albeit the fashionista risks the danger that by referring to a modernist socio-cultural value such as novelty and autonomy in an institutionalized manner, she or he is thereby in danger of signalling that they are in fact anti-modern, traditionalist. A gratuitous (post-modernist) bricolage of whatever a designer dreams up is not what happens (Thompson and Haytko 1995).[7] New fashions appear more quickly than ever before (*The Economist* 2004; Crane 2000) and the designs draw on an ever-wider array of sources, but the ideals and values represented there do not change. Fashion is on the cutting edge: presenting novel ideas and imitating ideas from the past, producing unicity and demarcation (see, Simmel 1957 [1904], p. 545). Consumption is thus, inevitably, an active and creative undertaking (Thompson and Haytko 1995; Robins 1994; Dolfsma 2004, 2008b).

The values that the different styles of fashion reflect are modernist. Simmel's (1957 [1904], p. 557) claim that the content of fashion '*in abstracto*' is irrelevant abandons one to a situation in which it is impossible to understand the dynamics of consumption patterns and which is consequently altogether unproductive (compare Dolfsma 2004). Thus, one would not consider the socio-cultural values underlying consumption, and their possibly paradoxical nature. One would not observe that fashion and fashion discourses offer a continuous juxtaposition of 'opposing values and beliefs' (Thompson and Haytko 1995, p. 15), and one would thus misunderstand the phenomenon. An adherence to unchanged socio-cultural values has resulted in the 'changed nature of fashion change', which has become 'more complex, erratic' (Crane 2000, p. 167). The different dynamics do not indicate a sea-change, although some might claim that they do. Elizabeth Wilson in her book *Adorned in Dreams – Fashion and Modernity* (1985, p. 5) has put it thus: 'Changes in fashion styles not only represent reaction against what went before; they may be self-contradictory too.'

The paradoxes of modernist consumption – manifest for fashion as well as in pop music – are the result of the hankering after the socio-cultural values of authenticity, freedom, novelty, speed, success, autonomy, independence, pleasure, success, youth and the like, values that need to be communicated in a way that is understandable to others (Thompson and Haytko 1995, p. 22; compare Coşgel 1997). Appearance is a crucial element of this consumption (Finkelstein 1991; Baudrillard 1981). Within an 'interpretative community' a 'socially negotiated set of rules of interpretation and aesthetic standards' is needed (Thompson and Haytko 1995; see also Dolfsma 2004). The rules of interpretation are shared by a community that constructs what might be called a 'generalized other, who is consistently characterized as a conformist who is highly sensitive to the opinions of peers' (Thompson and Haytko 1999, p. 22). A real or assumed generalized other is the release valve for pent up tensions arising from institutional tensions, or inherently conflicting modernist values (Dolfsma 2002, 2004). Or, as Wilson (1985, p. 6) observes '[d]espite its apparent irrationality, fashion cements social solidarity and imposes group norms, while deviations in dress are usually experienced as shocking and disturbing'. Thus vulnerability and anxiety are significant factors for consumers (Robins 1994). The dynamics of the phenomenon of fashion – the necessary finiteness of each trend – is to be understood in those terms (Simmel 1957 [1904]). Observable fashion trends thus do not constitute or reflect a break with modernism. Indeed they are a clear expression of it (Thompson and Haytko 1995; Berman 1982). Fashion sometimes referred to as post-modern fashion is, in this respect, no different from the immediate post-war 'New Look' or the 'Anti-Fashion' of the 1970s. Different values may be emphasized, but they are all firmly modernist (Enlightenment) values.

Advertisements for fashion products emphasize this point. Over and over, they reflect a hankering after modernist values such as freedom, escape (from traditions), independence, success. Which values are stressed and to what extent varies, but while the way in which such values are expressed (institutionalized) also differs, the advertisements are intended always to persuade their target audience of the specific relation between the values and a type of behaviour on their part.

Buying, using and wearing specific (perhaps 'designer') apparel is thus a way of signalling certain socio-cultural values, even though the products offered might not be the most distinguished and up-market (*The Economist* 2002). These are modernist values, and consumers express them in routinized or institutionalized ways so the message conveyed can be understood by relevant others. This is, of course, well appreciated in the marketing efforts made to try to establish the connection between significant modernist values and particular products. Scholars who stress the post-modernist nature of consumption indeed point to the role of marketing. But this does not obviate the point that the values involved are modernist, and the message needs to be (broadly) understandable – not only to others involved in fashion, but also to people who are not deeply involved. Paradoxically, it is within these two essentials that the grounds for the demise of each particular fashion lie. As more people start to pick up on a fashion, the very reason for its existence and attractiveness is undermined. The point about fashion is, of course, to distinguish one individual from others, to demonstrate autonomy and the like. The search for a new fashion is part and parcel of the phenomenon of fashion. Trying to create a fashion is, then, trying to walk a tightrope – too much novelty will result in a consumption good which sends a message that cannot be understood, while too much commonality means not signalling the proper, modernist values. Fashion, thus, is not the quintessential post-modern kind of consumption, but a thoroughly modernist one making undeniably clear the tensions with which modernity is imbued.

9.4 Consumption and the good life

Friedman (1990, p. 327) argues that consumption is the 'constituent of selfhood, of social identity'; it defines identity, the nature of power, of sickness and well-being (see also Douglas and Isherwood 1979). In consuming people signal to others, but consumption is not just an instrumental activity, although the idea that consuming is (merely) instrumental is not an unusual position; Campbell (1987) calls it 'Veblenesque', after Veblen (1899). Frank (1985), Bourdieu (1984) and others also take this position. Goods are, however, also consumed for what they represent, irrespective of what effects consuming them offers; as Friedman (1994, p. 169) notes: 'consumption is a material realization, or attempted realization, of the image of the good life'. Campbell (1987, p. 89) writes:

> Individuals do not so much seek satisfaction from products, as pleasure from the self-illusory experience which they construct from their

> associated meanings. The essential activity of consumption is thus not the actual selection, purchase or use of products, but the imaginative pleasure-seeking to which the product image lends itself.

To understand the dynamics of consumption patterns it is necessary to acknowledge the form that a specific consumption pattern takes (see Wilson 1985). It is essential thus to be aware of and able to analyse the socio-cultural values with which consumption goods are imbued. I have argued this for pop music elsewhere, showing for that case too that such values are expressed in routines and institutions (Dolfsma 2004, see also Frith 1983).

While, in everyday life people recognize the role that socio-cultural values play in economic processes, with a few exceptions, economists do not. One of the few schools of thought in economics that takes basic underlying socio-cultural values into account is that of institutional economics (Hodgson 1998). Many have contributed to the theory of institutional change, although not all of these would acknowledge the role socio-cultural values play. However, rather than developing this part of the argument, I have considered two separate but related arguments in this chapter. First, I have argued that a type of consumption that is considered by many to be particularly representative of post-modernity (and is thus incomprehensible) is in fact thoroughly modernist. Don Slater's (1997, p. 9, italics in original) comment that 'consumer culture is bound up with the *idea* of modernity' must be fully supported. Second, I have shown that analysing such a phenomenon by looking at the way in which socio-cultural values are institutionalized to determine behaviour (summarized in the Social Value Nexus) offers a clear and persuasive theoretical perspective through which to try to understand even fragmented and fickle consumption phenomena such as that of fashion.

10
Institutionalist Law and Economics and Values: the Case of Personal Bankruptcy Law[1]

> Bankruptcy is perhaps the greatest and most humiliating calamity which can befall an innocent man.
>
> (Adam Smith 1981 [1776], II iii 29)

From an evolutionary economics perspective bankruptcies may be seen as an important selection mechanism. Bankruptcy has, however, not received much attention in the economics literature. As the quotation from Smith, above, intimates, bankruptcy is an unpleasant process for individuals, their families and for wider society. Bankruptcy laws differ widely across countries and even within a federalized country such as the USA. Filing practices within a country also differ substantially across regions as well as among social groups (Fay et al. 2002). Bankruptcy is, thus, not the uncomplicated selection mechanism in the economic realm it sometimes is believed to be.

This chapter discusses how one may *evaluate* bankruptcy regimes from an economic perspective. It contrasts the instrumental rationality approach of the Chicago (law and economics) school with the instrumental valuation principle (IVP) from original institutional economics (OIE) in the context of personal bankruptcy.

10.1 Personal bankruptcy

The number of personal bankruptcies has been increasing in most developed countries over the years. Although there is clear evidence that malevolence is only involved in a minority of cases,[2] personal bankruptcies tend to be framed by the general public, creditors and filers alike as failures of self-control (see Starr 2007). Some mainstream economists also frame personal bankruptcies as such (Fay et al. 2002).[3]

Uniquely US citizens can choose two different ways of declaring bankruptcy (Efrat 2001): Chapter 7 and Chapter 13. Under Chapter 7, debtors surrender all their un-exempted assets to a trustee; the trustee liquidates and repays creditors. Unsecured debts such as credit card debts, instalment loans, medical bills and damage claims are discharged. Government-backed student loans, child support and alimony, and recent income taxes are not eligible for discharge. Homes tend to be exempted. Chapter 7 is an attractive avenue for filing for bankruptcy; 70 per cent of US filings are under this chapter (CBO 2000). Chapter 13 is intended for filers who earn a regular income. Filers do not surrender assets; instead a repayment schedule, usually over a 3–5 year period, is arranged through due legal process.

As may be expected, there is a wide variety of institutional arrangements associated with bankruptcy. Some arrangements reflect the historical antipathy towards those unfortunate enough to experience bankruptcy (Kilpi 1998).[4] US type Chapter 13 arrangements tend to be the norm in most developed economies. In the Netherlands and the UK, for example, bankrupts must accept a repayment plan in effect drawn up by the creditors or their trustees: the opposite of the US system.[5] While a judge can force creditors to cooperate, creditors have many instruments to help them to secure their interests.[6] Potentially, many lenders are not only motivated by the prospect of asset recovery, but also by a sense of grievance (Jungmann et al. 2001; Kilpi 1998). In general, few assets are exempted. Any income above a legally defined minimum must be surrendered. There is no material incentive for insolvents to earn additional income. In more liberal judicial systems debts tend to be discharged after three years. In less liberal systems bankruptcy can amount to debt-bondage (peonage) when insolvents are denied their autonomy indefinitely.

10.2 A Chicago interpretation of personal bankruptcy

The dominant Chicago approach to law and economics usurped the Ely-Commons inspired institutional law and economics some time ago (Mercuro and Medema 2006). The Chicago approach, typified especially by Becker, Posner and Coase, reduces Commons's rich delineation of transactions into one essentially consisting of commodity exchange in an overarching ubiquitous market. The defining feature of Becker and Posner's approach is a price-theoretic analysis of law (Engelmann 2005; Mercuro and Medema 2006). Posner in particular has justified this in terms of explaining legal and business practices within the parameters of 'basic economic theory' (Posner 1978, p. 931). He avows the efficiency of common law on the basis that judges select legal rules that generate efficient outcomes within the cost constraints of administering the legal system.[7] He declares: 'It is *as if* the judges wanted to adopt the rules, procedures, and case outcomes that would maximize society's wealth' (Posner 1990, p. 356, original emphasis). Legal rules are analogous to prices that influence rational individuals' incentive structures. Contracts, supported by common law, are a key efficiency source in the market system.

Criminality and breaches of contract will occur when the associated costs are outweighed by the benefits. For an individual in this situation, bankruptcy would represent efficient breach of contract. Individual declarations of bankruptcy will vary with its 'price'. William Waller's (2001) review of neoclassical studies of bankruptcy in the USA reveals that they generally support an increase in the relative price of Chapter 7 bankruptcy as a means of reducing returns. Clearly the underlying objective in this literature is to attenuate the attractiveness of contractual breach. High 'returns' to bankruptcy filing will mean that contracts will be easily breached, impeding the efficient operation of the market as transaction costs increase. Market exchange becomes less attractive, *ceteris paribus*. What to Chicago school law and economics is a statement of fact, in the eyes of uncritical observers becomes a morally reprehensible act.

Given its utilitarian roots, a Chicago school evaluation of bankruptcy is thus consequentialist (Kilpi 1998) within an individualist analytical frame. Becker and Posner's rhetoric of universal commodification renders a conflation of all value into exchange value.[8] Deontological aspects are either merely assumed to be adequately embodied by exchange value, and hence the consequences of exchange and action, or assumed away. Exchange value furnishes the central defining feature of commodities: as a commodity is an entity that may be potentially monetized, is produced *for* sale in a market (Polanyi 1944), therefore property rights to the entity can be defined and transferred. Bankruptcy as breach of contract adversely impacts on the enforcement of property rights: the creditor is either totally bereft of, or only partially receives, her/his due rewards. The exchange value of the entity transferred is no longer an accurate evaluation of the value that is actually exchanged.

Interestingly, Waller's (2001, p. 878) review of the mainstream literature reveals that rational choice models fail to explain observable behaviour such as the sudden declaration of bankruptcy by those with good credit ratings and no history of delayed or missed payments, borrowing to save, and why there are not more bankruptcy declarations in the USA, since almost any creditworthy household would gain financially. He thus makes clear that the rational choice approach is beset with explanatory problems. The broader institutionalist IVP offers a richer analytical and policy potential.

10.3 Some observations on IVP

IVP recognizes individuals and practices as embedded in an institutional environment, and can thus be argued to provide a framework for policy analysis. IVP is both sensitive to a given institutional environment shaping individuals and is able to question that environment. The principle embodies pluralistic values (Samuels 1995) and offers criteria for selecting alternative institutional 'furnitures' as Veblen likes to call them. An OIE analysis of law understands the broader context of both the law and the broader context of people's life-worlds. Favouring scientific inquiry and social well-being, the instrumental use of knowledge may guide policy formulation, generally favouring inclusion, egalitarianism and technical progress. The fact that the incidence of personal bankruptcies is rising is not merely to be understood as the result of financial mismanagement by the individuals concerned. Financial deregulation has eased lending and extended credit, which combined with the social pressures of conspicuous consumption embodied by a consumer society constitute important sources of personal indebtedness. Are (all) individuals able to make the kind of rational decisions the Chicago school law and economics tradition assumes? The Chicago approach reduces social interactions to the trading of commodities, implying a single institutional form: ubiquitous markets where self-interested, calculating agents maximize utility.

From Dewey's theory of knowledge and his adumbration of the means-end continuum, value adopts a processual or ethical dialectical quality (Waller and Robertson, 1993). Dewey argued: 'All conduct that is not simply either blindly impulsive or mechanically routine seems to involve valuations. The problem of valuation is thus closely associated with the problem of the structure of the sciences of *human* activities and *human* relations' (1939, p. 383, original emphasis). This is in direct contrast to other principles of value, such as utilitarianism, where the acceptance of 'given wants' would seem to infer an ethical relativism but in fact may engender an ethical absolutism. Specifically, Tool (1993, p. 126) argues that society distinguishes between admissible and inadmissible wants, and therefore, 'any unwillingness to uncritically accept the market satisfaction of wants evades judgmental responsibility'. This can result in ethical absolutism that favours the status quo as it is seen as optimal by definition.

By contrast IVP is not absolute, but provides a *framework* of discourse and policy analysis, and embodies pluralistic values (Samuels 1995, 1998). It does not imply a particular pattern of ownership or governance, and, '[a]ccordingly, it is neither identified with nor supportive of any Grand Alternatives, the isms of political economy – capitalism, socialism, communism – all of which offer timeless, institutionally defined economic models' (Tool 1993, p. 126). Instead, it provides *criteria* for the selection of alternative institutional structures. IVP draws a clear association between scientific inquiry and social well-being, with institutions being evaluated on the basis of the instrumental use of knowledge. As for Dewey, intelligence is an instrument for the advancement of social well-being (Samuels 1995); institutional change *should* be governed by intelligent action guided by the desired future consequences of that action (ends-in-view), and this should be facilitated by widespread participation in decision-making processes that reflect the pluralism of society (Atkinson 1987; Samuels 1995; Tool 1993, 1995, among others). Tool (1995, p. 23, emphasis added), following Foster, designates the following as the essence of IVP: '... do or choose that which provides for the *continuity* of human life and the *noninvidious* re-creation of community through the instrumental use of knowledge'.

The principle as a process of valuation provides a mode of discourse as opposed to a calculus of 'best solutions' of valuation that can be conclusively reached (Samuels 1998). The worth of actions, measures and institutional arrangements and the problems of policy have to be addressed through inquiry (Avio 2004).

Yet, as Klein (1995) and Avio recognize, the principle of instrumental valuation resonates considerable ambiguity. What is the basis of judgement? Whose judgement counts? What are the guiding principles?[9] This ambiguity may be inevitable given that the principle refers to a process of valuation: value emerges following inquiry and discourse. As Klein observes, for Hayek this could mean avoidance of 'serfdom', for Marx a classless society, and for some contemporary economists the freeing of the market. Thus: 'The problem is in giving teeth to the notion of reasonableness ... we might be left with very inadequate reeds on which to rely' (Klein, 1995, pp. 134 and 138).

10.4 Extending IVP: dealing with risk

Empirical studies, even those for the country where both data and studies are most abundant (the USA), are inconclusive with regard to the effects of policy reforms on the number of filings for bankruptcy (CBO 2000).[10]

Taking out a loan is 'simply behaving in the culturally approved manner', in a society where 'commerce is seen as essential to society' (Waller 2001, pp. 872, 875–6). Criminalizing the debtor in cases of insolvency is, however, still very common in many countries (Efrat 2001; Kilpi 1998), even if the creditor shares the blame for credit losses. The vast majority of credit has, to be sure, been extended voluntarily by a creditor (Kilpi 1998, p. 95). Creditors – and policymakers who have enabled easy credit – who wish to ignore this, and seek to retrieve the assets at any costs are driven mostly by what Galbraith has called the 'Puritan Ethos'. While denying discharge of debt through bankruptcy cannot be defended on utilitarian grounds, because the costs this creates for the parties involved and society at large are much higher than the benefits, this certainly cannot be defended from a deontological perspective. If both debtors and creditors are to be blamed for bankruptcy, and if insolvency is caused mainly by circumstances beyond the control of debtors, the state has a duty to protect its citizens from overly prolonged hardship and certainly from autarky (Kilpi 1998; Waller 2001). Welfare state provision offers a guaranteed minimum for living, but does not provide restitution of an agent's autonomy.

While government policy on bankruptcy law has not achieved the aims of reducing the number of bankruptcies, the quantity of assets involved in bankruptcy or the extent of fraud (CBO 2000; Jungmann et al. 2001; Jungmann 2006; Kilpi 1998),[11] the people involved have been affected. Reforms making bankruptcy more 'expensive', have 'lower[ed] the losses associated with defaults', or even 'ma[d]e the most profitable form of lending in the credit industry even more profitable' (Waller 2001, p. 875). In terms of Table 10.1, there is a progressive shift from cell II (USA) or cell IV (Europe) to cell I.[12] This is a movement that does not favour society broadly (CBO 2000).

It takes a broader perspective to evaluate the full effects of changes in bankruptcy law (see Moss 1992). Extending cell IV, I suggest that it endorses an analysis that looks at the effects of public policy in terms of how risks are dealt with. Indeed, bankruptcy law can be seen as a means for society to deal with risks (Zywicki 2005). Risks may be *reduced, shared* (by seeking scale), or they may be *shifted* (reallocated) (compare Moss 1992).

The way in which risks are handled in society allows for a critical perspective of existing institutional 'furnitures'. How a society deals with risks that may befall individuals should be considered from an overall perspective, not on a law-by-law basis. US bankruptcy law could well be regarded as an alternative to the welfare system that is in place in many

Table 10.1 Dealing with risks

Risks		**Solved by:**	
		Individual	**Society**
Caused by:	**Individual choices and behaviour**	I Individual responsibility ('you reap what you sow')	II Solidarity (Sharing risks)
	External circumstances	III Individual solidarity (accept risks)	IV Collective solidarity

Source: Adapted from Schmid (2006).

European countries. Lenient bankruptcy law allows or even causes the risks of insolvency to be shared by forcing creditors to increase interest rates to compensate for the increased risks they face. As European countries continue to pursue neo-liberal policies the Keynesian welfare state is at best attenuated. These countries do not tend to emulate US bankruptcy law, however, which in effect means a shift of risks from the state to individuals, under the guise of the claim that individuals are to blame for their adverse financial circumstances. In Table 10.1 there is a shift from cell IV to cell I.

Changes to bankruptcy law can thus be evaluated from the perspective of dealing with risks. In 1978, the liberal Bankruptcy Code was enacted in the USA. Given the foregoing, this law is a clear case of risk sharing: both creditors and debtors had to bear the brunt of insolvency; risks are shared by a larger group of actors. Legally, the move in the Netherlands in 1998 to have automatic discharge of debts three years after filing, even if creditors do not agree, is a breakthrough. In terms of risks, it means a shift from debtors to creditors. Recent, post-1978, changes in the means-testing rule or changes in (homes) exemption, included in most bankruptcy laws, such as the 2005 Bankruptcy Abuse Prevention and Consumer Protection Act, signed by the Bush administration, tend to make filing for bankruptcy less likely and less attractive. Risks are shifted to citizens (compare Waller 2001). The 2005 bill 'presumes abuse' if a debtor earns more than a certain income – a Chapter 7 filing may then be converted into a Chapter 13 filing. The rule, or the informal routine of prohibiting bankrupts' borrowing capabilities (or only at highly unattractive conditions), is a rule meant to reduce risks, but one that may just shift risks. Restricting the access to certain kinds of credit lines (such as credit cards[13]) of particular groups of people (such as high risk or low income borrowers; DeJarnatt 1999) would reduce risks too, but may be unpalatable for other reasons. They would also not be favoured by the credit industry.

10.5 Some concluding remarks

This chapter has discussed some recent developments in bankruptcy law. Bankruptcy law is a means for society to deal with risks, but is equally an arena for moral debate. At the same time it might provide an alternative to a welfare system (Sullivan et al. 1989), and to some extent reflects a society's valuation of entrepreneurship. I have discussed the way in which countries have chosen to formulate policies regarding personal bankruptcy from a welfare perspective, arguing that the Chicago school law and economics tradition, based in utilitarian ethics, does not allow one to make much of an evaluation. IVP offers greater analytical latitude beyond the rationalistic and individualistic properties underpinning contemporary reform. I have, however, suggested that in cases such as that of policies related to personal bankruptcy, the criteria that IVP suggests can be further elaborated. Effects of policy on the way in which risks manifest themselves is what I draw attention to, distinguishing risk sharing, shifting and reducing.

11
Conclusions

While attention on the role of institutions in the economy has increasingly permeated the communication of economists in recent years, the positivist inclination has not. Discussions of the concept of institutions have thus been informed by ideas from either Newtonian physics or from biology (Hodgson and Knudsen 2006; special issues of the *Journal of Evolutionary Economics* 2006 and the *Journal of Economic Methodology* 2004). Is the biological metaphor the proper one for evolutionary economics to pursue, given that it leads to the incorporation of more from biology as an academic discipline than would be called for? Is the economy, the subject of analysis for economists, not fundamentally different from a biological or a natural system? I argue that social systems are different from physical ones and that such an acknowledgement has consequences of a theoretical nature (compare Leydesdorff 2006a, 2006b).

The complexity of economy and society is man-made, the result of the creation and manipulation of symbols in processes of interaction between agents (Dolfsma 2008a). As such, it is a complexity that is not of a fundamentally recent kind – as if it were the result of ICT or modern technology or what is oft-times referred to as the knowledge economy. The economy as a complex system evolves endogenously. Coordination and selection of what is valuable, for instance, but not exclusively through the market, is necessarily institutionalized, aligns action, expectations and meanings. This brings us to a fundamental critique levelled at evolutionary economics (see also Leydesdorff 2006a; Andersen 1994), not addressed till now: variation and selection are not completely separate, and the selection environment is not undifferentiated. The economy and its agents being forward looking, purposeful, anticipatory, '[e]mpirical observable phenomena inform us about cases that have occurred historically, but not about what could have occurred' therefore '[t]he historical observables themselves cannot provide sufficient control for the quality of theorizing about meaning' (Leydesdorff 2006a, p. 103). Starting from given, historically emerged institutional structures would entail ignoring the probabilistic nature of a system; it would entail ignoring counterfactuals that agents could or actually have imagined and that have informed communications and decision-making processes.

This is not to deny the physical or biological nature of agents (individuals) in a system, but it does suggest that they are not limited by these dimensions of their existence. Social systems and biological systems are different because, in the former, meanings are created as effects of and preconditions for communicative behaviour. This line of argument does raise some serious questions about issues that are rather central to institutional and evolutionary theory. Communication of information of a symbolic nature then takes a central position in conceptualizations. Symbolic communication, the argument here is, refers to socio-cultural values and is institutionalized. The Social Value Nexus might offer a way of understanding this.

Notes

2. Market and Society: How Do They Relate, and How Do They Contribute to Welfare?

1. With John Finch and Robert McMaster.
2. Within the mainstream, some seem to hold the position that economy and society constitute two separate physical realms. After Robbins (1932), as economics tended to be defined not in terms of realm but in terms of method applied, the identification of realm and discipline holds less water than it used to. Economy and society are now separated in terms of motives, as economics is defined such that sociological or psychological elements, for instance, are believed to be irrelevant.
3. In some instances, however, it is clear that, however one looks at it, the growth of the market does encroach on society with clearly negative effects on well-being, if not welfare. An example is provided by the work of Schor (1992, 1998) who shows that the pressures in a modern consumption society are such that people tend to work much longer hours even as they grow richer, ending up with a much-curtailed social and family life. Schor claims that well-being is lowered in the process. Frank (2000) adds that welfare is lowered as well.
4. Van Staveren (2001) distinguishes three value-domains (freedom, justice, care) that would seem to relate to three 'places' (market, state, care). This is similar to Granovetter's position in Figure 2.2. If one severs domains from 'places' one is likely to hold that in each domain all or many possibly incongruent values can be found. This position would be more akin to that of Figure 2.3, and would signify a considerably different position.
5. Hodgson (1999, p. 269) defines markets as 'institutionalised exchanges, where a consensus over prices and other information may be established'. Hodgson observes that not all exchanges take place in markets, an important exception being what he calls relational exchange based on 'on-going ties of loyalty rather than competitive open-market deals'.
6. Reference to any standard health economics text indicates that health and health-care are considered to be 'special commodities' (see for instance, Folland et al. 1997 and McGuire et al. 1988).
7. Drawing from Polanyi's (1944) notion of a 'commodity fiction', and Marx's (1990) notable 'commodity fetishism', a commodity can be defined in terms of a thing that may be potentially monetized, sold for money, and therefore property rights to the entity can be defined and transferred (Fine 2002; Polanyi 1944).
8. Parts of the feminist literature also stress how the nature of care can change through institutional change, see, for example, Folbre and Nelson (2000).

3. Institutions, Institutional Change and Language

1. With John Finch and Robert McMaster.

2. Flaherty (2000) develops her concept of 'limited inquiry and intelligent adaptation' while examining the manufacture of semiconductors. Her concern is that members of a firm seek to stimulate experimentation but are also aware of the potentially damaging and disorganizing consequences of experiment with organizational procedures. Hence, experiments are means of social coordination.
3. We would loosely define a *boundary* as an institution or set of institutions that separates two or more relatively homogeneous entities (Chick and Dow, 2005). Boundaries are a means of connection as well as a means of distinction, such that boundaries are simultaneously buffers and bridges (Thompson 1967). Star and Griesemer (1989, p. 393) – in a paper that has become a standard reference in organization studies – argue that boundary (objects) 'are both plastic enough to adapt to local needs and the constraints of the several parties employing them, yet robust enough to maintain a common identity across sites'.
4. Can there ever be proper 'I-intention'? Pragmatically intentions anticipate actions that are necessarily social and communicative. However, 'we-intentionality' carries obligations in a manner not conveyed by 'I-intentions'. 'I intend to go for walk' does not carry the same communicative and normative properties as 'we intend to go for a walk', even though it may be an invitation to others to come along and thus constitute a weak form of we-intentionality. Returning to our theme of experimentation, this I-intention is also social because it is communicated – perhaps non-verbally – to some intended other. Garbo's 'I want to be alone' (in the 1932 film, *Grand Hotel*) is communicated to some other(s) and also means that others have some obligation to allow her to be alone.
5. Famously Veblen delineated different types of institutions, acerbically classifying monarchy and the papacy as 'imbecile institutions'. See Dunn (2005) for a discussion of the diversity and evolution of the institutional furniture of 'democracy'.

4. Structure, Agency and the Role of Values in Processes of Institutional Change

1. With Rudi Verburg.
2. A practice is '... any form of activity specified by a system of rules [institutions] which defines offices, roles, moves, penalties, defenses, and so on, and which gives activity its structure' (Rawls 1955, p. 3).
3. Compare Carrithers (1990), Dunbar (1998), Givón (2005); see also Searle (2005). The human brain seems particularly attuned to complex social behaviour, especially in relation to the use of language to understand and express higher-order intentions.
4. In earlier work, Hayden (1982) positions himself within a more evaluative tradition, discussing his contribution to work on Veblen's dichotomy.
5. Zilber (2004, p. 236) emphasizes this easily ignored category of 'interpretation as an active choice'. A given institutional setting always leaves room for individuals to exert their agency, no institutional 'script' is completely closed

(Akrich 1992; Gioia and Poole 1984; Barley and Tolbert 1997; Philips et al. 2004).

6. Beckert (1999, p. 784) pertinently says that 'highly stable environments make it possible to look for strategic alternatives' to be take advantage of by what he calls 'institutional entrepreneurs'.
7. Emphasizing interpretation and perception implies an understanding of knowledge that does not equate it to accumulated pieces of information, the Bayesian view of knowledge and knowledge acquisition (Berger and Luckmann 1966; Bandura 1986; Dolfsma 2004, 2008a).
8. Boulding (1956, p. 75) makes this point as well, referring to what he calls 'image' ('the total cognitive, affective, and evaluative structure of the [individual], or its internal view of itself and the universe'): 'To a very large extent changes in the image come about through the impact on society of unusually creative, charismatic or prophetic individuals.'
9. See Peterson (1990) and Burnett (1993). Combined market share for the few big record companies fell by some 40 per cent in just three years as rock music emerged around 1955.
10. As perceived by many players in Europe. Given that Medicare and Medicaid do provide collective coverage for health-care in the US for large groups of citizens, and also as a number of presidential candidates perceive of the European system as an example to imitate, this characterization might not be accurate.

5. 'Silent Trade' and the Supposed Continuum between OIE and NIE

1. With Antoon Spithoven.
2. As a third example, in addition to references to Herodotus and Polanyi, Basu et al. (1987) refer to medieval cities shutting themselves off from the surrounding countryside in order to keep the plague out. In private communication, Eric Jones indicates that in London the Winchester plague plaque gives notice to the effect that when the city had closed its gates during the plague, coins in payment for food brought by country folk were placed in vinegar in a basin outside the Westgate. Although contact between those involved was prevented, this example of trading food with farmers is no instance of silent trade as extensive prior exchange had happened, creating converging mental models and settling prices.
3. Middlemen, brokering between parties, met with each party, although not necessarily at the same time.
4. Modern trade, for instance of foreign exchange or of commodity futures, using computer screens and IT does not involve personal contact and operates across large geographical distances. As Knorr Cetina and Bruegger (2002) convincingly show, highly institutionalized kinds of communication are involved in this kind of trade. What is more, the relations between traders are more personal and more moral than one would be inclined to expect.
5. Consider, however, that Denzau and North (1994, p. 14 fn.6) claim that 'we are extremely unlikely to ever learn the true model': this is in stark contrast with Bayesian views of learning.

6. Knowledge Coordination and Development via Market, Hierarchy and Gift Exchange

1. With Rene van der Eijk.
2. IPRs include patents, copyrights and trademarks.
3. In line with Bourdieu's (1980) argument about the 'production of belief'.
4. Classically, literature has emphasized that the exchange of gifts in many cases is motivated by calculative self-interest (for example, Blau 1964; Heath 1976; Homans 1974; Mauss 2000 [1954]). A gift, however, *can* represent a free gift (Malinowski 1996), a completely disinterested gesture without expectation of reciprocity. According to Vandevelde (2000, p. 15): 'the logic of the gift thus can be reduced neither to disinterestedness or altruisms, nor to strict calculative egotism'.
5. The Book of Proverbs in the Bible, which is said to contain the wisdom of King Solomon, says that: 'A man's gift makes room for him and brings him before great men' (Proverbs, 18:16).
6. A tryad is a relationship between at least three actors who are either directly or indirectly connected with one another, resulting in a closure of the network where specific norms are created and enforced (Simmel 1964). Coleman (1994) also indicates that in such a situation of redundancy the costs of punishment of norm-transgressing behaviour by one party can be split between the other two, making norm-following behaviour more likely.
7. Reputation is information on past behaviour, communicated by a third party, that the focal actor has about the supposed trustworthiness of an exchange party. A party's reputation – even if incorrect – if sufficient alternatives exist for the focal actor will decrease the uncertainty associated with potential future coordination between the two (Kreps 1990). This is particularly important in cases of genuine uncertainty, such as in connection with newly established firms or in the case of knowledge development (Ferrary 2003).
8. Although the norm of reciprocity may be seen as a universal moral norm, it may operate differently in different contexts and is not unconditional. According to Noonan ([1984], taken from Steidlmeier, 1999, p. 4): 'Reciprocity is in any society a rule of life, and in some societies at least it is *the* rule of life.'
9. A social reality captured by the proverb 'never look a gift horse in the mouth'. Which can be translated as 'never criticize or express displeasure at a gift' (Seidl and McMordie 1978).
10. Or, to put it another way, 'The reciprocity domain involves the management of costs and benefits between functional equals' (Bugental 2000).

7. Making Knowledge Work: Intra-firm Networks, Gifts and Innovation

1. This figure is from Aalbers et al. (2006); also consult this source for a discussion of data collection and analysis that is entailed in this kind of approach.
2. R. Aalbers and W. Dolfsma (2004), 'Crossing Internal Borders: Inter-Divisional Communication Networks at Siemens Netherlands', ECCH (RSM) teaching case 404-090-1.

8. Path Dependence, Initial Conditions and Routines in Organizations: the Toyota Production System Re-examined

1. With Hugo van Driel.
2. In fact, Goldstone himself in an earlier publication (1991, p. 60) defines events as constituting initial conditions.
3. Kogut and Zander (1996) talk about 'higher-order principles'. Their analysis is largely along similar lines, but stresses identity, symbolic communication, and dialogue more than we do in our more mundane account.
4. Ohno (1988, p. 31) writes that he made the first step towards JIT in 1949–50; the timeline on the inside cover of this book mentions the start of 'withdrawal by subsequent processes' in 1948, while two-machine handling was introduced as early as 1947. Cusumano (1985, pp. 262–307), who interviewed Ohno, mentions 1948 as the start of his innovations.
5. A well-documented study shows that Toyota did not invent just-in-time production, but that such a 'hand-to-mouth' system, originating from *c.* 1905, was applied by the large American car makers in the 1920s and 1930s on a large scale, only to be abandoned soon after (Schwartz and Fish 1998; see also Williams et al. 1995, pp. 33, 35; and Cusumano, 1985, p. xx).
6. In 1952, when there were serious plans for his return to the company, Kiichiro unexpectedly died.
7. The bottom-up or 'democratic' nature of decision-making at Toyota should not be idealized. In relation to its development of electronics capabilities Toyota felt: '... that only a top-to-bottom Japanese-style program of learning-by-doing could infuse its entire organization with the skills and values essential to making electronics a genuine "core competence" ...' (Ahmadjian and Lincoln 2001, p. 689).

9. Paradoxes of Modernist Consumption: Reading Fashions

1. Etymologically, 'individual' derives from the Latin *individuum* – indivisible – and further back from the Greek '*atomos*' – impossible to cut.
2. The idea of a sea-change is itself, of course, modernist. Change, in a modernist conception, is almost inherently good as it is a break with the past and with traditions, creating something new for a better future.
3. See also Veblen (1899), but contrast Campbell (1987).
4. This does not mean that an actual observer will be there to receive the message. Observers may not be present, they may be imaginary, or the conspicuous consumption can be directed at the self. The latter is an instance of the well-known phenomenon of self-reward in social psychology, corroborated empirically (Bandura 1986).
5. Bush (1987, p. 1106) suggests a 'principle of minimal dislocation' suggesting that institutions that are under pressure for change will change such that the effects of the change on the setting as a whole are minimized.
6. Although fashion is associated by many an observer with femininity (Ireland 1987; Simmel 1957 [1904]), for the most part because women are believed to espouse the modernist value of rationality to a lesser degree (Bordo 1987), men have been at least as involved in consuming fashion as women (Breward 1999; Edwards 1997; Crane 2000).

7. This would amount to an Adornian position without the negative connotations about consumers being manipulated into purchasing whatever is on offer (Adorno 1941).

10. Institutionalist Law and Economics and Values: the Case of Personal Bankruptcy Law

1. With Robert McMaster.
2. It is reported that, in the USA, 'no more than 5 percent' of filers could repay all of their debt yet filed for personal bankruptcy (CBO 2000, p. 24). At the same time, again for the USA, 15 per cent of the population could benefit from filing for bankruptcy yet does not; only 0.7 per cent of the adult population actually does so (ibid., p. 21).
3. Buckley and Brinig (1998) find that economic factors play a marginal role in the decision to file for bankruptcy, and point to social factors such as the strength of filers' social networks.
4. Among the filers are many small, start-up firms that have no legal title. There is a well-known overly confident feeling among (starting) entrepreneurs about their own chances for success. Entrepreneurs in the USA who own a firm that has no legal title can choose to file under Chapter 11, as any other business, and thus find their personal assets exempted from a bankruptcy. The USA may well be more economically dynamic partly because of its more lenient bankruptcy law.
5. According to Efrat (2001), extensively comparing personal bankruptcy law and practice around the world, the USA, the UK and the Netherlands are all in the 'liberal camp' of countries with lenient bankruptcy law.
6. In order to qualify, potential filers must obtain a statement from their municipality relating the causes for their financial problems. A repayment plan will be announced several times in a newspaper. A trustee can have all personal surface mail directed through her. When creditors discharge a debtor, any remaining debt will remain publicly registered even if it is uncollectible; this will affect the debtor's ability to obtain future loans, leaving her in a state of semi-autarky.
7. Thus, '... common law adjudication brings the economic system closer to the results that would be produced by effective competition – a free market operating without significant externality, monopoly, or information problems' (Posner 1983, pp. 4–5).
8. The conception of the commodity is central to both Marx's (1990) and Polanyi's (1944) investigations of capitalism. Marx considered that commodities as entities possess both exchange and use values. The use value of something is only realized in its use or consumption (Marx 1990). The inference here is that the usefulness of something cannot be assessed ex ante. Moreover, usefulness cannot be quantified, whereas exchange value can: the former adopts a qualitative property. Exchange value does not reflect the social relationships governing the production or consumption of commodities, and accordingly can only offer a limited explanation of bankruptcy (compare Tilman 1998).

9. Klein notes various judgemental criteria, from Veblen's 'enhancing human life', John Commons's 'reasonable value', Ayres's 'toward a reasonable society', to Tool's Veblenian invidious-noninvidious distinction. Tool cites Veblen in his delineation of invidious and non-invidious. Invidious refers to a comparison of individuals on the basis of providing some value or relative worth. Thus, invidious distinctions relate to judgements on the basis of race, gender, wealth, power, tradition and so on: '[t]hose groups and individuals against whom invidious distinctions are directed are denied options, entitlements, and the full development of their capabilities (for example, access to education, occupation, or income). In consequence, the development of individuals' creative potential and productive capacities (and their self-worth) are arrested or eroded' (Tool 1993, pp. 122–3).
10. Changing exemption rules, means testing rules and so on has had negligible effects on the number of personal bankruptcies or the amounts of money involved in bankruptcy procedures (Sullivan et al. 1989). Both of these are mainly associated with macroeconomic developments or unpredictable changes in personal circumstances (such as illness and unemployment) (Kilpi 1998). What is more, people from all walks of life equally file for personal bankruptcy (CBO 2000; Kilpi 1998; Sullivan et al. 1989).
11. The belief that fraud is prevalent in bankruptcy cases is unfounded. Even in liberal countries such as Canada and the USA only just over 2 per cent of bankruptcy cases involve fraud (Kilpi 1998). Only a small fraction of people filing might have been able to repay their original debt. Repeat bankruptcy is not a reality (Sullivan et al. 1989).
12. There are costs involved with bankruptcies. What bankruptcy law in effect does is to spread these costs across everybody who takes loans via increased interest premiums or reduced availability of credit in the market. To the extent that not only those taking (new) loans are affected, but indeed everybody in a society shares the costs, the movement has been from cell IV to cell I, rather than from II to I. There is, however, little empirical evidence, at least for the USA about such costs (CBO 2000).
13. Scholars have ascribed higher indebtedness by increasing numbers of households to increased availability of credit cards (Ausubel 1997; Waller 2001; Sullivan 2000). Zywicki (2005, pp. 1496–7) claims that this is due to a substitution from other high-interest kinds of credit into credit card debt, and possibly a sign of a 'downward spiral of a defaulting borrower', possibly indicating (malevolent) strategic behaviour on the filer's part as such debt is unsecured and will be discharged in bankruptcy.

References

Aalbers, R., W. Dolfsma and O. Koppius (2006), 'Not Just with your Friends: Knowledge Transfer in Organizations', working paper, Erasmus University Rotterdam.

Abreu, D. (1988), 'On the Theory of Infinitely Repeated Games with Discounting', *Econometrica*, 56(2): 383–96.

Adams, J.S. (1965), 'Inequity in Social Exchange', in L. Berkowitz (ed.), *Advances in Experimental Social Psychology*, vol. 2, New York: Academic Press, pp. 267–99.

Adler, P.S. (2001), 'Market, Hierarchy, and Trust: the Knowledge Economy, and the Future of Capitalism', *Organization Science*, 12(2): 215–34.

Adler, P.S. and S.W. Kwon (2000), 'Social Capital: the Good, the Bad and the Ugly', in E. Lesser (ed.), *Knowledge and Social Capital: Foundations and Applications*, Boston: Butterworth-Heinemann, pp. 89–116.

—— (2002), 'Social Capital: Prospects for a New Concept', *Academy of Management Review*, 27(1): 17–40.

Adler, P.S., B. Goldoftas and D.I. Levine (1999), 'Flexibility versus Efficiency? A Case Study of Model Changeover in the Toyota Production System', *Organization Science*, 10(1): 43–68.

Adorno, T.W. (1941), 'On Popular Music', *Studies in Philosophy and Social Science*, 9: 17–48.

Agrawal, A.K., I.M. Cockburn and J. McHale (2003), 'Gone but not Forgotten: Labor Flows, Knowledge Spillovers and Enduring Social Capital', NBER Working Paper No. 9950.

Ahmadjian, C.L. and J.R. Lincoln (2001), 'Keiretsu, Governance, and Learning: Case Studies in Change for the Japanese Automotive Industry', *Organization Science*, 12: 683–701.

Akerlof, G.A. (1982), 'Labor Contracts as Partial Gift Exchange', *Quarterly Journal of Economics*, 97: 543–69.

Akrich, M. (1992), 'The De-Scription of Technical Objects', in W.E. Bijker and J. Law (eds), *Shaping Technology/Building Society*, Cambridge, MA and London: MIT Press, pp. 205–24.

Alchian, A.A. (1977), 'Why Money?' *Journal of Money, Credit and Banking*, 9(1), Part 2: 133–40.

Aldous, J. (1962), 'Urbanization, the Extended Family, and Kinship Ties in West Africa', *Social Forces*, 41(1): 6–12.

Allaire, Y. and M.E. Firsiroty (1984), 'Theories of Organizational Culture', *Organization Studies*, 5(3): 193–226.

Allen, T.J. (1977), *Managing the Flow of Technology: Technology Transfer and the Dissemination of Technological Information within the R&D Organization*, Cambridge, MA: MIT Press.

Allen, T.J. and S.I. Cohen (1969), 'Information Flow in Research and Development Laboratories', *Administrative Science Quarterly*, 14: 12–19.

Anand, N. and R.A. Peterson (2000), 'When Market Information Constitutes Fields: Sensemaking of Markets in the Commercial Music Industry', *Organization Science*, 11(3): 270–84.

Ancona D. and D. Caldwell (1992), 'Bridging the Boundary: External Activity and Performance in Organizational Teams', *Administrative Science Quarterly*, 37: 634–65.

Andersen, E.S. (1994), *Evolutionary Economics: Post-Schumpeterian Contributions*, London: Pinter.

Ankerloo, D. and G. Palermo (2004), 'Anti-Williamson', *Cambridge Journal of Economics*, 28: 413–29.

Archer, M.S. (1988), *Culture and Agency: the Place of Culture in Social Theory*, Cambridge: Cambridge University Press.

Arrow, K.J. (1984), 'Information and Economic Behavior', in *Collected Papers of Kenneth J. Arrow: the Economics of Information*, Cambridge, MA: The Belknap Press of Harvard University Press, pp. 136–52.

—— (1974), *The Limits of Organization*, New York: Norton.

—— (1972), 'Gifts and Exchanges', *Philosophy and Public Affairs*, 1: 343–62.

Arthur, B.A. (1989), 'Competing Technologies, Increasing Returns, and Lock-in by Historical Events', *Economic Journal*, 99: 116–31.

Atkinson, G. (1987), 'Instrumentalism and Economic Policy: the Quest for Reasonable Value', *Journal of Economic Issues*, 21: 189–202.

Ausubel, L.M. (1997), 'Credit Card Defaults, Credit Card Profits and Bankruptcy', *American Bankruptcy Law Journal*, 71: 249–70.

Avio, K.L. (2004), 'A Modest Proposal for Institutional Economics', *Journal of Economic Issues*, 38: 715–45.

—— (2002), 'Three Problems of Social Organisation: Institutional Law and Economics Meets Habermasian Law and Democracy', *Cambridge Journal of Economics*, 26: 501–20.

Avner, O. (1997), 'Between the Gift and the Market: the Economy of Regard', *Economic History Review*, 50(3): 450–76.

Axelrod, R. (1984), *The Evolution of Cooperation*, New York: Basic Books.

Back, K.W. (1986), 'Modernism and Fashion', in M.R. Solomon (ed.), *The Psychology of Fashion*, Lexington, MA: Heath, pp. 3–14.

Bandura, A. (1986), *Social Foundations of Thought and Action: a Social Cognitive Theory*, Englewood Cliffs, NJ: Prentice-Hall.

Barber, B. (1977), 'Absolutization of the Market', in G. Bermant (ed.), *Markets and Morals*, Washington, DC: Heminsphere.

Barley, S.R. and P.S. Tolbert (1997), 'Institutionalization and Structuration: Studying the Links between Action and Institution', *Organization Studies*, 18(1): 93–117.

Barnard, C.I. (1968), *The Functions of the Executive*, 30th anniversary edn, Cambridge, MA: Harvard University Press.

Bassanini, P. and G. Dosi (2001), 'When and How Chance and Human Will Can Twist the Arms of Clio', in R. Garud and P. Karnøe (eds), *Path Dependence and Creation*, Mahwah, NJ: Erlbaum, pp. 41–68.

Basu, Kaushik, Erik Jones and Ekkehart Schlicht (1987), 'The Growth and Decay of Custom', *Explorations in Economic History*, 24: 1–21.

Baudrillard, J. (1981), *For a Critique of the Political Economy of the Sign*, St Louis, MO: Telos.

Becker, M.C. (2004), 'Organizational Routines', *Industrial and Corporate Change*, 13: 643–77.

Beckert, J. (2002), *Beyond the Market*, Princeton, NJ: Princeton University Press.

—— (1999), 'Agency, Entrepreneurs, and Institutional Change: the Role of Strategic Choice and Institutionalized Practice in Organizations', *Organization Studies*, 20(5): 777–99.
Belk, R. (1995), 'Studies in the New Consumer Behaviour', in D. Miller (ed.) *Acknowledging Consumption*, London and New York: Routledge, pp. 58–95.
—— (1979), 'Gift-Giving Behavior', in J. Sheth (ed.), *Research in Marketing*, Volume 2, Greenwich, CT: JAI Press, pp. 95–126.
Benders, J. and M. Morita (2004), 'Changes in Toyota Motors' Operations Management', *International Journal of Production Research*, 42(3): 433–44.
Berger, P.L. and T. Luckmann (1966), *The Social Construction of Reality*, New York: Anchor Books.
Berman, M. (1982), *All That is Solid Melts into Thin Air*, New York: Simon & Schuster.
Beyer, J. (2005), 'Pfadabhängigkeit ist nicht gleich Pfadabhängigkeit. Wider den impliziten Konservatismus eines gängigen Konzepts', *Zeitschrift für Soziologie*, 34(1): 5–21.
Biggart, N.W. and R. Delbridge (2004), 'Systems of Exchange', *Academy of Management Review*, 29(1): 28–49.
Blau, P. (1964), *Exchange and Power in Social Life*, New York: Wiley.
Boeker, W.P. (1988), 'Organizational Origins: Entrepreneurial and Environmental Imprinting at the Time of Founding', in G.A. Carrol (ed.), *Ecological Models of Organizations*, Cambridge, MA: Ballinger, pp. 33–51.
Bordo, S. (1987), *The Flight to Objectivity*, New York: State University of New York Press.
Böröcz, J. (1995), 'Social Change by Fusion', Department of Sociology, Rutgers University.
Boulding, K.E. (1981), *A Preface to Grants Economics: the Economics of Love and Fear*, New York: Praeger.
—— (1956) *The Image: Knowledge of Life in Society*, Binghampton, NY: University of Michigan Press.
Bourdieu, P. (1986), 'Forms of Capital', in J.G. Richardson (ed.), *Handbook of Theory and Research for the Sociology of Education*, New York: Greenwood Press, pp. 241–58.
—— (1984), *Distinction: a Social Critique of the Judgment of Taste*, Cambridge, MA: Harvard University Press.
—— (1977), *Outline of a Theory in Practice*, Cambridge: Cambridge University Press.
Bourdieu, P. and R. Nice (1980), 'The Production of Belief: Contribution to an Economy of Symbolic Goods', *Media, Culture & Society*, 2: 261–93.
Bouty, I. (2000), 'Interpersonal and Interaction Influences on Informal Resource Exchanges between R&D Researchers across Organizational Boundaries', *Academy of Management Journal*, 43(1): 50–65.
Bovill, [Jim] E.W. (1929), 'The Silent Trade of Wangara', *Journal of the Royal African Society*, 29(113): 27–38.
Bowles, S. (2007), 'Social Preferences and Public Economics', Working Paper No. 496, Dipartimento di Economica Politica, Università degli Studi di Siena, January.
Bowles, S. and H. Gintis (1998), 'The Moral Economy of Communities: Structured Populations and the Evolution of Pro-Social Norms', *Evolution and Human Behavior*, 19: 3–25.

Bradach, J.L. and R.G. Eccles (1989), 'Price, Authority, and Trust: From Ideal Types to Plural Forms', *Annual Review of Sociology*, 15: 97–118.

Breward, C. (1999), *The Hidden Consumer: Masculinity, Fashion and City Life 1860–1914*, Manchester and New York: Manchester University Press.

Brown, J.S. and P. Duguid (2001), 'Knowledge and Organization', *Organization Science*, 12(2): 198–213.

—— (1991), 'Organizational Learning and Communities of Practice', *Organization Science*, 2(1): 40–57.

Buckley, F.H. and M.F. Brinig (1998), 'The Bankruptcy Puzzle', *Journal of Legal Studies*, 27: 187–207.

Bugental, D.B. (2000), 'Acquisition of the Algorithms of Social Life: a Domain-Based Approach', *Psychological Bulletin*, 126(2): 187–219.

Burman, Patrick (1979), 'Variations on a Dialectical Theme', *Philosophy of the Social Sciences*, 9: 357–75.

Burnett, R. (1993), 'The Popular Music Industry in Transition', *Popular Music and Society*, 17: 87–114.

Burns, T.R. (1986), 'Actors, Transactions, and Social Structure', in U. Himmelstrand (ed.), *Sociology: the Aftermath of Crisis*, London: Age, pp. 8–37.

Burt, R.S. (2004), 'Structural Holes and Good Ideas', *American Journal of Sociology*, 110: 442–55.

—— (1992), *Structural Holes*, Cambridge, MA: Harvard University Press.

Bush, P.D. (2008), 'Culture, Values, and Institutions', in J. Davis and W. Dolfsma (eds), *The Elgar Companion of Socio-Economics*, Cheltenham, UK and Northampton, MA, USA: Edward Elgar, pp. 153–70.

—— (1987), 'The Theory of Institutional Change', *Journal of Economic Issues*, 21(3): 1075–116.

Campbell, C. (1987), *The Romantic Ethic and the Spirit of Modern Consumerism*, Oxford: Basil Blackwell.

Carrier, J. (1991), 'Gifts, Commodities, and Social Relations: a Maussian View of Exchange', *Sociological Forum*, 6(1): 119–36.

Carrithers, M. (1990), 'Why Humans Have Cultures', *Man*, 25(2): 189–206.

CBO (Congressional Budget Office) (2000), *Personal Bankruptcy: a Literature Review*, Washington DC: CBO.

Cheal, D. (1986), 'The Social Dimensions of Gift Behaviour', *Journal of Social and Personal Relationships*, 3: 423–39.

Chick, V. and S.C. Dow (2005), 'Open and Closed Systems', *Journal of Economic Methodology*, 12(3): 363–81.

Child, J. and D. Faulkner (1998), *Strategies of Cooperation*, Oxford: Oxford University Press.

Cicourel, A. (1973), *Cognitive Sociology: Language and Meaning in Social Interaction*, Harmondsworth: Penguin.

Coase, R. H. (1988 [1937]), *The Firm, the Market, and the Law*, Chicago: University of Chicago Press.

—— (1937), 'The Nature of the Firm', *Economica*, 4: 386–405.

Cohen, J.B. (1949), *Japan's Economy in War and Reconstruction*, Minneapolis: Minnesota Press.

Cohen, P.S. (1968), *Modern Social Theory*, London: Heinemann.

Cohen, W.M. and D.A. Levinthal (1990), 'Absorptive Capacity: a New Perspective on Learning and Innovation', *Administrative Science Quarterly*, 35: 128–52.

Cohendet, P., F. Creplet, M. Diani, O. Dupouet and E. Schenk (2004), 'Matching Communities and Hierarchies within the Firm', *Journal of Management and Governance*, 8: 27–48.

Coleman, J.S. (1994), *Foundations of Social Theory*, Cambridge, MA: Belknap Press.

—— (1988), 'Social Capital: in the Creation of Human Capital', *American Journal of Sociology*, 94 (Supplement): S95–S120.

Cook, K. and R. Emerson (1984), 'Exchange Networks and the Analysis of Complex Organizations', in S. Bacharach and E. Lawler (eds), *Research on the Sociology of Organizations*, Greenwich, CT: JAI Press.

Coriat, B. (2000), 'The "Abominable Ohno Production System": Competences, Monitoring, and Routines in Japanese Production Systems', in G. Dosi, R.R. Nelson and S.G. Winter (eds), *The Nature and Dynamics of Organizational Capabilities*, Oxford: Oxford University Press, pp. 213–43.

Coşgel, M. (1997), 'Consumption Institutions', *Review of Social Economy*, 55(2): 153–71.

—— (1994), 'Audience Effects in Consumption', *Economics and Philosophy*, 10: 19–30.

—— (1992), 'Rhetoric in the Economy: Consumption and Audience,' *Journal of Socio-Economics*, 21: 363–77.

Cosmas Indicopleustes (1897), *Christian Topography* [AD 55], first series no. 98, the Hakluyt Society, online edn, http://www.sacred-texts.com/earth/ct/ct00.htm (accessed 16 April 2009).

Cowan, R., P.A. David and D. Foray (2000), 'The Explicit Economics of Knowledge Codification and Tacitness', *Industrial and Corporate Change*, 9(2): 211–53.

Cowen, T. (1998), *In Praise of Commercial Culture*, Cambridge, MA: Harvard University Press.

Crane, D. (2000), *Fashion and its Social Agendas*, London and Chicago: University of Chicago Press.

—— (1997), 'Globalization, Organizational Size, and Innovation in the French Luxury Fashion Industry', *Poetics*, 24: 393–414.

Cross, R., S. Borgatti and A. Parker (2002), 'Making Invisible Work Visible: Using Social Network Analysis to Support Human Networks', *California Management Review*, 44(2): 25–46.

Cusumano, M.A. (1985), *The Japanese Automobile Industry*, Cambridge, MA: Harvard University Press.

Cutler, David M. (2002), 'Equality, Efficiency, and Market Fundamentals: the Dynamics of International Medical-Care Reform', *Journal of Economic Literature*, 40 (September 2002): 881–906.

Dahlqvist, J., P. Davidsson and J. Wiklund (2000), 'Initial Conditions as Predictors of New Venture Performance: a Replication and Extension of the Cooper et al. Study', *Enterprise & Innovation Management Studies*, 1 (1): 1–17.

Dahrendorf, R. (1959), *Class and Class Conflict in Industrial Society*, London: Routledge & Kegan Paul.

Daito, E. (2000), 'Automation and the Organization of Production in the Japanese Automobile Industry', *Enterprise & Society*, 1(March): 139–78.

Darr, A. (2003), 'Gifting Practices and Inter-organizational Relations: Constructing Obligations Networks in the Electronics Sector', *Sociological Forum*, 18(1): 31–51.

Davenport, T.H. (1997), 'Ten Principles of Knowledge Management and Four Case Studies', *Knowledge and Process Management*, 4(3): 187–208.

David, P.A. (1994), 'Why are Institutions the "Carriers Of History"? Path Dependence and the Evolution of Conventions, Organizations and Institutions', *Structural Change and Economic Dynamics*, 5: 205–20.

—— (1985), 'Clio and the Economics of QWERTY', *American Economic Review*, 75(2): 332–7.

Davis, J.B. (2004), 'The Conception of the Individual in Non-Cooperative Game Theory', Tinbergen Institute Discussion Papers 03-095/2.

—— (2003), *The Theory of the Individual in Economics: Identity and Value*, London: Routledge.

Davis, J.B. and M. Klaes (2003), 'Reflexivity: Curse or Cure', *Journal of Economic Methodology*, 10: 329–52.

Davis, J. and R. McMaster (2004), 'The Individual in Mainstream Health Economics: a Case of Persona Non-grata?' paper presented at the 2004 EAEPE Conference, University of Crete.

De Moraes Farias, Paulo F. (1974), 'Silent Trade: Myth and Historical Evidence', *History in Africa: a Journal of Method*, 1(1): 9–24.

Deckop, J.R., C.C. Cirka and L.M. Andersson (2003), 'Doing Unto Others: the Reciprocity of Helping Behavior in Organizations', *Journal of Business Ethics*, 47: 101–13.

DeJarnatt, S.L. (1999), 'Once is not Enough: Preserving Consumers' Rights to Bankruptcy Protection', *Indiana Law Journal*, 74: 455–512.

Demsetz, H. (1991), 'The Theory of the Firm Revisited', in O.E. Williamson and S.G. Winter (eds), *The Nature of the Firm*, Englewood Cliffs, NJ: Prentice-Hall, pp. 159–78.

Denzau, A.T. and D.C. North (1994), 'Shared Mental Models: Ideology and Institutions', *Kyklos*, 47(1): 3–31.

Dewey, J. (1966 [1916]), *Democracy and Education*, New York: Free Press.

—— (1945 [1922]), *Human Nature and Conduct: an Introduction to Social Psychology*, New York: Henry Holt and Company.

—— (1939), 'Theory of Valuation', in O. Neurath, R. Carnap and C. Morris (eds), *Foundations of the Unity of Science*, Vol. 2, Nos. 1–9, Chicago: University of Chicago Press.

DiMaggio, P.J. and W.E. Powell (1983), 'The Iron Cage Revisited: Institutional Isomorphism and Collective Rationality in Organizational Fields', *American Sociological Review*, 48(2): 147–60.

Djelic, M.-L. and S. Quack (2007), 'Overcoming Path Dependency: Path Generation in Open Systems', *Theory and Society*, 36: 161–86.

Dolfsma, W. (2008a), *Knowledge Economies: Innovation, Organization and Location*, London: Routledge.

—— (2008b), *Consuming Symbolic Goods*, London: Routledge.

—— (2006), 'Appropriability in Services', ERIM Report ERS-2005-021-ORG.

—— (2004), *Institutional Economics and the Formation of Preferences*, Cheltenham, UK and Northampton, MA, USA: Edward Elgar.

—— (2002) 'Mediated Preferences: How Institutions Affect Consumption', *Journal of Economic Issues*, 36(2): 449–57.

—— (1998) 'Labor Relations in Changing Capitalist Economies: the Meaning of Gifts in Social Relations', *Journal of Economic Issues*, 32(2): 631–8.

Dolfsma, W. and C. Dannreuther (2003), 'Subjects and Boundaries: Contesting Social Capital-Based Policies', *Journal of Economic Issues*, 37(2): 405–13.

Dolfsma, W. and L. Leydesdorff (2009), 'The Citation Field of Evolutionary Economics', *Journal of Evolutionary Economics*, forthcoming.
Dopfer, K. (1991), 'Toward a Theory of Economic Institutions: Synergy and Path Dependency', *Journal of Economic Issues*, 25(2): 535–50.
Dore, R. (1983), 'Goodwill and the Spirit of Market Capitalism', *British Journal of Sociology*, 34(4): 459–82.
Douglas, M. (1986), *How Institutions Think*, Syracuse: Syracuse University Press.
Douglas, M. and B. Isherwood (1979), *The World of Goods*, New York: W.W. Norton.
Doz, Y.L. (1996), 'The Evolution of Cooperation in Strategic Alliances: Initial Conditions or Learning Processes?' *Strategic Management Journal*, 17 (Summer) (Special Issue): 55–83.
Dunbar, R.I.M. (1998), 'The Social Brain Hypothesis', *Evolutionary Anthropology*, 6(5): 178–90.
Dunn, J. (2005), *Setting the People Free: the Story of Democracy*, London: Atlantic Books.
Durkheim, E. (1964 [1893]), *The Division of Labor in Society*, NY: The Free Press.
—— (1947[1895]), *Les Règles de la Méthode Sociologique*, Paris: Alcan.
Dyer, J.H. and K. Nobeoka (2000), 'Creating and Managing a High-Performance Knowledge-Sharing Network: the Toyota-Case', *Strategic Management Journal*, 21: 345–67.
The Economist (2007), 'Briefing Toyota: a Wobble on the Road to the Top', 10–16 November.
—— (2006), 'The Business of Giving: a Survey of Wealth and Philanthropy', 25 February.
—— (2004) 'Rags and Riches: a Survey of Fashion', 6 March.
—— (2002), 'Luxury Goods', 22 March.
Edwards, T. (1997), *Men in the Mirror*, London: Cassell.
Efrat, R. (2001), 'Global Trends in Personal Bankruptcy', *American Bankruptcy Law Journal*, 76(1): 81–109.
Elster, J. (1989), *The Cement of Society: a Study of Social Order*, Cambridge: Cambridge University Press.
Engelmann, S.G. (2005), 'Posner, Bentham and the Rule of Economy', *Economy and Society*, 34: 32–50.
Enthoven, A. (1988), 'Managed Competition of Alternative Delivery Systems', in W. Greenberg (ed.), *Competition in the Health Care Sector*, Durham, NC: Duke University Press, pp. 83–99.
Fay, S., E. Hurst and M.J. White (2002), 'The Household Bankruptcy Decision', *American Economic Review*, 92(3): 706–18.
Fear, J. (2001), 'Thinking Historically about Organizational Learning', in M. Dierkes, A. Berthoin Antal, J. Child and I. Nonaka (eds), *Handbook of Organizational Learning and Knowledge*, Oxford: Oxford University Press, pp. 162–91.
Feldman, M. (2003), 'A Performative Perspective on Stability and Change in Organizational Routines', *Industrial and Corporate Change*, 12: 727–52.
Ferrary, M. (2003), 'The Gift Exchange in the Social Networks of Silicon Valley', *California Management Review*, 45(4): 120–38.
Finch, J. (2004), 'Whatever Happened to Parsons and Smelser's Economic Sociology?' mimeo, University of Aberdeen.
—— (1997) ' "Verstehen", Ideal Types and Situational Analysis, and the Problem of Free Will', *Journal of Institutional and Theoretical Economics*, 153: 737–47.

Fine, B. (2002), *The World of Consumption*, 2nd edn, London: Routledge.
Finkelstein, J. (1991), *The Fashionable Self*, Cambridge: Polity Press.
Firat, A.F. and C.J. Schultz II (1997), 'From Segmentation to Fragmentation: Markets and Market Strategies in the Postmodern Era', *European Journal of Marketing*, 31: 183–207.
Firat, A. and A. Venkatesh (1993), 'Postmodernity: the Age of Marketing', *International Review of Research in Marketing*, 10: 227–49.
Fiske, A.P. (1992), 'The Four Elementary Forms of Sociality: Framework for a Unified Theory of Social Relations', *Psychological Review*, 99(4): 689–723.
Fitzgerald, R. (2004), 'The New Zealand Health Reforms: Dividing the Labour of Care', *Social Science and Medicine*, 58: 331–41.
Flaherty, M.-T. (2000), 'Limited Inquiry and Intelligent Adaptation in Semiconductor Manufacturing', in G. Dosi, R.R. Nelson and S.G. Winter (eds), *The Nature and Dynamics of Organizational Capabilities*, Oxford and New York: Oxford University Press, pp. 99–123.
Foa, E. and U.G. Foa (1980), 'Resource Theory: Interpersonal Behavior as Exchange', in K. Gergen, M. Greenberg and R. Willis (eds), *Social Exchange: Advances in Theory and Research*, New York: Plenum, pp. 77–94.
Folbre, N. and J. Nelson (2000), 'For Love or Money – or Both?' *Journal of Economic Perspectives*, 14: 123–40.
Folland, S., A.C. Goodman and M. Stano (1997), *The Economics of Health and Health Care*, 2nd edn, Upper Saddle River, NJ: Prentice-Hall.
Foray, D. (1997), 'The Dynamic Implications of Increasing Returns', *International Journal of Industrial Organization*, 15: 733–52.
Foucault, M. (1982), 'The Subject and Power', in H.L. Dreyfus and P. Rainbow (eds), *Michel Foucault: Beyond Structuralism and Hermeneutics*, Chicago: University of Chicago Press, pp. 208–26.
Fox, A. (1974), *Beyond Contract: Work, Power and Trust Relations*, London: Faber and Faber.
Frank, R.H. (2000), *Luxury Fever*, Princeton, NJ: Princeton University Press.
—— (1985), *Choosing the Right Pond*, New York and Oxford: Oxford Uuniversity Press.
Freeman, C. (1991), 'Networks of Innovators: a Synthesis of Research Issues', *Research Policy*, 20: 499–514.
Frey, B.S. (1997), 'A Constitution of Knaves Drives out Civic Virtues', *Economic Journal*, 107(443): 1043–53.
Friedman, J. (1994), 'The Political Economy of Elegance', in J. Friedman (ed.), *Consumption and Identity*, London: Harwood, pp. 167–87.
—— (1990), 'Being in the World', *Theory, Culture and Society*, 7: 311–28.
Frith, S. (1996), *Performing Rite*, New York: Oxford University Press.
—— (1983), *Sound Effects*, London: Constable.
Fruin, W.M. (1992), *The Japanese Enterprise System*, Oxford: Clarendon Press.
Fujimoto, T. (1999), *The Evolution of a Manufacturing System at Toyota*, Oxford: Oxford University Press.
—— (1995), 'A Note of the Origin of the "Black Box Parts" Practice in the Japanese Motor Vehicle Industry', in S. Shiomi and K. Wada (eds), *Fordism Transformed: the Development of Production Methods in the Automobile Industry*, Oxford: Oxford University Press, pp. 184–216.

Furukawa, R. and A. Goto (2006), 'The Role of Corporate Scientists in Innovation', *Research Policy*, 35: 24–36.
Galbraith, J.R. (1973), *Designing Complex Organizations*, Reading, MA: Addison-Wesley.
Garrard, T.F. (1982), 'Myth and Metrology: the Early Trans-Saharan Gold Trade', *Journal of African History*, 23(4): 443–61.
George, A.L. and A. Bennett (2005), *Case Studies and Theory Development in the Social Sciences*, Cambridge, MA: MIT Press.
Giddens, A. (1984), *The Constitution of Society*, Berkeley: University of California Press.
Gilson, L. (2003), 'Trust and the Development of Health Care as a Social Institution', *Social Science & Medicine*, 56: 1453–68.
Gioia. D.A. and P.P. Poole (1984), 'Scripts in Organizational Behavior', *Academy of Management Review*, 9(3): 449–59.
Givón, T. (2005), *Context as Other Minds: the Pragmatics of Sociality, Cognition and Communication*, Amsterdam: Benjamins.
Goldstone, J. (1998a), 'Initial Conditions, General Laws, Path-Dependence, and Explanation in Historical Sociology', *American Journal of Sociology*, 104: 829–45.
—— (1998b), 'The Problem of the "Early Modern" World', *Journal of Economic and Social History of the Orient*, 41: 249–84.
—— (1991), *Revolution and Rebellion in the Early Modern World*, Berkeley and Los Angeles: University of California Press.
Gordon, A. (1985), *The Evolution of Labour Relations in Japan: Heavy Industry, 1853–1955*, Cambridge, MA: Harvard Uuniversity Press.
Gordon, J.R. (1993), *Macroeconomics*, New York: HarperCollins College Publishers.
Gouldner, A.W. (1960), 'The Norm of Reciprocity: a Preliminary Statement', *American Sociological Review*, 25: 161–78.
Granovetter, M. (1985), ' Economic Action and Social Structure: the Problem of Embeddedness', *American Journal of Sociology*, 91: 481–510.
—— (1973), 'The Strength of Weak Ties', *American Journal of Sociology*, 78: 1360–80.
Grant, R.M. (1996), 'Towards a Knowledge-Based Theory of the Firm', *Strategic Management Journal*, 17: 109–22.
Greif, A. (2006), *Institutions and the Path to the Modern Economy*, Cambridge: Cambridge University Press.
Grit, K. and W. Dolfsma (2007), 'Sp(l)itting Images: Introducing Market Mechanisms in Healthcare', Erasmus University, BMG, mimeo.
—— (2002), 'Dynamics of the Dutch Health Care System', *Review of Social Economy*, 60(3): 377–401.
Groenewegen, J.G., F. Kerstholt and A. Nagelkerke (1995), 'On Integrating New and Old Institutionalism: Douglass North Building Bridges', *Journal of Economic Issues*, 29(2): 467–75.
Grønning (1997), 'The Emergence and Institutionalization of Toyotism: Subdivision and Integration of the Labour Force at the Toyota Motor Corporation from the 1950s to the 1970s', *Economic and Industrial Democracy*, 18: 423–55.
Gulati, R. (1995), 'Does Familiarity Breed Trust', *Academy of Management Journal*, 38: 85–112.
Haack, S. (2004), 'Pragmatism, Old and New', *Contemporary Pragmatism*, 1: 3–41.
Halberstam, D. (1986), *The Reckoning*, New York: Avon Books.

Hamilton, W. (1932), 'Institutions', in E.R.A. Seligman and A. Johnson (eds), *Encyclopedia of the Social Sciences*, vol. 8, New York: Macmillan, pp. 84–9.

Hamilton-Grierson, [Philip] J. (1904), 'Book Notices: the Silent Trade', *Bulletin of the American Geographical Society*, 36(11): 710–11.

Hampson, I. (1999), 'Lean Production and the Toyota Production System', *Economic and Industrial Democracy*, 20: 369–91.

Hansen, M.T. (1999), 'The Search-Transfer Problem: the Role of Weak Ties in Sharing Knowledge', *Administrative Science Quarterly*, 44(1): 82–111.

Harper, David A. (2004), 'Trade, Language and Communication', New York University, http://www.econ.nyu.edu/dept/austrian/Trade&Comm.pdf (accessed 27 July 2007).

Hay, C. and D. Wincott (1998), 'Structure, Agency and Historical Institutionalism', *Political Studies*, 46: 951–7.

Hayden, F. Gregory (1988), 'Values, Beliefs, and Attitudes in a Sociotechnical Setting', *Journal of Economic Issues*, 22(2): 415–26.

—— (1982), 'Social Fabric Matrix: From Perspective to Analytical Tool', *Journal of Economic Issues*, 16(3): 637–62.

Hayek, F. (1945), 'The Use of Knowledge in Society', *American Economic Review*, 35: 519–30.

Hays, S. (1994), 'Structure and Agency and the Sticky Problem of Culture', *Sociological Theory*, 12(1): 57–72.

Heath, A.F. (1976), *Rational Choice and Social Exchange: Critique of Exchange Theory*, New York: Cambridge University Press.

Heide, J.B. and A.S. Miner (1992), 'The Shadow of the Future: Effects of Anticipated Interaction and Frequency of Contact on Buyer-Seller Cooperation', *Academy of Management Review*, 35: 265–91.

Heider, K.G. (1969), 'Visiting Trade Institutions', *American Anthropologist* (new series) 71(3): 462–71.

Hellriegel, D. and J.W. Slocum (1996), *Management*, Cincinnati, OH: South-Western College Publishing.

Henderson, W., T. Dudley-Evans and R. Backhouse (eds) (1993), *Economics and Language*, London and New York: Routledge.

Hendrikse, G.W.J. and F.T. Schut (2004), 'Towards New Governance Structures in Dutch Health Care', *Acta Hospitalis*, 44(1): 5–20 [in Dutch].

Hennart, J. (1993), 'Explaining the Swollen Middle: Why Most Transactions are a Mix of "Market" and "Hierarchy"', *Organization Science*, 4(4): 529–47.

Herodotus (1988), *The History* [440 BC], translated David Grene, Chicago: University of Chicago Press.

Herskovits, M.J. (1940), *The Economic Life of Primitive Peoples*, New York and London: Alfred A Knopf.

Hicks, D. (1995), 'Published Papers, Tacit Competencies and Corporate Management of the Public/Private Character of Knowledge', *Industrial and Corporate Change*, 4(2): 401–24.

Hill, C.W.L. (1990), 'Cooperation, Opportunism and the Invisible Hand: Implications for Transaction Cost Theory', *Academy of Management Review*, 15(3): 500–13.

Hino, S. (2006), *Inside the Mind of Toyota*, New York: Productivity Press (original Japanese edition from 2002).

Hirschman, Albert O. (1977), *The Passions and the Interests.* Princeton, NJ: Princeton University Press.
Hitlin, S. and J.A. Piliavin (2004), 'Values: Reviving a Dormant Concept', *Annual Review of Sociology*, 30: 359–93.
Hobbes, T. (1986 [1651]), *Leviathan,* ed. C.B. Macpherson, Harmondsworth: Penguin.
Hodgson , G.M. (2006), 'What are Institutions?' *Journal of Economic Issues*, 40(1): 1–25.
—— (2005), 'Knowledge at Work', *Review of Social Economy*, 63(4): 547–65.
—— (2004), *The Evolution of Institutions: Agency, Structure and Darwinism in American Institutionalism*, London: Routledge.
—— (2003), 'The Hidden Persuaders: Institutions and Individuals in Economic Theory', *Cambridge Journal of Economics*, 27: 159–75.
—— (1999), *Economics and Utopia: Why the Learning Economy is not the End of History*, London and New York: Routledge.
—— (1998), 'The Approach of Institutional Economics', *Journal of Economic Literature*, 36: 166–92.
—— (1993), *Economics and Evolution*, Ann Arbor: University of Michigan Press.
—— (1988), *Economics and Institutions*, Oxford: Polity Press.
Hodgson, G.M. and T. Knudsen (2006), 'Why We Need a Generalized Darwinism: and Why a Generalized Darwinism is not Enough', *Journal of Economic Behavior and Organization*, 61(1): 1–19.
Hofstede, Geert (1991), *Cultures and Organizations: Software of the Mind*, London: HarperCollins Business.
—— (1980), *Culture's Consequences*, Newbury Park, CA: Sage.
Homans, G.C. (1974), *Social Behavior: its Elementary Forms*, New York: Harcourt Brace Jovanovich.
—— (1958), 'Social Behavior as Exchange', *American Journal of Sociology*, 63, 597–606.
—— (1950), *The Human Group*, New York: Harcourt Brace.
Howlett, M. and J. Rayner (2006), 'Understanding the Historical Turn in the Policy Sciences: a Critique of Stochastic, Narrative, Path Dependency and Process-Sequencing Models of Policy-Making Over Time', *Policy Sciences*, 39(1): 1–18.
Humphrey, C. and S. Hugh-Jones (1992), *Barter, Exchange and Value*, Cambridge: Cambridge University Press.
Hunter, D.J. (1996), 'The Changing Roles of Health Care Personnel in Health and Health Care Management', *Social Science & Medicine*, 43(5): 799–808.
Huysman, M. and D. de Wit (2004), 'Practices of Managing Knowledge Sharing: Towards a Second Wave of Knowledge Management', *Knowledge and Process Management*, 11(2): 81–92.
Iammarino, S. (2005), 'An Evolutionary Integrated View of Regional Systems of Innovation: Concepts, Measures and Historical Perspectives', *European Planning Studies*, 13(4): 497–519.
Iannello, K.P. (1992), *Decisions without Hierarchy*, New York: Routledge.
Inglehart, R. (1990), *Culture Shift in Advanced Industrial Society*, Princeton, NJ: Princeton University Press.
Ingram, P. and K. Clay (2000), 'The Choice-within-Constraints New Institutionalism and Implications for Sociology', *Annual Review of Sociology*, 26: 525–46.

Ingram, P. and P. Roberts (2000), 'Friendship among Competitors in the Sydney Hotel Industry', *American Journal of Sociology*, 106(2): 387–423.

Ireland, P.J. (1987), *Encyclopedia of Fashion Details*, London: B.T. Batsford.

Jackson, W.A. (2005), 'Capabilities, Culture and Social Structure', *Review of Social Economy* 63(1): 101–24.

Jacques, E. (1990), 'In Praise of Hierarchy', *Harvard Business Review*, 68: 127–33.

Jameson, F. (1988), 'Postmodernism and Consumer Society', in E.A. Kaplan (ed.), *Postmodernism and its Discontents*, London: Verso, pp. 13–29.

Jessop, B. (2001), 'Regulationist and Autopoieticist Reflections on Polanyi's Account of Market Economies and the Market Society', *New Political Economy*, 6: 213–32.

—— (2000), 'Institutional (Re)Turns and the Strategic-Relational Approach', *Environment and Planning A*, 33: 1213–35.

Johnson, V. (2007), 'What is Organizational Imprinting? Cultural Entrepreneurship in the Founding of the Paris Opera', *American Journal of Sociology*, 113(1): 97–117.

Jordan, B. and N. Fuller (1975), 'On the Non-Fatal Nature of Trouble: Sense-Making and Trouble-Making in Lingua Franca Talk', *Semiotica*, 13: 11–31.

Journal of Economic Methodology (2004), special issue 'Ontological Issues in Evolutionary Economics', ed. M. Klaes, 11(2).

Journal of Evolutionary Economics (2006), special issue 'Evolutionary Concepts in Economics and Biology', ed. U. Witt, 16(5).

Jungmann, N. (2006), *De Wsnp: bedoelde en onbedoelde effecten op het minnelijke traject*, Amsterdam: Amsterdam University Press.

Jungmann, N., E. Niemeijer and M.J. ter Voert (2001), *Van schuld naar een schone lei – Evaluatie Wet Schuldsanering natuurlijke personen*, Den Haag: WODC.

Kaiser, S.B., R.H. Nagasawa and S.S. Hutton (1991), 'Fashion, Postmodernity and Personal Appearance: a Symbolic Interactionist Formulation', *Symbolic Interaction*, 14(2): 165–85.

Kamiya, S. (1976), *My Life with Toyota*, Toyota Motor Sales Company, no place given (translated from the Japanese).

Karni, E. and D. Schmeidler (1990), 'Fixed Preferences and Changing Tastes', *American Economic Review*, 80 (2): 262–7.

Katz, L.M and H.S. Rosen (1994), *Microeconomics*, Boston, MA: Irwin.

Kawahara, A. (1997), *The Origin of Competitive Strength*, no place given, original Japanese edn 1995.

Kenney, M. and U. von Burg (1999), 'Technology, Entrepreneurship and Path Dependence: Industrial Clustering in Silicon Valley and Route 128', *Industrial and Corporate Change*, 8(1): 67–103.

Kilduff, M. and D.J. Brass (2001), 'The Social Network of High and Low Self-Monitors: Implications for Workplace Performance', *Administrative Science Quarterly*, 46(1): 121–46.

Kilpi, J. (1998), *The Ethics of Bankruptcy*, London: Routledge.

King, A. (1999), 'Against Structure: a Critique of Morphogenetic Social Theory', *Sociological Review*, 47(2): 199–227.

Klamer, A. (ed.) (1996), *The Value of Culture*, Ann Arbor: University of Michigan Press.

—— (1995), 'The Conception of Modernism in Economics', in S. Dow and J. Hillard (eds), *Keynes, Knowledge and Uncertainty*, Cheltenham, UK and Northampton, MA, USA: Edward Elgar, pp. 318–33.

Klein, Philip (1995), 'Instrumental Valuation in Democratic Society', in C.M.A. Clark (ed.), *Institutional Economics and the Theory of Social Value*, Norwell, MA: Kluwer, pp. 97–112.

Klein Woolthuis R., B. Hillebrand and B. Nooteboom (2005), 'Trust, Contract and Relationship Development', *Organization Studies*, 26(6): 813–40.

Kloosterman, R.C and C. Quispel (1990), 'Not Just the Same Old Show on my Radio: an Analysis of Black Music among Whites in the South of the United States of America, 1920 to 1960', *Popular Music* 9(2): 151–64.

Kluckhohn, Clyde (1962[1951]), 'Values and Value-Orientations in the Theory of Action', in Talcot Parsons and Edward A. Shils (eds), *Toward a General Theory of Action*, Cambridge, MA: Harvard University Press, pp. 388–433.

Kogut, B. and U. Zander (1996), 'What do Firms do?' *Organization Science*, 7(5): 502–18.

—— (1992), 'Knowledge of the Firm, Combinative Capabilities, and the Replication of Technology', *Management of Technology*, 3(2): 383–97.

Kohn, A. (1993), *Punished by Reward: the Trouble with Gold Stars, Incentive Plans, A's, Praise and Other Bribes*, Boston, MA: Houghton Mifflin.

Komter, A.E. (1996), *The Gift: an Interdisciplinary Approach*, Amsterdam: Amsterdam University Press.

Knorr Cetina, K. and U. Bruegger (2002), 'Global Microstructures: the Virtual Societies of Financial Markets', *American Journal of Sociology*, 107(4): 905–50.

Kreiner, K. and M. Schultz (1993), 'Informal Collaboration in R&D', *Organization Studies*, 14(2): 189–209.

Kreps, D.M. (1990), 'Corporate Culture and Economic Theory', in J. Alt and K. Shepsel (eds), *Perspectives on Positive Political Economy*, Cambridge: Cambridge University Press, pp. 90–143.

Kreps, D., P. Milgrom and R. Wilson (1982), 'Rational Cooperation in the Finitely Repeated Prisoner's Dilemma', *Journal of Economic Theory*, 27: 245–52.

Kriauciunas, A. and P. Kale (2006), 'The Impact of Socialist Imprinting and Search on Resource Change: a Study of Firms in Lithuania', *Strategic Management Journal*, 27: 659–79.

Kula, W. (1986), *Measure and Men*, trans. R. Szreter, Princeton NJ: Princeton University Press.

Laiou, Angeliki E. (2002), *The Economic History of Byzantium*, Vol. 2, Washington DC: Dumbarton Oaks Research Library and Collection.

Larsen, D. and J.J. Watson (2001), 'A Guide Map to the Terrain of Gift Value', *Psychology & Marketing*, 18(8): 889–906.

Lawler, E., S. Thye and J. Yoon (2000), 'Emotion and Group Cohesion in Productive Exchange', *American Journal of Sociology*, 106: 616–57.

Lawson, Anthony (1987), 'The Relative/Absolute Nature of Knowledge and Economic Analysis', *Economic Journal*, 97: 951–70.

Lawson, T. (2003), *Reorienting Economics*, London: Routledge.

—— (1997), *Economics and Reality*, London: Routledge.

Le Grand, J. (2003), *Motivation, Agency, and Public Policy: of Knights and Knaves, Pawns and Queens*, Oxford and New York: Oxford University Press.

Lefebre, H. (1995), *Introduction to Modernity*, London: Verso.

Levi-Strauss, C. (1996), 'The Principle of Reciprocity', in A.E. Komter (ed.), *The Gift: an Interdisciplinary Perspective,* Amsterdam: Amsterdam University Press, pp. 18–25.

Levinthal, D.A. and J.G. March (1993), 'The Myopia of Learning', *Strategic Management Journal*, 14: 95–112.

Lewenhaupt, T. and C. Lewenhaupt (1989), *Crosscurrents: Art, Fashion, Design (1890–1989)*, New York: Rizzoli.

Leydesdorff, L. (2006a), *The Knowledge-based Economy: Modelled, Measured, Simulated*, Boca Raton: Universal Publishers.

—— (2006b), 'The Knowledge-Based Economy and the Triple Helix Model', in W. Dolfsma and L. Soete (eds), *Understanding the Dynamics of a Knowledge Economy*, Cheltenham, UK and Northampton, MA, USA: Edward Elgar, pp. 42–76.

Lichtblau, K. (1999), 'Differentiations of Modernity', *Theory, Culture and Society*, 16(3): 1–30.

Light, D.W. (2001a), 'Managed Competition, Governmentality and Institutional Response in the United Kingdom', *Social Science & Medicine*, 52(8): 1167–81.

—— (2001b), 'Comparative Institutional Response to Economic Policy: Managed Competition and Governmentality', *Social Science & Medicine*, 52(8): 1151–66.

Lopes, H. and J.C. Caldas (2008), 'Firms: Collective Action and its Supportive Values', in J. Davis and W. Dolfsma (eds), *Companion to Social Economics*, Cheltenham, UK and Northampton, MA, USA: Edward Elgar, pp. 305–25.

Lovelock, C.H. (1984), 'Developing and Implementing New Services', in W.R. George and C.E. Marshall (eds), *Developing New Services*, Chicago, IL: American Marketing Association, pp. 44–64.

Luhmann, N. (1995), *Social Systems*, trans. John Bednarz Jr with Dirk Baecker, Stanford CA: Stanford University Press [originally published in German in 1984].

Lukes, S. (1971), 'The Meaning of "Individualism"', *Journal of the History of Ideas*, 32: 45–66.

Madhaven, R. and R. Grover (1998), 'From Embedded Knowledge to Embodied Knowledge: New Product Development as Knowledge Management', *Journal of Marketing*, 62: 1–12.

Maguire, S. and C. Hardy (2006), 'The Emergence of New Global Institutions: a Discursive Perspective', *Organization Studies*, 27(1): 7–29.

Mahoney, J. (2000), 'Path Dependence in Historical Sociology', *Theory and Society*, 29: 507–48.

Maitland, I. (2002), 'The Human Face of Self-Interest', *Journal of Business Ethics*, 38: 3–17.

Malinowski, B. (1922), *Argonauts of the Western Pacific*, London: George Routledge & Sons.

—— (1996), 'The Principle of Give and Take', in A.E. Komter (ed.), *The Gift: an Interdisciplinary Perspective,* Amsterdam: Amsterdam University Press, pp. 15–17.

Marquis, C. (2003), 'The Pressure of the Past: Network Imprinting in Intercorporate Communities', *Administrative Science Quarterly*, 48: 655–89.

Marx, K. (1990), *Capital*, Vol. 1, Harmondsworth: Penguin.

Mass, W. and A. Robertson (1996), 'From Textiles to Automobiles: Mechanical and Organizational Innovation in the Toyoda Enterprises, 1895–1933', *Business and Economic History*, 25(2): 1–37.

Mauss, M. (1954 [2000]), *The Gift*, New York: Norton.

McCloskey, D. and A. Klamer (1995), 'One Quarter of GDP is Persuasion', *American Economic Review*, 85(2): 191–5.
McGuire, A., J. Henderson and G. Mooney (1988), *The Economics of Health Care: an Introductory Text*, London: Routledge and Kegan Paul.
McMaster, R. (2002), 'A Socio-Institutionalist Critique of the 1990s' Reforms of the UK's National Health Service', *Review of Social Economy*, 60(3): 403–33.
Mercuro, N. and S.G. Medema (2006), *Economics and Law: From Posner to Post-Modernism and Beyond*, 2nd edn, Princeton and Oxford: Princeton University Press.
Merton, R. (1968), 'The Matthew Effect in Science', *Science*, 159(3819): 56–63.
Miles, R. and C. Snow (1986), 'Organizations: New Concepts for New Forms', *California Management Review*, 28: 62–73.
Milgrom, P. and J. Roberts (1990), 'The Economics of Modern Manufacturing: Technology, Strategy and Organization', *American Economic Review*, 80(3): 511–28.
Miller, D. (1995), 'Consumption as the Vanguard of History', in D. Miller (ed.), *Acknowledging Consumption*, London and New York: Routledge, pp. 1–57.
Mintzberg, H. (1979), *The Structuring of Organizations*, Englewood Cliffs, NJ: Prentice-Hall.
Mirowski, Ph. (1989), *More Heat than Light: Economics as Social Physics, Physics as Nature's Economics*, Cambridge: Cambridge University Press.
Molm, L.D. (2003), 'Theoretical Comparisons of Forms of Exchange', *Sociological Theory*, 21(1): 1–17
Moran, P. and S. Ghosal (1996), 'Value Creation by Firms', *Academy of Management Proceedings*, 35–9.
Morris-Suzuki, T. (1994), *The Technological Transformation of Japan*, Cambridge: Cambridge University Press.
Moss, D.A. (1992), *When All Else Fails: Government as the Ultimate Risk Manager*, Cambridge, MA: Harvard University Press.
Munir, K. and N. Phillips (2005), 'The Birth of the Kodak Moment: Institutional Entrepreneurship and the Adoption of New Technologies', *Organization Studies*, 26(11): 1665–87.
Nahapiet, J. and S. Ghosal (1998), 'Social Capital, Intellectual Capital, and the Organizational Advantage', *Academy of Management Review*, 23(20): 242–66.
Neale, W.C. (1987), 'Institutions', *Journal of Economic Issues*, 21(3): 1177–206.
Nelson, J.P. (1999), 'Consumer Bankruptcy and Chapter Choice', *Contemporary Economic Policy*, 17(4): 552–66.
Nelson, R.R. (2004), 'The Market Economy, and the Scientific Commons', *Research Policy*, 33(3): 455–71.
—— (1959), 'The Simple Economics of Basic Scientific Research', *Journal of Political Economy*, 57: 297–306.
Nelson, R.R. and B.N. Sampat (2001), 'Making Sense of Institutions as a Factor of Shaping Economic Performance', *Journal of Economic Behavior and Organization*, 44: 233–56.
Nelson, R.R. and S.G. Winter (1982), *An Evolutionary Theory of Economic Change*, Cambridge, MA: The Belknap Press.
New, S.J. (2007), 'Celebrating the Enigma: the Continuing Puzzle of the Toyota Production System', *International Journal of Production Research*, 45(16): 3545–54.

Nightingale, P. (2003), 'If Nelson and Winter are Only Half Right about Tacit Knowledge, Which Half? A Searlean Critique of "Codification"', *Industrial and Corporate Change*, 12: 149–83.

Nishiguchi, T. (1994), *Strategic Industrial Sourcing*, New York: Oxford University Press.

Nohara, H. (1999), 'The Historic Reversal of the Division of Labour?' in J.P. Durand, P. Stewart and J.J. Castillo (eds), *Teamwork in the Automobile Industry*, Basingstoke: Macmillan, pp. 37–53.

Nooteboom, B. (2002), *Trust: Forms, Foundations, Functions, Failures and Figures*, Cheltenham, UK and Northampton, MA, USA: Edward Elgar.

—— (2000), *Learning and Innovation in Organizations and Economies*, Oxford: Oxford University Press.

North, D.C. (1996), 'Economics and Cognitive Science', http://129.3.20.41/eps/eh/papers/9612/9612002.pdf (accessed 5 September 2007).

—— (1991), 'Institutions', *Journal of Economic Perspectives*, 5(1): 97–112.

—— (1990), *Institutions, Institutional Change and Economic Performance*, Cambridge: Cambridge University Press.

—— (1955), 'Location Theory and Regional Economic Growth', *Journal of Political Economy*, 63(3): 243–58.

Nye, F. I. (1979), 'Choice, Exchange and the Family', in W.R. Burr. R. Hill, F. I. Nye and I. L. Reiss (eds), *Contemporary Theories about the Family*, Vol. 2, New York: Free Press, pp. 1–41.

O'Hara, Ph. (2000), *Marx, Veblen and Contemporary Institutional Political Economy: Principles and Unstable Dynamics of Capitalism*, Cheltenham, UK and Northampton, MA, USA: Edward Elgar.

O'Neill, J. (1998), *The Market: Ethics, Knowledge and Politics*, London: Routledge.

Obstfeld, D. (2005), 'Social Networks, the *Tertius Iungens* Orientation, and Involvement in Innovation', *Administrative Science Quarterly*, 50: 100–30.

Odaka, K., K. Ono and F. Adachi (1988), *The Automobile Industry in Japan*, Tokyo: Kinokuniya Company Ltd.

Ohno, T. (1988), *Toyota Production System*, Cambridge, MA: Productivity Press (translated from Japanese edn of 1978).

Okayama, R. (1987), 'Industrial Relations in the Japanese Automobile Industry 1945–1970: the Case of Toyota', in S. Tolliday and J. Zeitlin (eds), *The Automobile Industry and its Workers*, New York: St Martin's Press, pp. 168–89.

Organization for Economic Co-operation and Development (2001), *Science, Technology and Industry Outlook 2001*, Paris: OECD.

Osterloh, M. and B. Frey (2000), 'Motivation, Knowledge Transfer, and Organizational Forms', *Organization Science*, 11(5): 538–50.

Ostrom, E. and T.K. Ahn (2003), *Foundations of Social Capital*, Cheltenham, UK and Northampton, MA, USA: Edward Elgar.

Ouchi, W.G. (1980), 'Markets, Bureaucracies, and Clans', *Administrative Science Quarterly*, 25(1): 129–41.

—— (1979), 'A Conceptual Framework for the Design of Organizational Control', *Management Science*, 25(9): 833–48.

Page, S.E. (2006), 'Path Dependence', *Quarterly Journal of Political Science*, 1(1): 87–115.

Parkhe, A. (1993), 'Strategic Alliance Structuring: a Game Theoretic and Transaction Cost Examination of Inter-Firm Cooperation', *Academy of Management Journal*, 36: 794–829.
Parsons, T. (1968 [1937]), *The Structure of Social Action*, New York: The Free Press.
—— (1951), *The Social System*, New York: The Free Press.
Parsons, T. and E.A. Shils (eds) (1951), *Toward a General Theory of Action*, Cambridge MA: Harvard University Press.
Parsons, T. and N.J. Smelser (1956), *Economy and Society: a Study in the Integration of Economic and Social Theory*, London: Routledge & Kegan Paul.
Parto, S. (2005), 'Economic Activity and Institutions: Taking Stock', *Journal of Economic Issues*, 39: 21–52.
Pesendorfer, W. (1995), 'Design Innovation and Fashion Cycles', *American Economic Review*, 85: 771–92.
Peters, T. (1987), *Thriving on Chaos*, London: Pan Books.
Peterson, R.A. (1990), 'Why 1955? Explaining the Advent of Rock Music', *Popular Music*, 9: 97–116.
Philips, N., T.B. Lawrence and C. Hardy (2004), 'Discourse and Institutions', *Academy of Management Review*, 29(4): 635–52.
Pierson, P. (2004), *Politics in Time*, Princeton and Oxford: Princeton University Press.
Pil, F.K. and T. Fujimoto (2007), 'Lean and Reflective Production: the Dynamic Nature of Production Models', *International Journal of Production Research*, 45(16): 3741–61.
Podolny, J.M. (1993), 'A Status-Based Model of Market Competition', *American Journal of Sociology*, 98: 829–72.
Polanyi, K. (1966), *Dahomey and the Slave Trade*, Seattle: University of Washington Press.
—— (1963), 'Ports of Trade in Early Societies', *Journal of Economic History*, 23(1): 30–45.
—— (1944), *The Great Transformation*, Boston: Beacon Press.
Porter, M.E. (1991), 'Towards a Dynamic Theory of Strategy', *Strategic Management Journal*, 12: 95–117.
Porter, T. (1992), 'Quantification and the Accounting Ideal in Science', *Social Studies of Science*, 22: 633–52.
Portes, A. (1998), 'Social Capital: its Origins and Applications in Modern Sociology', *Annual Review of Sociology*, 24: 1–24.
Posner, R.A. (1990), *The Problems of Jurisprudence*, Cambridge, MA: Harvard University Press.
—— (1983), *The Economics of Justice*, Cambridge, MA: Harvard University Press.
—— (1978), 'The Chicago School of Antitrust Analysis', *University of Pennsylvania Law Review*, 127: 335–58.
Potts, J. (2000), *The New Evolutionary Microeconomics: Complexity, Competence and Adaptive Behaviour*, Cheltenham, UK and Northampton, MA, USA: Edward Elgar.
Powell, W. (1990), 'Neither Market nor Hierarchy: Network Forms of Organization', *Research in Organization Behavior*, 12: 295–336.
Powell, W.W. and P.J. DiMaggio (eds) (1991), *The New Institutionalism in Organizational Analysis*, Chicago: University of Chicago Press.

Powell, W.W., K.W. Koput and L. Smith-Doerr (1996), 'Interorganizational Collaboration and the Locus of Innovation: Networks of Learning in Biotechnology', *Administrative Science Quarterly*, 41(1), pp. 116–45.

Putnam, R.D. (2000), *Bowling Alone: the Collapse and Revival of American Community*, New York: Simon & Schuster.

Rangan, S. (2000), 'The Problem of Search and Deliberation in Economic Action: When Social Networks Really Matter', *Academy of Management Review*, 25(4): 813–28.

Rawls, J. (1955), 'Two Concepts of Rules', *Philosophical Review*, 64: 3–32.

Reagans, R. and B. McEvily (2003), 'Network Structure and Knowledge Transfer: the Effects of Cohesion and Range', *Organization Science*, 13(3): 232–48.

Ring, P.S. and A. van de Ven (1992), 'Structuring Cooperative Relationships between Organizations', *Strategic Management Journal*, 13: 483–98.

Robbins, L. (1932), *An Essay on the Nature and Significance of Economic Science*, London: Macmillan.

Robichaud, D., H. Giroux and J.R. Taylor (2004), 'The Metaconversation: the Recursive Property of Language as a Key to Organizing', *Academy of Management Review*, 29: 617–34.

Robins, K. (1994), 'Forces of Consumption', *Media, Culture & Society*, 16: 449–68.

Rokeach, M. (1979), 'From Individual to Institutional Values', in M. Rokeach (ed.), *Understanding Human Values*, New York: Free Press, pp. 47–70.

Romer, P. (2002), 'When Should We Use Intellectual Property Rights?' *American Economic Review*, 92(2): 213–16.

Romme, A.G.L. (1996), 'A Note on the Hierarchy-Team Debate', *Strategic Management Journal*, 17(5): 411–17.

Rook, D.W. (1999), 'Ritual', in P.E. Earl and S. Kemp (eds), *The Elgar Companion to Consumer Research and Economic Psychology*, Cheltenham, UK and Northampton, MA, USA: Edward Elgar, pp. 506–11.

Rose-Ackerman, S. (1998), 'Bribes and Gifts', in A. Benner and L. Putterman (eds), *Economics, Values and Organization*, Cambridge: Cambridge University Press, pp. 296–328.

Rosenbaum, E.F. (2000), 'What is a Market? On the Methodology of a Contested Concept', *Review of Social Economy*, 58(4): 455–82.

Rousseau, D.M. (1990), 'Assessing Organizational Culture: the Case for Multiple Methods', in B. Schneider (ed.), *Organizational Climate and Culture*, San Francisco: Jossey-Bass, pp. 153–92.

Rousseau, D.M. and J.M. Parks (1993), 'The Contracts of Individuals and Organizations', *Research in Organizational Behavior*, 15: 1–43.

Rutherford, M.H. (1995), 'The Old and the New Institutionalism: Can Bridges be Built?' *Journal of Economic Issues*, 29(2): 443–51.

—— (1994), *Institutions in Economics: the Old and the New Institutionalism*, Cambridge: Cambridge University Press.

—— (1989), 'What is Wrong With the New Institutional Economics (and What is Still Wrong With the Old)?' *Review of Political Economy*, 1: 299–318.

Ryan, M.S. (1966), *Clothing: a Study in Human Behavior*, New York: Holt, Rinehart and Winston.

Saga, I. and M. Hanada (1999), 'Nissan: Recent Evolution of Industrial Relations and Work Organization', in J.P. Durand, P. Stewart and J.J. Castillo (eds), *Teamwork in the Automobile Industry*, Basingstoke: Macmillan, pp. 54–82.
Sahlins, M.D. (1996), 'On the Sociology of Primitive Exchange', in A.E. Komter (ed.), *The Gift: an Interdisciplinary Perspective*, Amsterdam: Amsterdam University Press, pp. 26–38.
Sako, M. (2004), 'Supplier Development at Honda, Nissan and Toyota', *Industrial and Corporate Change*, 13: 281–308.
Samuels, Warren J. (1998), 'The Historical Quest for Principles of Valuation', in S. Fayazmanesh and M.R. Tool (eds), *Institutionalist Method and Value*, Cheltenham, UK and Northampton, MA, USA: Edward Elgar, pp. 112–29.
—— (1995), 'The Instrumentalist Value Principle and its Role', in C.M.A. Clark (ed.), *Institutional Economics and the Theory of Social Value*, Norwell, MA: Kluwer, pp. 97–112.
Sanchez, R. and J.T. Mahoney (1996), 'Modularity, Flexibility and Knowledge Management in Product and Organization Design', *Strategic Management Journal*, 17: 63–76.
Scharpf, F. (1997), *Games Real Actors Play*, Boulder, CO: Westview.
Schein E.H. (1992), *Organizational Culture and Leadership*, 2nd edn, San Francisco: Jossey-Bass.
—— (1965), *Organization Psychology*, New York: Prentice-Hall, Englewood Cliffs.
Schmid, A. Allan (2004), *Conflict and Cooperation: Institutional and Behavioral Economics*, Malden, MA, Oxford (UK), Victoria (Australia): Blackwell.
Schmid, G. (2006), 'Social Risk Management through Transitional Labour Markets', *Socio-Economic Review*, 4: 1–33.
Schor, J. (1998), *The Overspent American*, New York: Basic Books.
—— (1992), *The Overworked American*, New York: Basic Books.
Schulz, M. (2003), 'Pathways of Relevance: Exploring Inflows of Knowledge into Subunits of Multinational Corporations', *Organization Science*, 14(4): 440–59.
Schumpeter, J. (1934 [1978]), *The Theory of Economic Development*, London: Oxford University Press.
Schwartz, B. (1996), 'The Social Psychology of the Gift', in A.E. Komter (ed.), *The Gift: an Interdisciplinary Perspective*, Amsterdam: Amsterdam University Press, pp. 69–80.
Schwartz, H. (2004), 'Down the Wrong Path: Path Dependence, Increasing Returns, and Historical Institutionalism', unpublished paper, Department of Politics, University of Virginia, http://people.virginia.edu/~hms2f/Path.pdf (accessed 16 April 2009).
Schwartz, M. and A. Fish (1998), 'Just-in-time Inventories in Old Detroit', *Business History*, 48(1): 90–118.
Scott, W.R. (1995), *Institutions and Organizations*, Thousands Oaks, CA: Sage.
—— (1992), *Organizations: Rational, Natural and Open Systems*, New York: Harper.
Searle, J.R. (2005), 'What is an Institution?' *Journal of Institutional Economics*, 1: 1–22.
—— (1995), *The Construction of Social Reality*, Harmondsworth: Penguin.
Senge, P.M. (1990), *The Fifth Discipline*, New York: Doubleday Currency.
Sewell Jr, W.H. (1992), 'A Theory of Structure: Duality, Agency, and Transformation', *American Journal of Sociology*, 98(1): 1–29.

Shapiro, S.P. (1987), 'The Social Control of Impersonal Trust', *American Journal of Sociology*, 93: 623–58.

Sherry, J.F. (1991), 'Postmodern Alternatives', in T.S. Robertson and H. Kassarjian (eds), *Handbook of Consumer Research*, Englewood Cliffs, NJ: Prentice Hall, pp. 548–91.

—— (1983), 'Gift Giving in Anthropological Perspective', *Journal of Consumer Research*, 10(2): 157–68.

Shimokawa, K. (1994), *The Japanese Automobile Industry: a Business History*, London: The Athlone Press.

—— (1987), 'Product and Labour Strategies in Japan', in S. Tolliday and J. Zeitlin (eds), *The Automobile Industry and its Workers*, New York: St Martin's Press, pp. 224–43.

Shingo, S. (1989), *A Study of the Toyota Production System from an Industrial Engineering Viewpoint*, Cambridge MA: Productivity Press.

Shiomi, H. (1995), 'The Formation of Assembler Networks in the Automobile Industry: the Case of Toyota Motor Company (1955–1980)', in H. Shiomi and K. Wada (eds), *Fordism Transformed: the Development of Production Methods in the Automobile Industry*, Oxford: Oxford University Press, pp. 28–48.

Simmel, G. (1996), 'Faithfulness and Gratitude', in A.E. Komter (ed.), *The Gift: an Interdisciplinary Perspective*, Amsterdam: Amsterdam University Press, pp. 39–48.

—— (1964), *Conflict and the Web of Group Affiliations* (trans. Kurt H. Wolff and Reinhard Bendix), New York: The Free Press.

—— (1957 [1904]), 'Fashion', *American Journal of Sociology* 62(6): 541–58.

Simon, H.A. (1991), 'Bounded Rationality and Organizational Learning', *Organization Science*, 2: 125–34.

Sjöstrand, Sven-Erik (ed.) (1993), *Institutional Change, Theory and Empirical Findings*, Armonk, NY: M.E. Sharpe.

Slater, D. (1997), *Consumer Culture and Modernity*, Cambridge, MA: Polity Press/Blackwell.

Smart, A. (1993), 'Gifts, Bribes, and Guanxi: a Reconsideration of Bourdieu's Social Capital', *Cultural Anthropology*, 8(3): 388–408.

Smith, A. (1982 [1759]), *The Theory of Moral Sentiments*, Indianapolis: Liberty Press

—— (1981 [1776]), *An Inquiry into the Nature and Causes of the Wealth of Nations*, Indianapolis: Liberty Press .

Soete, L. and B. ter Weel (2005), *The Economics of the Digital Society*, Cheltenham, UK and Northampton, MA, USA: Edward Elgar.

Spear, S. and H.K. Bowen (1999), 'Decoding the DNA of the Toyota Production System', *Harvard Business Review*, 77(5): 97–106.

Sproles, G.B. and L.D. Burns (1994), *Changing Appearances: Understanding Dress in Contemporary Society*, New York: Fairchild.

Star, S.L. and J.R. Griesemer (1989), 'Institutional Ecology, "Translations" and Boundary Objects: Amateurs and Professionals in Berkeley's Museum of Invertebrate Zoology, 1907–39', *Social Studies of Science*, 19: 387–420.

Starpoli, C. (1998), 'Cooperation in R&D in the Pharmaceutical Industry', *Technovation*, 18(1): 13–23.

Starr, J.A. and I.C. Macmillan (1990), 'Resource Cooptation via Social Contracting: Resource Acquisition Strategies for New Ventures', *Strategic Management Journal*, 11: 79–92.

Starr, M. (2007), 'Saving, Spending and Self-Control', *Review of Radical Political Economy*, 39(2): 214–29.
Steele, V. (1997), *Fifty Years of Fashion*, New Haven and London: Yale University Press.
Steidlmeier, P. (1999), 'Gift Giving, Bribery and Corruption: Ethical Management of Business Relationships in China', *Journal of Business Ethics*, 20: 121–32.
Stevenson, W.B. and M.C. Gilly (1991), 'Information Processing and Problem Solving: the Migration of Problems through Formal Positions and Networks of Ties', *Academy of Management Journal*, 34: 918–28.
Stewart, T.A. and A.P. Raman (2007), 'Lessons from Toyota's Long Drive', *Harvard Business Review*, 85(7/8): 74–83.
Stigler, G. (1968), 'Competition', in D.L. Sills (ed.), *International Encyclopedia of the Social Sciences*, vol. 3, New York: Macmillan.
Stiglitz, J.E. (1994), *Whither Socialism?* Cambridge, MA: MIT Press.
Stinchcombe, A. (1968), *Constructing Social Theories*, New York: Harcourt Brace.
—— (1965), 'Social Structure and Organizations' in J.G. March (ed.), *Handbook of Organizations*, Chicago: Rand McNally, pp. 142–93.
Streeck, W. and K. Theelen (2005), 'Introduction: Institutional Change in Advanced Political Economies', in W. Streeck and K. Theelen (eds), *Beyond Continuity: Institutional Change in Advanced Political Economies*, Oxford: Oxford University Press, pp. 1–39.
Sugimori, Y., K. Kusunoki, F. Cho and S. Uchikawa (1977), 'Toyota Production System and Kanban System', *International Journal of Production Research*, 15(6): 553–64.
Sullivan, T.A., E. Warren and J.L. Westbrook (1989), *As We Forgive Our Debtors: Bankruptcy and Consumer Credit in America*, New York: Oxford University Press.
Sundström, Lars (1965), *The Trade of Guinea*, Lund: Håkan Ohlssons Boktryckeri.
Swaminathan, A. (1996), 'Environmental Conditions at Founding and Organizational Mortality: a Trial-by-Fire Model', *Academy of Management Journal*, 39(5): 1350–77.
Swanson, J.T. (1975), 'The Myth of Trans-Saharan Trade during the Roman Era', *International Journal of African Historical Studies*, 8(4): 582–600.
Swedberg, R., U. Himmelstrand and G. Brulin (1990), 'The Paradigm of Economic Sociology', in S. Zukin and P. DiMaggio (eds), *Structures of Capital: the Social Organization of the Economy*, Cambridge: Cambridge University Press, pp. 57–86.
Sydow J., G. Schreyögg and J. Koch (2005), 'Organisational Paths: Path Dependency and beyond', paper prepared for the 21st EGOS colloquium, Berlin, Germany.
Szulanski, G. (1996), 'Exploring Internal Stickiness: Impediments to the Transfer of Best Practice within the Firm', *Strategic Management Journal*, 17: 27–43.
Szulanski, G. and R.J. Jensen (2004),'Overcoming Stickiness: an Empirical Investigation of the Role of the Template in the Replication of Organizational Routines', *Managerial and Decision Economics*, 25(6–7): 347–63.
Telser, L.G. (1980), 'A Theory of Self-Enforcing Agreements', *Journal of Business*, 53: 27–44.
Thelen, K. (2004), *How Institutions Evolve: the Political Economy of Skills in Germany, Britain, the United States, and Japan*, Cambridge: Cambridge University Press.

Thompson, C. and D.L. Haytko (1995), 'Speaking of Fashion: Consumers' Uses of Fashion Discourses and the Appropriation of Countervailing Cultural Meanings', *Journal of Consumer Research*, 24(1): 15–42.

Thompson, James D. (1967), *Organizations in Action: Social Science Bases of Administrative Theory*, New York: McGraw-Hill.

Thorelli, H.B. (1986), 'Networks: Between Markets and Hierarchies', *Strategic Management Journal*, 7(1): 37–51.

Tilman, Rick (1998), 'John Dewey as User and Critic of Thorstein Veblen's Ideas', *Journal of the History of Economic Thought*, 20 (1998): 145–60.

Tool, M.R. (1995), *Pricing, Valuation and Systems: Essays in Neoinstitutional Economics*, Cheltenham, UK and Northampton, MA, USA: Edward Elgar.

—— (1993), 'The Theory of Instrumental Value: Extensions, Clarifications' in M.R. Tool (ed.), *Institutional Economics: Theory, Method, Policy*, Dordrecht: Kluwer, pp. 119–59.

—— (1991), 'Contributions to an Institutional Theory of Price', in G.M. Hodgson and E. Screpanti (eds), *Rethinking Economics*, Aldershot: Edward Elgar, pp. 19–39.

Togo, Y. and W. Wartman (1993), *Against all Odds: the Story of the Toyota Motor Corporation and the Family that Created it*, New York: St Martin's Press.

Totsuka, H. (1995), 'The Transformation of Japanese Industrial Relations: a Case Study of the Automobile Industry' in S. Babson (ed.), *Lean Work: Empowerment and Exploitation in the Global Auto Industry*, Detroit: Wayne State University Press, pp. 108–28.

Toyoda, Eiji (1987), *Toyota Fifty Years in Motion: an Autobiography by the Chairman Eiji Toyoda*, Tokyo and New York: Kodansha International (translation from Japanese edn of 1985).

Toyota. A History of the First 50 years (1988), Toyota Motor Corporation, Toyota City (translation).

Towill, D.R. (2007), 'Exploiting the DNA of the Toyota Production System', *International Journal of Production Research*, 45(16): 3619–37.

Tsai, W. and S. Ghosal (1998) 'Social Capital and Value Creation: the Role of Intra Firm Networks', *Academy of Management Journal*, 41 (4): 464–76.

Ueda, H. (1997), 'The Subcontracting System and Business Groups: the Case of the Japanese Automotive Industry', in T. Shiba and M. Shimotani (eds), *Beyond the Firm*, Oxford: Oxford University Press, pp. 215–42.

Uehara, E. (1990), 'Dual Exchange Theory, Social Networks, and Informational Support', *American Journal of Sociology*, 96: 521–57.

Ullmann-Margalit, Edna (1977), *The Emergence of Norms*, Oxford: Clarendon Press.

Van den Berg, Bernard and Wolter Hassink (2008), 'Cash Benefits in Long-term Home Care', *Health Policy*, 88(2): 209–21.

Van der Eijk, R., W. Dolfsma and A. Jolink (2009), 'On a Source of Social Capital: Gift Exchange', *Journal of Business Ethics*, forthcoming.

Van der Geest, S. and K. Finkler (2004), 'Hospital Ethnography: Introduction', *Social Science and Medicine*, 59: 1995–2001.

Van Raaij, W.F. (1993), 'Postmodern Consumption', *Journal of Economic Psychology*, 14: 541–63.

Van Staveren, I. (2001), *The Values of Economics: an Aristotelian Perspective*, London: Routledge.

Vandevelde, A. (2000), 'Reciprocity and Trust as Social Capital', in A. Vandevelde (ed.), *Over Vertrouwen en Bedrijf*, Leuven: Acco, pp. 133–42 [in Dutch].

Veblen, T.B. (1969 [1919]), *The Place of Science in Modern Civilization and Other Essays*, New York: Capricorn Books.
—— (1961), 'The Limitations of Marginal Utility', in Thorstein Veblen, *The Place of Science in Modern Civilization*, New York: Russell & Russell, pp. 231–51.
—— (1899), *The Theory of the Leisure Class*, New York: Macmillan.
Venkatesh, A. (1999), 'Postmodernism and Consumption', in P.E. Earl and S. Kemp (eds), *The Elgar Companion to Consumer Research and Economic Psychology*, Cheltenham, UK and Northampton, MA, USA: Edward Elgar, pp. 458–63.
Von Hippel, E. (1994), ' "Sticky Information" and the Locus of Problem Solving', *Management Science*, 40(4): 429–39.
—— (1987), 'Cooperation between Rivals: Informal Know-How Trading', *Research Policy*, 16: 291–302.
Wada, K. (2006), 'The Fable of the Birth of the Japanese Automobile Industry: a Reconsideration of the Toyoda-Platt Agreement of 1929', *Business History*, 48(1): 90–118.
Wada, K. and T. Yui (2002), *Courage and Change: the Life of Kiichiro Toyoda*, Toyota Motor Corporation, Toyota City (translation).
Waller, W. (2004), 'Institutions as Boundaries and Valuational Metrics', paper presented at the AFEE meetings, 3–5 January 2004 San Diego, CA.
—— (2001), 'Kickin'em While They're Down: Consumer Bankruptcy Reform', *Journal of Economic Issues*, 35(4): 871–88.
Waller, W.J. and L.R. Robertson (1993), 'Commentary [on Tool]', in M.R. Tool (ed.), *Institutional Economics: Theory, Method, Policy*, Kluwer: Dordrecht.
Walster, E., E. Berscheid and G.W. Walster (1973), 'New Directions in Equity Research', *Journal of Personality and Social Psychology*, 25(2): 151–76.
Walzer, M. (1983), *Spheres of Justice*, New York: Basic Books.
Weber, M. (1978), *Economy and Society*, Berkeley: University of California Press.
—— (1964 [1922]), *The Theory of Social and Economic Organisation*, ed. T. Parsons, New York: The Free Press.
Weigelt, K. and C. Camerer (1988), 'Reputation and Corporate Strategy: a Review of Recent Theory and Applications', *Strategic Management Journal*, 9: 443–54.
Wenger, E.C. (1998) *Communities of Practice: Learning, Meaning and Identity*, Cambridge: Cambridge University Press.
Wenger, E.C. and W. Snyder (2000), 'Communities of Practice: the Organizational Frontier', *Harvard Business Review*, 78(1): 139–45.
Wildavsky, A. (1987), 'Choosing Preferences by Constructing Institutions', *American Political Science Review*, 81: 3–21.
Williams, B. (1988), 'Formal Structures and Social Reality', in D. Gambette (ed.), *Trust: Making and Breaking of Cooperative Relations*, Oxford: Blackwell.
Williams, K., C. Haslam, S. Johal and J. Williams (1994), *Cars: Analysis, History, Cases*, Providence: Berghahn.
Williams, K., C. Haslam, S. Johal, J. Williams, A. Adoroff and R. Willis (1995), 'Management Practice or Structural Factors: the Case of America versus Japan in the Car Industry', *Economic and Industrial Democracy*, 16: 9–37.
Williamson, O.E. (2000), 'The New Institutional Economics: Taking Stock, Looking Ahead', *Journal of Economic Literature*, 38: 595–613.
—— (1998), 'Transaction Cost Economics: How it Works: Where it is Headed', *De Economist*, 146(1): 23–58.

—— (1993), 'Transaction Cost Economics and Organization Theory', *Industrial and Corporate Change*, 2(2):107–56.

—— (1985), *The Economic Institutions of Capitalism: Firm Markets, Relational Contracting*, New York: Free Press.

—— (1975), *Markets and Hierarchies: Analysis and Antitrust Implications*, New York: Free Press.

Williamson, Oliver E., Geoffrey M. Hodgson and David Gindis (2007), 'An Interview with Oliver Williamson', *Journal of Institutional Economics*, 3(3): 373–86.

Wilson, E. (1985), *Adorned in Dreams: Fashion and Modernity*, London: Virago.

Wilson, Matthew (2006), 'Comment on Geoffrey M. Hodgson's "What are institutions?"' *Journal of Economic Issues*, 40(4): 1153–7.

Wittgenstein, L. (1954), *Philosophische Untersuchungen*, Frankfurt: Suhrkamp.

Womack, J.P., D.T. Jones and D. Jones (1990), *The Machine that Changed the World*, New York: Macmillan.

Wrenn, M. (2006), 'Agency and Mental Models in Heterodox Economics', *Journal of Economic Issues*, 40(2): 483–91.

Wrong, D. (1961), 'The Oversocialised Conception of Man in Modern Sociology', *American Sociological* Review, 26: 183–93; reprinted in (1976), *Skeptical Sociology*, New York: Columbia University Press.

Zeitlyn, D. (2003), 'Gift Economies in the Development of Open Source Software', *Research Policy*, 32(7): 1287–91.

Zelizer, V.A (1997), *The Social Meaning of Money*, Princeton, NJ: Princeton University Press.

—— (1985), *Pricing the Priceless Child*, New York: Basic Books.

—— (1979), *Morals and Markets*, New York: Columbia University Press.

Zilber, T.B. (2004), 'Institutionalization as Interplay between Actions, Meanings, and Actors', *Academy of Management Journal*, 45(1): 234–54.

Zucker, L.G. (1986), 'Production of Trust: Institutional Sources of Economic Structure, 1840–1920', *Research in Organizational Behavior*, 8: 53–111.

Zywicki, T.J. (2005), 'An Economic Analysis of the Consumer Bankruptcy Crisis', *Northwestern University Law Review*, 99(4): 1463–541.

'En toen kwam er een olifant met een lange snuit, en die blies het verhaal uit'

Index